Lecture Notes in Computer Science   11150

Commenced Publication in 1973
Founding and Former Series Editors:
Gerhard Goos, Juris Hartmanis, and Jan van Leeuwen

More information about this series at http://www.springer.com/series/7408

Ferhat Khendek · Reinhard Gotzhein (Eds.)

System Analysis and Modeling

Languages, Methods, and Tools for Systems Engineering

10th International Conference, SAM 2018
Copenhagen, Denmark, October 15–16, 2018
Proceedings

 Springer

Editors
Ferhat Khendek
Concordia University
Montreal, QC
Canada

Reinhard Gotzhein
University of Kaiserslautern
Kaiserslautern
Germany

ISSN 0302-9743   ISSN 1611-3349   (electronic)
Lecture Notes in Computer Science
ISBN 978-3-030-01041-6   ISBN 978-3-030-01042-3   (eBook)
https://doi.org/10.1007/978-3-030-01042-3

Library of Congress Control Number: 2018955148

LNCS Sublibrary: SL2 – Programming and Software Engineering

This Springer imprint is published by the registered company Springer Nature Switzerland AG
The registered company address is: Gewerbestrasse 11, 6330 Cham, Switzerland

Preface

The System Analysis and Modeling (SAM) Conference provides an open arena for participants from academia and industry to present and discuss the most recent innovations, trends, experiences, and concerns in modeling, specification, and analysis of distributed, communication, and real-time systems using the Specification and Description Language (SDL) and Message Sequence Charts (MSC) notations from the International Telecommunication Union (ITU-T), as well as related system design languages such as UML, ASN.1, TTCN-3, SysML, and the User Requirements Notation (URN). This 10th SAM conference (http://sdl-forum.org/Events/SAM2018/) was held in Copenhagen, Denmark, October 15–16, 2018. It was collocated with the ACM/IEEE 21st International Conference on Model-Driven Engineering Languages and Systems (MODELS 2018).

This year's edition of SAM was under the theme "Languages, Methods, and Tools for Systems Engineering," including languages and methods standardized by the ITU-T, and domain-specific languages. This volume contains the papers presented at SAM 2018. In total, 14 high-quality papers were selected from 24 submissions, for a selection rate of 58%. Each paper was reviewed by at least three Programme Committee members and discussed during the online Programme Committee meeting. The selected papers cover a wide spectrum of topics related to system design languages and system modeling and engineering, grouped into five technical sessions. The first session is devoted to modeling for the cloud, the papers in the second session discuss notations and their semantics, while papers in the third session propose methods for the modeling and analysis of performance, safety, and realizability. Papers in session four are related to the requirement modeling notations while the last session was on collaborative modeling. In addition to the selected papers, the program of SAM 2018 included two inspiring keynotes by Dr. Azimeh Sefidcon (Ericsson, Sweden) and Professor Juergen Dingel (Queen's University, Canada).

SDL Forum Society

The SDL Forum Society is a not-for-profit organization that, in addition to running the System Analysis and Modeling (SAM) Conference series of events (once every two years), also:

- Runs the System Design Languages Forum (SDL Forum) series, every two years between SAM conference years
- Is a body recognized by ITU-T as co-developing system design languages in the Z.100 series (SDL), Z.120 series (MSC), Z.150 series (URN), and other language standards
- Promotes the ITU-T System Design Languages

For more information on the SDL Forum Society, see http://www.sdl-forum.org.

August 2018   Ferhat Khendek
                                                     Reinhard Gotzhein

Organization

Program Co-chairs

Ferhat Khendek (Secretary, SDL Forum Society) — Concordia University, Canada

Reinhard Gotzhein (Chairman, SDL Forum Society) — University of Kaiserslautern, Germany

Publicity Chair

Mohamed Aymen Saeid — Concordia University, Canada

Program Committee

Shaukat Ali	Simula Research Laboratory, Norway
Daniel Amyot	University of Ottawa, Canada
Ludovic Apvrille	Telecom ParisTech - Sophia-Antipolis, France
Tibor Csöndes	Ericsson, Hungary
Juergen Dingel	Queen's University, Canada
Joachim Fischer	Humboldt University Berlin, Germany
Emmanuel Gaudin	PragmaDev, France
Abdelouahed Gherbi	Université du Québec, Canada
Jens Grabowski	University of Göttingen, Germany
Wahab Hamou-Lhadj	Concordia University, Canada
Jameleddine Hassine	KFUPM, Saudi Arabia
Øystein Haugen	SINTEF, Norway
Steffen Herbold	University of Göttingen, Germany
Gábor Kovács	Budapest University of Technology and Economics, Hungary
Alexander Kraas	T-Systems, Germany
Finn Kristofferson	Cinderella, Denmark
Zoltan Micskei	Budapest University of Technology and Economics, Hungary
Birger Møller-Pedersen	University of Oslo, Norway
Gunter Mussbacher	McGill University, Canada
Ileana Ober	University of Toulouse, France
Iulian Ober	University of Toulouse, France
Rick Reed	TSE, UK
Houari Sahraoui	Université de Montréal, Canada

Edel Sherratt   University of Wales Aberystwyth, UK
Maria Toeroe   Ericsson, Canada
Tao Yue   Simula Research Laboratory, Norway

Additional Reviewers

E. Batot
H. Lu
P. Makedonski
D. Weber
T. Weigert
M. Zhang

Acknowledgements

The SAM conference was made possible by the dedicated work and contributions of many people and organizations. We thank the authors of submitted papers, the keynote speakers, the members of the Programme Committee, and the members of the SDL Forum Society Board.

Furthermore, we thank the MODELS Organizing Committee for the effective support during the preparation and smooth realization of the SAM conference.

The submission and review process was run with EasyChair.org; and we thank the people behind the EasyChair conference system. We thank Springer for once again publishing the conference proceedings in their LNCS series.

Contents

Modeling Data Protection Vulnerabilities of Cloud Systems Using Risk Patterns

Alexander Palm$^{(\boxtimes)}$, Zoltán Ádám Mann, and Andreas Metzger

paluno – The Ruhr Institute for Software Technology,
University of Duisburg-Essen, Essen, Germany
{alexander.palm,zoltan.mann,andreas.metzger}@paluno.uni-due.de

Abstract. Ensuring the protection of sensitive data is important for the adoption of cloud services. Cloud systems are becoming increasingly complex and dynamic, leading to various potential scenarios for attackers to get access to sensitive data. To handle such data protection risks, the concept of risk patterns was introduced previously. A risk pattern models a structural fragment of cloud systems that should not appear in the running system because it would lead to high data protection risks. At deployment and at run time, graph pattern matching and dynamic reconfiguration methods can be used to ensure that the run-time model of the cloud system contains no instance of the risk patterns. The previous work left it open, however, how and to what extent real data protection vulnerabilities can be modeled in the form of risk patterns. Therefore, this paper focuses on the design of risk patterns based on vulnerabilities described in the literature. Based on an analysis of 87 papers, we determined 45 risk patterns. Our findings (i) demonstrate that risk patterns can indeed capture many of the vulnerabilities described in the cloud literature, (ii) give insight into the typical structure of risk patterns, and (iii) show the limits of the applicability of the risk pattern approach.

Keywords: Cloud computing · Data protection · Privacy
Run-time model · Risk pattern

1 Introduction

Cloud computing is increasingly popular, thanks to the benefits it brings to both providers and users of cloud services. However, outsourcing sensitive data to the cloud puts the data at a risk, which many users of cloud services are not ready to accept [16].

Data protection in the cloud is hard because cloud systems are increasingly complex and dynamic. They consist of many different physical and virtual machines, as well as various applications and their software components, all of which interact and may dynamically reconfigure during run time [1,9,15,30]. In addition, a multitude of stakeholders may be involved, such as service consumers, cloud providers, data subjects, data controllers, and actual end users.

© Springer Nature Switzerland AG 2018
F. Khendek and R. Gotzhein (Eds.): SAM 2018, LNCS 11150, pp. 1–19, 2018.
https://doi.org/10.1007/978-3-030-01042-3_1

Due to such complex interactions, a cloud system may expose vulnerabilities that enable attackers to gain access to sensitive data stored in the cloud. Moreover, since the attributes and interactions of the cloud entities continuously change, *data protection vulnerabilities* may arise during operation. By data protection vulnerability, we mean the possibility of unauthorized access to sensitive data. This is not the same as a system vulnerability (e.g., if a vulnerable system neither stores nor has access to sensitive data, then there is no data protection vulnerability), but system vulnerabilities may lead to data protection vulnerabilities which put sensitive data at risk.

To identify and mitigate data protection risks in complex and dynamic cloud systems, we have introduced the concept of risk patterns in our earlier work [26]. That approach was based on two types of artefacts:

- A model of the – current or planned – configuration of the cloud system, including infrastructure elements, middleware, applications, data, and the involved actors;
- A set of *risk patterns*, which describe cloud configurations that would cause too high risks of data protection violation and hence must be avoided.

For modeling the configuration of the cloud system, a meta-model was proposed [17]. When a cloud system is to be deployed, the system designer creates the model of the planned configuration as an instance of the meta-model. When the configuration changes during the deployment process or later during the operation of the system, the model is updated accordingly, so that it always reflects the current state of the cloud system and can be used as a run-time model.

Risk patterns are expressed in a domain-specific language based on the same meta-model as the cloud model. Risk patterns model fragments of a cloud system by specifying the presence or absence of certain entities, attributes, or relations. Risk patterns capture forbidden fragments of a cloud system model that would exhibit overly high data protection risks. During deployment and at run time, the model of the cloud system is checked for the existence of fragments corresponding to risk patterns. If an instance of a risk pattern is found in the cloud model, a potential data protection vulnerability is identified, which may be mitigated with appropriate changes of the deployment or by run-time adaptation.

Our previous work [17,26] evaluated the risk pattern approach using two example risk patterns. The evaluation showed that, if the relevant data protection vulnerabilities are captured in the form of risk patterns, then these risk patterns can indeed be used to detect and mitigate the data protection risks during deployment and at run time. The prerequisite is a catalog of risk patterns capturing the relevant data protection vulnerabilities. Our previous work did not address in detail how risk patterns can be devised, leaving several questions open:

- Is it feasible to model a broad range of real data protection vulnerabilities in the form of risk patterns?

- What is the typical size and structure of risk patterns? (This is important as it impacts the applicability of graph pattern matching algorithms in terms of their computational complexity (which in turn is not part of this paper))
- For which kinds of data protection vulnerabilities is the risk pattern approach appropriate?

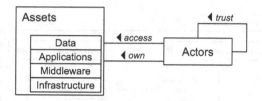

Fig. 1. Abstract view of the meta-model for cloud models [17]

This paper seeks to answer these questions by gaining experience with modeling risk patterns. Specifically, we review 87 papers from the cloud security literature (which were collected in a previous survey [3]) and identify the ones that describe relevant vulnerabilities in sufficient detail. Then, we devise risk patterns for the vulnerabilities described in these papers. This results in a total of 45 risk patterns.

Our findings show that most of the vulnerabilities that were described in sufficient detail in the respective papers could indeed be captured by appropriate risk patterns, thus demonstrating the general applicability of the risk pattern approach. All identified risk patterns share the same high-level structure and consist of 6 to 10 entities. This suggests that graph pattern matching can indeed be efficiently used to find risk patterns in cloud models. Also some limitations of the risk pattern approach are uncovered, relating to both the types of vulnerabilities that can be captured (e.g., vulnerabilities resulting from human and social aspects are not appropriate) and the underlying cloud meta-model (a very fine-grained meta-model can lead to a proliferation of many similar risk patterns to capture essentially the same vulnerability).

The remainder of this paper is organized as follows. In Sect. 2 we review the meta-model underlying the risk pattern approach. Section 3 then gives an overview of the methodology used to define the risk patterns and Sect. 4 presents the structure of risk patterns. In Sect. 5 we describe the risk patterns that we derived from the literature. Section 6 summarizes the lessons learned during the process, while Sect. 7 describes related work and Sect. 8 concludes the paper.

2   Cloud Meta-Model

In this section we briefly review the previously proposed meta-model [17]. The model of the cloud system, which plays a central role in the risk pattern approach, is an instance of this meta-model. Further, the risk patterns also reference entities, attributes, and relations from this meta-model.

The meta-model consists of the packages Actors and Assets (see Fig. 1). The Actors package defines the different data-specific roles (e.g., data subject, data controller) and cloud-specific roles (e.g., infrastructure provider) that a natural or legal person can have, and a trust relationship that can exist between different actors. An actor can also access and/or own assets, e.g. an actor can access a virtual machine.

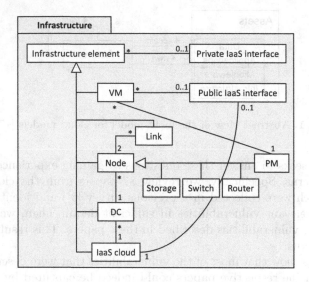

Fig. 2. Infrastructure sub-model of the meta-model for cloud models [17]

The Assets package is further divided into the sub-packages Data, Applications, Middleware and Infrastructure. The elements necessary to model the data that has to be protected are given by the data sub-package. The main element within this sub-package is the data object. Data can be stored in form of a stored data set or exchanged between different application components via a data flow element. The application sub-package comprises the elements needed to model software elements, like applications with different application components and connectors between them. Middleware elements, like web servers, application servers and database management systems are available in the middleware sub-package. The elements needed to model the infrastructure of a cloud system, like virtual machines (VMs), physical machines (PMs) and data centers (DCs) are given by the infrastructure sub-package. As an example, Fig. 2 shows the contents of the infrastructure sub-package. The full meta-model is shown in the Appendix.

3 Methodology

In this section we describe the methodology that we used to derive a catalog of risk patterns.

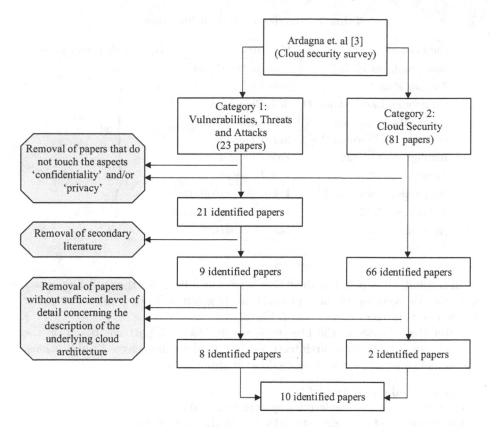

Fig. 3. Overview of the literature analysis

The starting point was a survey about cloud security [3]. From the categories defined in that survey paper, we focused on the categories 'vulnerabilities, threats and attacks' and 'cloud security', and analyzed all papers in those categories which mentioned the aspects *confidentiality* or *privacy*. In the publications of the first category, different attacks on cloud systems are described. Nearly all papers of this category (21 out of 23) touch the aspects confidentiality or privacy. Publications of the second category focus on security solutions and do not mention confidentiality or privacy to the extent the publications of the first category do (66 of 81 papers were considered relevant).

In the next step, we removed the secondary literature from the first category, leaving 9 out of 21 papers of this category. We analyzed all remaining papers for their level of detail concerning the description of an attack on or a vulnerability of a cloud system and the underlying cloud architecture. Only two papers of the category 'cloud security' described the underlying problem of the security solution in sufficient detail, so 64 papers were removed. In the category 'vulnerabilities, threats and attacks', 8 out of 9 papers were detailed enough.

Table 1. Overview of relevant literature

Publication	Category	No. of risk patterns
Somorovsky et al. [29]	Control Interfaces	12
Aviram et al. [4]	Side Channel	
Godfrey and Zulkernine [11]	Side Channel	
Green [12]	Side Channel	24
Okamura and Oyama [19]	Side Channel	
Ristenpart et al. [22]	Side Channel	
Zhang et al. [32]	Side Channel	
Rocha and Correia [23]	Privilege Exploitation	7
Sedayao et al. [27]	Privilege Exploitation	
Bernsmed et al. [5]	Service Mistrust	2

In the end, 10 papers remained that served as a basis for the modeling of risk patterns. An overview of these publications is given in Table 1 and an overview of the literature analysis is given in Fig. 3.

After the analysis of the literature, we derived risk patterns based on the relevant excerpts of cloud architectures described in the selected publications. The modeling of a risk pattern was done in three steps:

1. Analysis and description of the attack
2. Identification of the underlying system vulnerability
3. Identification of the relevant paths within the meta-model

After the analysis and description of the attack, the main goal was to identify the specific system vulnerability exploited by the attack. This includes the identification of elements of the meta-model suitable to model this vulnerability and in particular its attack point. After this, the sensitive data that should be protected are modeled and in the third step the relevant paths connecting the sensitive data with the attack point are identified.

4   Structure of Risk Patterns

A risk pattern is a sub-structure of a cloud system configuration, which threatens the protection of sensitive data and therefore has to be avoided [26]. A risk pattern can typically be divided into three parts (see Fig. 4):

- Part (a) represents the *personal data* that need to be protected. These data are always modeled by the same elements of the data package: a data record which is part of a stored data set, and an actor who is the data subject that the data belong to.

– Part (b) represents the *attack point* of the system vulnerability: the point of the configuration through which an attacker gets access to the system. This part of the risk pattern depends on the type of the modeled attack.

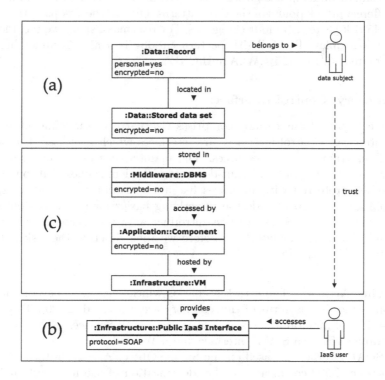

Fig. 4. An example risk pattern, structured into three parts

– Part (c) contains two *connections* between part (a) and part (b). One connection is between the sensitive data and the attack point, the other one between the actors. The possibilities for the first connection are determined by the underlying meta-model and depend on the 'distance' (within the meta-model) between parts (a) and (b). The second connection is always a mistrust relation between the data subject and the attacker. (Note: A dashed line implies that the according relation must not exist, whereas a solid line implies that the according relation must exist)

The attributes of the entities also play an important role. Sometimes vulnerabilities only differ in some attributes.

5   The Devised Risk Patterns

In this section we present how we modeled different types of vulnerabilities from the literature by different categories of risk patterns. The categorization is based on the different attack points of the risk patterns. Overall the risk pattern catalog includes 45 risk patterns in four categories. For reasons of space we include here only some examples. The full risk pattern catalog is available under https:// zenodo.org/record/1324125#.W2A2mrhCREY.

5.1   Category: Control Interfaces

The first category of our catalog comprises risk patterns modeling attacks on control interfaces. Control interfaces are interfaces which give users the opportunity of maintaining their resources. The maintenance of resources includes the instantiation, starting and shut-down of virtual machines. Although such interfaces are protected with measures like authorization and signatures, still vulnerabilities exist. To provide the underlying basics for the definition of the risk patterns of this category, we first introduce an attack scenario targeting a vulnerability of a control interface, before we then describe the risk patterns derived from this scenario.

Underlying Attacks. The attack scenarios which serve as a baseline for the definition of the risk patterns of this category are described in [29]. To provide the possibility of maintaining resources, Amazon Web Services (AWS) provides mainly two interfaces: a SOAP interface and a Web interface.

The SOAP interface is based on the Simple Object Access Protocol (SOAP) which uses an X.509 certificate for the identification of the user and an XML-based signature to enable authentication and prove the integrity of a message. Furthermore the SOAP messages themselves are based on XML. The authors of [29] proved that SOAP is vulnerable to so-called signature wrapping attacks. To perform a signature wrapping attack on SOAP, the attacker has to intercept a SOAP message exchanged between the user and the interface. Then the attacker can add an additional message body to the intercepted message and reuse the signature. This enables the attacker to perform arbitrary operations on the SOAP interface, because only the body referenced in the signature is verified for integrity, but the additional body is interpreted.

The Web interface enables an attacker to perform a so-called script injection attack on the cloud interface. As this attack is also founded in the underlying protocol (HTTP), the derived risk patterns are analogous to those of the aforementioned attack. Based on these attack scenarios, the usage of SOAP and HTTP can be considered as a data protection vulnerability of a cloud system and therefore is modeled as a risk pattern.

Risk Pattern Definition. The attack point of the risk patterns of this category is shown in Fig. 5 (Note: this is an excerpt of the corresponding risk pattern shown in Fig. 4). The interface is modeled as a 'Public IaaS Interface' entity from the Infrastructure package of the meta-model. The IaaS user accessing the interface may behave as the attacker of the attack scenario described above, thus gaining unauthorized access to sensitive data. The protocol of the interface can be identified by the attribute 'protocol', which is 'SOAP' in Fig. 5.

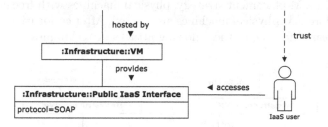

Fig. 5. Excerpt of a risk pattern of the category 'control interfaces'

The meta-model allows multiple possibilities for connecting the 'Public IaaS Interface' of Fig. 5 with the sensitive 'Data Record', i.e., multiple possibilities for the attacker to actually access sensitive data, depending on the specific cloud configuration. The risk pattern shown previously in Fig. 4 is one possibility, in which the access takes place through a chain of a virtual machine (VM), an application component, and a database management system (DBMS). The meta-model allows five further possibilities, described by the following chains of assets:

- VM → application component → local database
- VM → application server → application component → local database
- VM → DBMS
- VM → application server → DBMS
- VM → application server → application component → DBMS

These risk patterns capture different cloud configurations that exhibit a similar data protection vulnerability.

5.2 Category: Side Channels

The second category of our catalog includes risk patterns modeling side channel attacks. Side channels are based on a shared resource (e.g. CPU cache) which enables data leakage or is misused for communication between two virtual machines that are co-located on the same physical machine but belong to different users.

Underlying Attacks. Side channels can have two consequences: they can be misused for communication between otherwise isolated VMs [19,22] or for data leak [11,12,22,32]. Side channels always rely on multi-tenancy, which means that a physical machine is shared among different users.

How such co-location can be accomplished in Amazon EC2 is described in [22]. An attacker can instantiate lots of VMs of the same instance type and inside the same availability zone as the victim's VM. Doing this, there is a high probability that one of the instantiated VMs is on the same physical machine as the victim's one. The probability can even be increased if the instantiation process is launched right after the victim's instance is re-instantiated, because following Amazon EC2's VM placement strategy, physical machines with free capacity are filled first before new physical machines are started. After co-location is achieved, the way is cleared for one of the following attacks or techniques.

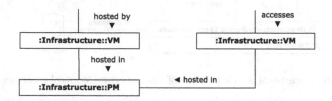

Fig. 6. Excerpt of an abstract risk pattern of the category 'side channels'

In [19] a technique called CCCV for the use of the CPU load as a side channel is described. The technique is possible if virtual CPUs (VCPUs) of different VMs share the same physical CPU. Assuming a spyware was injected into the victim's VM, the CPU load can be manipulated, so that data can be transfered adhering to the protocol described in [19]. This protocol is based on the fact that a high CPU load of one VM affects the performance of co-located VMs, and can thus be observed by them. A different attack where CPU load is misused as a side channel for communication is also described in [22].

The Prime+Trigger+Probe (PTP) technique uses a shared cache as side channel [11, 22]. As its name implies, PTP comprises three phases. Within the 'prime' phase, the attacker fills all lines of the shared cache and measures the time needed to read each of these lines. In the following 'trigger' phase, the attacker hands over the control of the shared cache to the victim's VM. The victim's VM then may change some lines of the cache and hand over control back to the attacker's VM. The change of cache lines results in cache misses when the attacker probes the cache during the 'probe' phase. This technique can be used to communicate between the two VMs [22] when a change of the cache is interpreted as the sending of a '1' and no change of the cache is interpreted as a '0'. Furthermore, this technique can be used to extract sensitive data such as private keys [12], because the attacker can possibly determine which operations were carried out by the victim's VM based on the changes of the access times of different cache lines and also based on which cache lines have been changed. A slightly different technique is described in [32] and a scenario stating possible consequences of such an attack is described in [4].

Risk Pattern Definition. As side-channel attacks always rely on a shared resource used by two co-located VMs and only differ in the type of resource used and in nuances of hardware settings, we introduced *abstract risk patterns* which can be made concrete through attributes of the concerned elements depending on the specific vulnerability that should be exploited. The attack point of the abstract risk patterns (and therefore also of all concrete risk patterns of this category) comprises two VMs being hosted on the same physical machine (see Fig. 6). The actor accessing one of the VMs (and thus serving as attacker) is not trusted by the data subject. Attributes used to concretize abstract risk patterns include 'hypervisor' to specify a certain hypervisor and 'cpu-scheduling' to specify a certain kind of CPU scheduler.

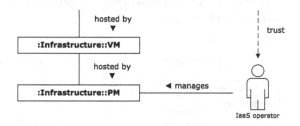

Fig. 7. Excerpt of a risk pattern of the category 'privilege exploitation'

5.3 Category: Privilege Exploitation

The third category of our catalog comprises risk patterns modeling privilege exploitation attacks. In privilege exploitation attacks, an administrator abuses their privileges to get access to sensitive data [23,27].

Underlying Attacks. Administrators of cloud systems normally have no rights to log on to client VMs. However, an administrator with root privileges can generate memory dumps of client VMs for troubleshooting. The administrator can also misuse this opportunity to extract private data (e.g., cryptographic keys) from such memory dumps [23]. Although data might be stored encrypted on permanent storage, the administrator can get access to the cleartext if the memory dump is generated at the right moment (i.e. when data are decrypted for processing). Because private keys are often stored as ASN.1-objects, an attacker just needs to search for typical byte sequences of ASN.1-objects within the memory dump. This attack becomes more difficult if secure hardware is used that prevents the memory from being dumped. In this case, an attacker may trigger a VM relocation first, and perform the attack when the VM is relocated on a physical machine which is not using this kind of hardware. A similar kind of attack is also possible on storage devices [27].

Risk Pattern Definition. The attack point of the risk patterns of this category is shown in Fig. 7. As all attacks of this category are based on an administrator abusing their privileges to access sensitive data, this situation is modeled in the risk patterns of this category. More specifically, an untrusted IaaS operator managing the physical machine on which the VM with the personal data of the data subject is hosted is accessing these data.

5.4 Category: Service Mistrust

The fourth category of our catalog comprises risk patters modeling the problem of mistrust within service compositions. Because service compositions consist of different services which are composed in a hierarchical fashion and belong to different providers, a data subject may not trust – and may not even know – some of the involved providers. An untrusted provider getting access to sensitive data constitutes a data protection risk.

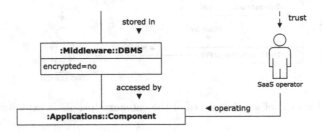

Fig. 8. Excerpt of a risk pattern of the category 'service mistrust'

Underlying Attacks. Bernsmed et al. [5] consider a scenario where a service provider might access personal data processed by its service. In service compositions, the situation of trust becomes more complex. Although there may be a chain-of-trust between the participating providers of a service compositions, a data subject whose data is processed by the composed service, does not necessarily trust all of the involved providers. The situation becomes even worse if the data subject does not even have knowledge about the participating providers. Therefore this situation is a data protection vulnerability and can be modeled as a risk pattern.

Risk Pattern Definition. The attack point of the risk patterns of this category is shown in Fig. 8. The situation is modeled by a SaaS (Software as a Service) operator that is responsible for the operation of an application component – which represents a service in a possibly larger composition of services – and therefore can access sensitive data processed by this application component.

6 Lessons Learned

Through the modeling of real data protection vulnerabilities in the form of risk patterns, we have gained insight into both the applicability of the risk pattern approach and the characteristics of typical risk patterns.

6.1 Applicability of the Risk Pattern Approach

Since we managed to represent several real data protection vulnerabilities in a natural way in the form of risk patterns, we can state that *the risk pattern approach is appropriate for modeling data protection vulnerabilities*. In particular, quite complex attack scenarios spanning multiple cloud layers could be modeled, and also very different kinds of attacks.

That said, it is important to note that the attacks described in several papers could not be reasonably modeled in the form of risk patterns. In some cases, this was due to a lack of detail about the vulnerabilities in the respective papers (cf. Fig. 3), because those papers focused primarily on describing data protection techniques against some classes of attacks, rather than describing specific vulnerabilities in detail. However, there were also cases where the non-applicability of the risk pattern approach had other reasons, and these reasons shed some light on the limits of the applicability of the approach:

- Some vulnerabilities are not technical, but stem from human or organizational factors, e.g., lack of security training for personnel (e.g. the vulnerability described in [7] lies is the careless behaviour of users not cleaning their Amazone Machines Images of passwords before making them available for others). In contrast, risk patterns are appropriate for capturing forbidden socio-technical configurations that are at least partly *technical* in the way they expose data.
- Several papers focus on attacks and not on vulnerabilities, e.g., describing several ways an attacker could exploit some basic vulnerability. Risk patterns are not meant to capture specific attacks, but rather configurations that lead to high *risks* of successful attacks (therefore the risk patterns stemming from different side-channel attacks (cf. Sect. 5.2) only slightly differ.). Thus, the use of risk patterns is more proactive than, for instance, intrusion detection techniques [28].
- Several papers focus on system vulnerabilities which do not necessarily imply data breach (e.g. attacks compromising the availability of resources, cf. [6,13]). Although risk patterns could in principle also be used to model such system vulnerabilities, our focus was on *data protection* vulnerabilities, thus rendering some attacks irrelevant.
- Some papers describe vulnerabilities that are not cloud-related. While risk patterns could in principle also be used in other contexts, the currently used meta-model is *cloud-specific*, hence we only considered cloud-related vulnerabilities. However, we decided to differentiate between cloud-related side-channel attacks and the more general virtual machine escape (cf. [21]). The latter was not cloud-related for us and therefore excluded.
- Some papers describe unlikely attacks, i.e., attacks that work only under strong assumptions about the possibilities of the attacker. Risk patterns are supposed to be created in the course of risk assessment, covering the configurations that are considered to be *too risky* – not necessarily all configurations that might allow some attack under unlikely conditions. This also applies to some of the configurations we modeled in this paper.

The applicability of the approach is also strongly related to how cloud configurations can be modeled by using the types from the meta-model described in [17]. The experience with using the meta-model has shown that it is indeed a solid basis for modeling complex cloud configurations. In particular, the possibility of the meta-model to combine different hardware and software entities, data, and actors in a single model has proven invaluable, since all risk patterns span several of these categories. Some small extensions to the meta-model were also necessary, e.g., some new attributes and relationships between certain assets and actors had to be introduced (e.g. to model the direct access of an IaaS user to a virtual machine or a DBMS running directly on a virtual machine). This is normal; project-specific tailoring of the meta-model was also envisaged in [17].

6.2 Characteristics of Risk Patterns

As shown in Sect. 4, risk patterns have a common structure. All risk patterns that we devised follow this same structure. From a graph-theoretic point of view, a risk pattern defines a path from an attacker to the sensitive data (the path through which the attacker may be able to access the data), plus an additional path between the same two vertices encoding that the data belong to a data subject who does not trust the attacker. This means that instead of a general graph pattern matching problem as suggested in [26], only subgraphs of very limited structure (cycle graphs) must be searched for in the cloud model, which may require significantly less computation.

For assessing the computational implications, it is also an important finding that the risk patterns are quite small: all the devised risk patterns consist of 6 to 10 entities, with exactly two connections per entity.

Another aspect is the number of risk patterns. In particular, a single system vulnerability leads to multiple risk patterns: if an asset is compromised from which there are k different kinds of paths to the sensitive data, then potentially k risk patterns are needed to capture all possible data protection vulnerabilities stemming from the same system vulnerability (and it is possible to use different data protection mechanisms to protect each of those paths). It is important to note that the number k of different kinds of paths from an asset to the data depends on the meta-model and especially the possible connections between the different entities of it. With the meta-model used in this work, $k \leq 6$. Moreover, for some system vulnerabilities, indeed 6 different risk patterns were needed; for some other system vulnerabilities, a lower number of risk patterns was sufficient. If the meta-model were refined with further types and relationships, this could lead to higher values of k and thus to a proliferation of similar risk patterns (i.e. they only differ in the possible paths between the compromised asset and the sensitive data). Therefore, the level of detail of the meta-model constitutes an important trade-off between the accuracy of modeling cloud configurations and the effort for modeling the risk patterns.

7   Related Work

We discuss the work most relevant to ours along two aspects: (1) data protection risks of cloud services and (2) model-based approaches for cloud security and privacy.

7.1   Data Protection Risks of Cloud Services

Risk management covers the process of describing, detecting and mitigating risks. So far, only few frameworks for risk management of services have been presented [18].

Djemame et al. [8] propose a risk assessment framework for cloud computing which is designed to help cloud users and cloud providers assess risks during service deployment and operation. This approach focuses on the relationship between service providers and services. However, they do not state how risks may be monitored during operations. This is where risk patterns can help by specifying what cloud configurations to look for during operations to determine risky situations.

Meszaros and Buchalcevova [18] present a framework for online service risk management. They consider similar assets to ours and present a risk and threat model as basis. They focus on risk assessment and mitigation and propose techniques for risk monitoring. Our approach can be considered complementary to their work as our risk patterns capture specific configurations of cloud services and systems that would lead to high data protection risks.

Several authors have analyzed specific data protection risks in the context of cloud computing and services. Paquette et al. [20] analyzed the risks of cloud computing, focusing on the context of governmental use of cloud computing. Fernandes et al. [10] surveyed security issues in cloud computing as a potential source for data protection risks. These insights provide an important source of input for our approach as they help defining and specifying risk patterns by taking important data protection concerns into account. Our approach can be seen as a vehicle for capturing and utilizing this kind of knowledge.

7.2   Model-Based Approaches for Cloud Security and Privacy

Apvrille and Roudier introduced Attack Graphs based on the SysML-Sec framework [2]. Similar to risk patterns, also attack graphs are visual representations of security threats. However, attack graphs are used to model malicious attacks on – especially embedded – systems, whereas risk patterns encode cloud configurations that can potentially lead to data protection issues. That is, an attack graph models all the details of an attack, including the tools used and activities performed by an attacker, whereas a risk pattern models only the cloud configuration that could potentially be exploited, thereby enabling more general preventive measures. Attack graphs were applied to model a single attack, whereas we compiled a catalog of 45 risk patterns.

Watson and Little [31] introduced an approach to reason about the deployment of a distributed system and its impact on security. They state that not all deployment problems can be solved during design time, so run-time reasoning is needed. In contrast to our risk patterns, their approach requires the assignment of security levels to all assets, which can be difficult in some settings. In fact, risk patterns could help here: the number of risk patterns in which a given asset type appears may be used as an indication of the security requirements of that asset. Beyond the types of entities considered in that paper, we also explicitly consider actors. As shown in our paper, actors are important for accurately determining data protection concerns.

Similarly to our approach, the work of Schmieders et al. also applied model-based adaptive methods to data protection in the cloud [24,25]. That work, however, is limited to one specific type of privacy goals: geo-location constraints. Our work, in contrast, addresses data protection goals in a much broader sense.

Kritikos and Massonet proposed a domain-specific modeling language for modeling security aspects in cloud computing [14]. This includes security controls, security properties, security metrics, and security capabilities. In contrast, our work focuses on modeling the typical assets of cloud systems and their relationships, which are the possible attack surfaces and make up the configurations that may lead to data protection violations.

8   Conclusions and Future Work

In this paper, a catalog of risk patterns was elaborated on the basis of vulnerabilities described in the literature. The results demonstrate that our previously proposed risk pattern approach [26] in combination with the meta-model described in [17] is capable of modeling typical data protection vulnerabilities. The present work also sheds light on the limits of the applicability of the risk pattern approach and the typical characteristics of risk patterns.

Several directions for future work remain. First, the syntax and semantics of the *language* of risk patterns should be defined formally. The catalog of risk patterns elaborated in this work is an important input for the formal definition of the language, as it shows the different constructs that must be supported. Second, the *process* of devising risk patterns should be formalized based on the experience reported here, and then validated by using it to create further risk patterns. Third, an efficient *algorithm* should be devised and implemented to search for risk patterns in the cloud model, using the gained insights about the structure and size of risk patterns. Fourth, it should be investigated how the expressive power of the language could be increased by introducing *wildcards* or other mechanisms to compactly represent families of related risk patterns.

Acknowledgments. This work was partially supported by the European Union's Horizon 2020 research and innovation programme under grant 731678 (RestAssured).

A   Appendix

The following picture shows the underlying meta-model (without the packages 'Goals & Metrics' and 'Mechanisms'):

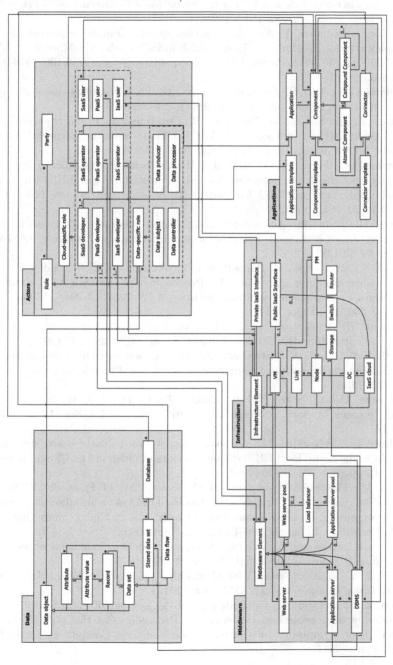

References

1. Ahvar, E., Ahvar, S., Mann, Z.Á., Crespi, N., Garcia-Alfaro, J., Glitho, R.: CACEV: a cost and carbon emission-efficient virtual machine placement method for green distributed clouds. In: IEEE International Conference on Services Computing (SCC), pp. 275–282. IEEE (2016)
2. Apvrille, L., Roudier, Y.: SysML-sec attack graphs: compact representations for complex attacks. In: Mauw, S., Kordy, B., Jajodia, S. (eds.) GraMSec 2015. LNCS, vol. 9390, pp. 35–49. Springer, Cham (2016). https://doi.org/10.1007/978-3-319-29968-6_3
3. Ardagna, C.A., Asal, R., Damiani, E., Vu, Q.H.: From security to assurance in the cloud: a survey. ACM Comput. Surv. 48(1), 2:1–2:50 (2015)
4. Aviram, A., Hu, S., Ford, B., Gummadi, R.: Determinating timing channels in compute clouds. In: Proceedings of the 2nd ACM Cloud Computing Security Workshop, CCSW 2010, Chicago, IL, USA, pp. 103–108, 8 Oct 2010
5. Bernsmed, K., Jaatun, M.G., Meland, P.H., Undheim, A.: Thunder in the clouds: security challenges and solutions for federated clouds. In: IEEE 4th International Conference on Cloud Computing Technology and Science (CloudCom), pp. 113–120. IEEE (2012)
6. Booth, G., Soknacki, A., Somayaji, A.: Cloud security: attacks and current defenses. In: 8th Annual Symposium on Information Assurance (ASIA'13), pp. 56–62 (2013)
7. Bugiel, S., Nürnberger, S., Pöppelmann, T., Sadeghi, A.R., Schneider, T.: Amazonia: when elasticity snaps back. In: Proceedings of the 18th ACM Conference on Computer and Communications Security, CCS 2011, Chicago, Illinois, USA, pp. 389–400, 17–21 Oct 2011
8. Djemame, K., Armstrong, D., Guitart, J., Macias, M.: A risk assessment framework for cloud computing. IEEE Trans. Cloud Comput. 4(3), 265–278 (2016)
9. Elrotub, M., Gherbi, A.: Virtual machine classification-based approach to enhanced workload balancing for cloud computing applications. Procedia Comput. Sci. 130, 683–688 (2018)
10. Fernandes, D.A.B., Soares, L.F.B., Gomes, J.V.P., Freire, M.M., Inácio, P.R.M.: Security issues in cloud environments: a survey. Int. J. Inf. Sec. 13(2), 113–170 (2014)
11. Godfrey, M., Zulkernine, M.: A server-side solution to cache-based side-channel attacks in the cloud. In: IEEE Sixth International Conference on Cloud Computing (Cloud), pp. 163–170. IEEE (2013)
12. Green, M.: The threat in the cloud. IEEE Secur. Priv. 11(1), 86–89 (2013)
13. Jensen, M., Schwenk, J., Gruschka, N., Iacono, L.L.: On technical security issues in cloud computing. In: IEEE International Conference on Cloud Computing, Cloud 2009, Bangalore, India, pp. 109–116, 21–25 Sept 2009
14. Kritikos, K., Massonet, P.: An integrated meta-model for cloud application security modelling. Procedia Comput. Sci. 97, 84–93 (2016)
15. Mann, Z.Á.: Multicore-aware virtual machine placement in cloud data centers. IEEE Trans. Comput. 65(11), 3357–3369 (2016)
16. Mann, Z.A., Metzger, A.: Optimized cloud deployment of multi-tenant software considering data protection concerns. In: Proceedings of the 17th IEEE/ACM International Symposium on Cluster, Cloud and Grid Computing, pp. 609–618. IEEE Press (2017)

17. Mann, Z.A., Metzger, A., Schoenen, S.: Towards a run-time model for data protection in the cloud. In: Modellierung 2018, pp. 71–86. Gesellschaft für Informatik e.V. (2018)
18. Meszaros, J., Buchalcevova, A.: Introducing OSSF: a framework for online service cybersecurity risk management. Comput. Secur. **65**, 300–313 (2017)
19. Okamura, K., Oyama, Y.: Load-based covert channels between Xen virtual machines. In: Proceedings of the 2010 ACM Symposium on Applied Computing, pp. 173–180. ACM (2010)
20. Paquette, S., Jaeger, P.T., Wilson, S.C.: Identifying the security risks associated with governmental use of cloud computing. Gov. Inf. Q. **27**(3), 245–253 (2010)
21. Pearce, M., Zeadally, S., Hunt, R.: Virtualization: issues, security threats, and solutions. ACM Comput. Surv. (CSUR) **45**(2), 17 (2013)
22. Ristenpart, T., Tromer, E., Shacham, H., Savage, S.: Hey, you, get off of my cloud: exploring information leakage in third-party compute clouds. In: Proceedings of the 16th ACM Conference on Computer and Communications Security, pp. 199–212. ACM (2009)
23. Rocha, F., Correia, M.: Lucy in the sky without diamonds: stealing confidential data in the cloud. In: IEEE/IFIP 41st International Conference on Dependable Systems and Networks Workshops (DSN-W), pp. 129–134. IEEE (2011)
24. Schmieders, E., Metzger, A., Pohl, K.: Architectural runtime models for privacy checks of cloud applications. In: Proceedings of the Seventh International Workshop on Principles of Engineering Service-Oriented and Cloud Systems, pp. 17–23 (2015)
25. Schmieders, E., Metzger, A., Pohl, K.: Runtime model-based privacy checks of big data cloud services. In: International Conference on Service-Oriented Computing, pp. 71–86 (2015)
26. Schoenen, S., Mann, Z.Á., Metzger, A.: Using risk patterns to identify violations of data protection policies in cloud systems. In: 13th International Workshop on Engineering Service-Oriented Applications and Cloud Services (WESOACS) (2017)
27. Sedayao, J., Su, S., Ma, X., Jiang, M., Miao, K.: A simple technique for securing data at rest stored in a computing cloud. In: Jaatun, M.G., Zhao, G., Rong, C. (eds.) CloudCom 2009. LNCS, vol. 5931, pp. 553–558. Springer, Heidelberg (2009). https://doi.org/10.1007/978-3-642-10665-1_51
28. Shameli-Sendi, A., Cheriet, M., Hamou-Lhadj, A.: Taxonomy of intrusion risk assessment and response system. Comput. Secur. **45**, 1–16 (2014)
29. Somorovsky, J., Heiderich, M., Jensen, M., Schwenk, J., Gruschka, N., Iacono, L.L.: All your clouds are belong to us: security analysis of cloud management interfaces. In: Proceedings of the 3rd ACM Cloud Computing Security Workshop (CCSW 2011), pp. 3–14 (2011)
30. Toeroe, M., Pawar, N., Khendek, F.: Managing application level elasticity and availability. In: 10th International Conference on Network and Service Management, pp. 348–351 (2014)
31. Watson, P., Little, M.: Multi-level security for deploying distributed applications on clouds, devices and things. In: IEEE 6th International Conference on Cloud Computing Technology and Science, pp. 380–385 (2014)
32. Zhang, Y., Juels, A., Reiter, M.K., Ristenpart, T.: Cross-VM side channels and their use to extract private keys. In: Proceedings of the 2012 ACM Conference on Computer and Communications Security, pp. 305–316. ACM (2012)

Scheduling Architectures for Scientific Workflows in the Cloud

Johannes Erbel[✉], Fabian Korte, and Jens Grabowski

University of Goettingen, Institute of Computer Science, Goettingen, Germany
{johannes.erbel,fkorte,grabowski}@cs.uni-goettingen.de

Abstract. Scientific workflows describe a sequence of tasks that together form a scientific experiment. When workflows are computation or data intensive, distributed systems are used. Especially, cloud computing has gained a lot of attention due to its flexible and scalable nature. However, most approaches set up a preconfigured computation clusters or schedule tasks to existing resources. In this paper, we propose the utilization of cloud runtime models and couple them with scientific workflows to create the required architecture of a workflow task at runtime. Hereby, we schedule the architecture state required by a workflow task in order to reduce the overall amount of data transfer and resources needed. Thus, we present an approach that does not schedule tasks to be executed on resources, but schedule architectures to be deployed at runtime for the execution of workflows.

Keywords: Workflow · Models at runtime · Cloud computing · OCCI

1 Introduction

For an easy and repeatable execution of experiments, scientists utilize workflows to model their experiments as a sequence of data processing tasks [3]. Hereby, the individual tasks are commonly scheduled for execution on a cluster of preconfigured computing resources which are for example provided by a cloud service. Cloud computing however, allows to provision compute, storage, and network resources on demand [9]. Combined, these resources serve as infrastructure for arbitrary applications to be deployed. Thus, cloud computing allows to dynamically deploy individual architectures for workflow tasks requiring specific application and infrastructure configurations. Meanwhile, a few workflow languages exist that annotate workflow models with architectural requirements. Even though some approaches dynamically deploy these required architectures at runtime [15], no runtime reflection is provided. Therefore, it is difficult to make use of runtime information and tune the workflow accordingly.

In this paper, we propose an approach that combines the benefits of design time and runtime models to dynamically schedule architectures in the cloud for

We thank the Simulationswissenschaftliches Zentrum Clausthal-Goettingen (SWZ) for financial support.

F. Khendek and R. Gotzhein (Eds.): SAM 2018, LNCS 11150, pp. 20–28, 2018.
https://doi.org/10.1007/978-3-030-01042-3_2

the execution of workflows. While, the design time model describes the order of workflow tasks and their architectural requirements, the runtime model reflects the state of the workflow and the running architecture. Based on these models, we propose a simulation procedure to derive optimized cloud architectures for successive tasks to reduce the amount of resources and data that has to be transferred.

The remainder of this paper is structured as follows. Section 2 provides an overview of basic concepts and related work. Section 3 summarizes problems to be solved in order to dynamically schedule cloud architectures for workflows. Section 4 presents the proposed approach and its different components, whereby the current state of the implementation is discussed in Sect. 5. Finally, Sect. 6 provides a summary and outlook into future work.

2 Background and Related Work

Workflows are typically expressed as *Directed Acyclic Graph* (DAG) or as *Directed Acyclic Graph* (DCG), if loops are supported [3]. Hereby, nodes represent tasks, whereas links describe either a control or dataflow between them. As workflows can be compute and data intensive, distributed architectures like grids and clouds are commonly utilized by workflow systems like Pegasus [4] and Taverna [17]. Hereby, the dynamic capabilities of such systems are often not utilized as tasks are scheduled on a preconfigured cluster of computing resources. However, cloud computing is a service that allows to rent virtualized resources on demand [9]. To provide a uniform access to such a service standards like the *Open Cloud Computing Interface* (OCCI) [12] and the *Topology and Orchestration Specification for Cloud Applications* (TOSCA) [11] emerged for which corresponding metamodels have been developed [10,11]. This trend led to models at runtime approaches [5,6] which deploy a modeled architecture and keep it in sync with the cloud.

Recent approaches make use of these matured cloud orchestration techniques to directly couple cloud architectures with workflow tasks. Qasha et al. [15] extend the TOSCA standard to support workflows. Hereby, they couple tasks to cloud resources and ensure the workflows reproducibility by using containers. Even though, they deploy the containers at runtime their approach is not model-driven and only considers a design time representation. Another approach by Beni et al. [2] presents a middleware which monitors the running workflow over metamodel reflections. In addition to the generation of a workflow deployment plan, they gather runtime information to optimize the infrastructure for the workflow for future executions. However, their reflection of a running workflow does not conform to any cloud standard. Furthermore, it only considers the running cloud infrastructure and does not reflect deployed components and applications. Finally, Flowbster a workflow system presented by Kacsuk et al. [7], deploys scaling architectures for the execution of workflows. Nonetheless, the approach is not model-driven, does not conform to any cloud standard, and directly deploys the architecture for the whole workflow.

3   Problem Statement

The related work shows that there is a need for architecture aware workflows. However, most approaches only consider design time representations. Thus, the runtime state of a workflow and its underlying architecture can not be reflected preventing its architecture awareness. Furthermore, there is no process that merges cloud architectures taking the requirements of parallel executing and successive tasks into account. Therefore, current approaches require an explicit modelling of how a workflow is executed on an infrastructure making a modular design impossible. Finally, it has to be calculated when the deployment process for a task's architecture has to be triggered. However, no approach exists that combines the execution time of a task with the time needed to reconfigure a cloud architecture. Summed up, we identified the following problems:

- **P1:** Only design time models are used to execute workflows in the cloud.
- **P2:** Approaches are needed to merge cloud architectures for workflow tasks.
- **P3:** There is no connection between task execution and deployment times.

4   Approach

To ensure the reproducibility of the workflow while managing its underlying architecture at runtime, a design time as well as a runtime model is required. While the design time model provides a static representation of the workflow and its required architecture, as depicted in Fig. 1, the runtime model is used to reflect the actual state of the workflow and the cloud. Based on the design time information, the architecture scheduler assembles cloud architecture models required in different time steps by the workflow and checks their viability over a simulation approach. These models are then passed to a models at runtime engine which synchronizes the described architecture with the cloud. As soon as the architecture for a task is available the corresponding task is executed. Thus, the architecture serves as extra dependency for the task execution in addition to the input data. To loosely couple the architecture scheduler with the task execution engine, their communication is handled only over the runtime model. In the following the workflow runtime model and architecture scheduler concept are presented in more detail.

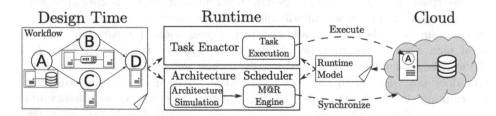

Fig. 1. Components to schedule architectures for workflow tasks

4.1   Workflow Runtime Model

To schedule cloud architectures for workflows, we propose the utilization of a
design time as well as a runtime model. While the design time model is capable of storing all the information about the workflow and its architecture, the
runtime model is used to reflect the actual state of the cloud and the workflow.
To represent both views, we utilize OCCI, a cloud standard by the *Open Grid
Forum* (OGF), which defines a uniform interface to manage cloud resources.
OCCI defines an extensible datamodel for which Merle et al. [10] created a
metamodel that got further enhanced in [18]. In addition to a classification and
identification mechanism, OCCI defines three core base types: `Entity`, `Resource`,
and `Link`, shown in Fig. 2. These core base types can be specialized to create
new types which in general form OCCI extensions. Additionally, OCCI *Mixins*
can be part of an extension which allow to dynamically add capabilities to specialized core types at runtime. In order to describe a task's cloud architecture
the infrastructure [13], platform [14], and placement extension [8] can be used.
These extensions define elements to describe how an `Application` consisting of
multiple `Components` is deployed on a set of *Virtual Machines* (VMs) and how
these machines are interconnected. On top of these extensions, we propose the
extension shown in Fig. 2. This extension allows to model workflows running on
top of architectures modeled with OCCI. Thus, already existing OCCI models
can be used as underlying architecture for a sequence of tasks to be executed,
as well as other extensions defined for OCCI.

The `Task` element represents a single workflow task and inherits from the
`Resource` type. This element gives information about a task's current state
and provides actions to start and stop its execution. Each `Task` is linked over
an `ExecutionLink` to an executable `Component` which may be part of a larger
`Application`. Hereby, the execution of the `Task` itself is triggered over the start
action every `Component` has to implement besides other lifecycle operations. As

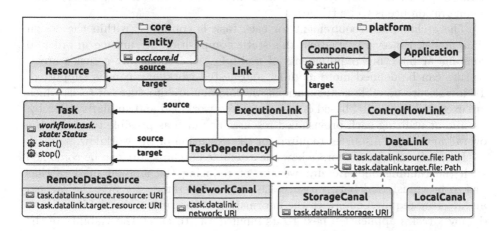

Fig. 2. OCCI workflow extension

the task execution order is predetermined, each `Task` can be directly reflected in the runtime model, whereas the architecture lying beneath the `Component` to be executed can be created at runtime. Thus, a loose coupling between the architecture and the workflow is provided. Additionally, this allows to update a workflow during its execution by adapting the task sequence or architecture requirements in the design time model. As a consequence, only the task sequence in the runtime model has to be updated as a task's architecture is extracted from the design time model shortly before it's execution.

To model a sequence of tasks, each `Task` can be linked over a `TaskDependency` to its successor. While `ControlflowLinks` only represent a simple control flow, `DataLinks` describe a control and dataflow. Because of that, a `DataLink` stores information about the source and target location of a file to be transferred which represents the in and output data of a `Task`. In addition to the workflow entities, we define three canal Mixins, a `NetworkCanal`, a `StorageCanal`, a `LocalCanal`. Using these, we can specify what kind of communication canal is used to transfer the data between two tasks. For example, the flow of data between two VMs using a network (`NetworkCanal`) or a storage (`StorageCanal`) or the flow of data within a VM (`LocalCanal`). Additionally, we specify the `RemoteDataSource` Mixin which is attached to a `DataLink` if the data is not directly located on the device hosting the executable `Component`.

4.2   Architecture Scheduler

The goal of the architecture scheduler is to compose an architecture model fitting the runtime needs of the workflow. The resulting model is then deployed over a models at runtime engine which compares the runtime state of the cloud to the desired state and performs required requests accordingly. To assemble such cloud architectures for different points in time, several questions need to be answered: *What* is required by the current and following tasks? *Where* can a task's application be deployed most efficiently? *When* does the new architecture configuration needs to be triggered?

The architecture requirement for each task is contained within the design time model. However, we adjust this static composition at runtime in order to combine architecture requirements of multiple tasks. This way a task's architecture can be defined more modular and nested workflows can be supported. To investigate possible configurations, we combine architectures of tasks which are executed in parallel based on their required workload and similarity. Hereby, we aim at utilizing each provisioned resource as much as possible to reduce the overall amount of resources required for the execution of the workflow.

In a next step, we elaborate how the assembled architecture can be combined with the running one. Hereby, we aim at reducing the amount of data that has to be transferred between successive tasks. Therefore, we fuse the merged architecture requirements with the information of the runtime model in order to deploy a task's application next to its input data. To check the viability of the resulting architecture model we perform a simulation which allows to evaluate performance metrics without an actual deployment.

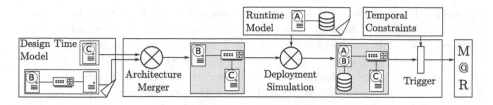

Fig. 3. Architecture Scheduler Example

To trigger the deployment of a new configuration, the task's execution time and the time to deploy the configuration is required. Therefore, we can estimate a task's execution time, e.g., based on the amount of input data [16]. Additionally, we can profile the required provisioning or deployment time of each element in a workflow's architecture. For example, we observe how long it takes to provision a VM, and the time to deploy an application on top of it. Using this information, we then estimate how long the execution of a complete deployment plan takes. Combined with the task's execution time we can then calculate when to deploy the new architecture or adapt the existing one.

An example of the described process is shown in Fig. 3. Here, task A is currently running, whereas B, C are followup tasks. Based on the architecture requirements of B and C, the scheduler assembles a suitable architecture for the following step. For example, the second virtual machine of task B is merged with the one of task C, as we historically recorded a low workload for both. Next the architecture proposal is simulated in the runtime environment context. Assume, task A and B both require a similar component and the data produced by A is required by B and stored locally. Thus, we reuse the machine that executed task A for B as no machine has to be started and no data has to be transferred. Finally, the reconfiguration process is triggered based on the estimated deployment time and the time for task A to be finished. In a next step, when A is finished, the storage and components not required anymore are deleted by removing them from the runtime model.

5   Current Status

As the proposed approach is work in progress, we discuss how the issues described in Sect. 3 are tackled. Therefore, we explain how the proposed approach is going to be implemented and validated.

P1: *Only design time models are used to execute workflows in the cloud.* To provide a runtime representation of a workflow, we propose an OCCI extension which allows to manage and reflect the workflow execution and the architecture over a standardized interface. To implement the proposed OCCI extension, we use the OCCIware tool chain [18]. This tool chain provides a graphical and textual editor to design OCCI extensions. Furthermore, it allows to automatically generate an implementation for an OCCI interface supporting the designed extension. Then we deploy the interface implementation of the workflow extension on an OCCIware runtime server which also supports the infrastructure [13], platform [14], and placement extension [8]. This runtime server is directly connected to the cloud system on which the workflow is executed and the task specific architectures are deployed. Hereby, the server directly maintains an OCCI runtime model reflecting the state of the workflow and the cloud. To proof the concept of the workflow extension, we are going to develop a set of compute and data intensive workflows. Moreover, these workflows will be designed in such a manner that they require a sequence of complex infrastructure and application configurations for their execution. Finally, we plan to test the execution of these workflows on a private cloud using a prototypical implementation of the proposed approach.

P2: *Approaches are needed to merge cloud architectures for workflow tasks.* To lower the workflow execution time, we strive to reuse parts of a running architecture to reduce the amount of resources and the amount of data that has to be transferred. First, we identify resources that have enough capacity to handle components of parallel executing tasks. For this purpose, we are going to investigate suitable scheduling approaches to assign tasks to resources. It should be noted that software configurations of different applications may interfere with each other. Thus, every application has to be completely separated from each other. Therefor, either containerized virtualization or separated runtime environments can be used. Secondly, we fuse the resulting architecture with the runtime model to place a component next to its data. Finally, we validate the resulting configuration by deriving performance measurements using the OCCI simulation extension [1]. To actually deploy the simulated model, we utilize the OCCI compliant models at runtime engine presented in a former work [5]. To investigate the benefits and drawbacks of combining architectures of successive and parallel tasks, we plan to execute workflows with and without the proposed merging approach. Hereby, we will measure and compare the execution time required by each workflow, as well as the amount of provisioned resources and data that had to be transferred.

P3: *There is no connection between task execution and deployment times.* To reduce the time between the execution of two successive tasks, it has to be calculated when the reconfiguration of the cloud architecture has to be triggered. Therefore, we combine estimates about a task's execution time with the time required to deploy or reconfigure components within the cloud architecture. Therefore, we combine existing approaches that estimate a task's execution time [16] with historical data about the deployment and provisioning time of each single element in the cloud architecture. Thus, the architecture required for the execution of each task is deployed as soon as the previous task finishes. In order to evaluate the estimated time to trigger a cloud reconfiguration, we are going to measure the amount of time a workflow is idle because of a task which is waiting for its architecture to be deployed.

6   Summary and Outlook

In this position paper, we propose an approach that dynamically schedules cloud architecture states for the execution of workflow tasks using runtime models in order to reduce the overall amount of data transfer and resources needed. Hereby, we identified that in addition to a design time a runtime model is required to manage and reflect the state of the workflow and its underlying architecture. In the future, we will concentrate on implementing the OCCI workflow extension. Thereafter, we focus on the deployment time for cloud architectures and fuse them with the execution time of workflow tasks. Then we test multiple scheduling approaches to combine architecture models and elaborate how the resulting model can be fused with the runtime model. Finally, we are going to assemble these components into the proposed approach and proof the concept based on a set of compute and data intensive workflows.

References

1. Ahmed-Nacer, M., Gaaloul, W., Tata, S.: Occi-compliant cloud configuration simulation. In: 2017 IEEE International Conference on Edge Computing (EDGE), pp. 73–81 (June 2017)
2. Beni, E.H., Lagaisse, B., Joosen, W.: Adaptive and reflective middleware for the cloudification of simulation & optimization workflows. In: Proceedings of the 16th Workshop on Adaptive and Reflective Middleware, ARM '17, pp. 2:1–2:6. ACM (2017)
3. Deelman, E., Gannon, D., Shields, M., Taylor, I.: Workflows and e-science: an overview of workflow system features and capabilities. Futur. Gener. Comput. Syst. **25**(5), 528–540 (2009)
4. Deelman, E., et al.: Pegasus: a framework for mapping complex scientific workflows onto distributed systems. Sci. Program. J. **13**(3), 219–237 (2005)
5. Erbel, J., Korte, F., Grabowski, J.: Comparison and runtime adaptation of cloud application topologies based on occi. In: Proceedings of the 8th International Conference on Cloud Computing and Services Science, CLOSER, vol. 1, pp. 517–525. INSTICC, SciTePress (2018)
6. Ferry, N., Chauvel, F., Song, H., Rossini, A., Lushpenko, M., Solberg, A.: Cloudmf: Model-driven management of multi-cloud applications. ACM Trans. Internet Technol. **18**(2), 16:1–16:24 (2018)
7. Kacsuk, P., Kovács, J., Farkas, Z.: The flowbster cloud-oriented workflow system to process large scientific data sets. J. Grid Comput. **16**(1), 55–83 (2018)
8. Korte, F., Challita, S., Zalila, F., Merle, P., Grabowski, J.: Model-driven configuration management of cloud applications with occi. In: Proceedings of the 8th International Conference on Cloud Computing and Services Science, CLOSER, vol. 1, pp. 100–111. INSTICC, SciTePress (2018)
9. Mell, P., Grance, T.: The NIST Definition of Cloud Computing (2011)
10. Merle, P., Barais, O., Parpaillon, J., Plouzeau, N., Tata, S.: A precise metamodel for open cloud computing interface. In: 2015 IEEE 8th International Conference on Cloud Computing, pp. 852–859 (June 2015)
11. OASIS: Topology and Orchestration Specification for Cloud Applications (2013). http://docs.oasis-open.org/tosca/TOSCA/v1.0/TOSCA-v1.0.html. Accessed 27 July 2018

12. OGF: Open Cloud Computing Interface - Core (2016). https://www.ogf.org/documents/GFD.221.pdf. Accessed 27 July 2018
13. OGF: Open Cloud Computing Interface - Infrastructure (2016). https://www.ogf.org/documents/GFD.224.pdf. Accessed 27 July 2018
14. OGF: Open Cloud Computing Interface - Platform (2016). https://www.ogf.org/documents/GFD.227.pdf. Accessed 27 July 2018
15. Qasha, R., Cala, J., Watson, P.: Dynamic deployment of scientific workflows in the cloud using container virtualization. In: 2016 IEEE International Conference on Cloud Computing Technology and Science (CloudCom), pp. 269–276 (Dec 2016)
16. da Silva, R.F., et al.: Toward fine-grained online task characteristics estimation in scientific workflows. In: Proceedings of the 8th Workshop on Workflows in Support of Large-Scale Science, WORKS '13, pp. 58–67. ACM (2013)
17. Wolstencroft, K., et al.: The taverna workflow suite: designing and executing workflows of web services on the desktop, web or in the cloud. Nucl. Acids Res. **41**(W1), W557–W561 (2013)
18. Zalila, F., Challita, S., Merle, P.: A model-driven tool chain for OCCI. In: Panetto, H. (ed.) OTM 2017. LNCS, vol. 10573, pp. 389–409. Springer, Cham (2017). https://doi.org/10.1007/978-3-319-69462-7_26

CREST - A DSL for Reactive Cyber-Physical Systems

Stefan Klikovits[✉], Alban Linard, and Didier Buchs

Software Modeling and Verification (SMV) Group,
Faculty of Science University of Geneva, Geneva, Switzerland
{Stefan.Klikovits,Alban.Linard,Didier.Buchs}@unige.ch

Abstract. This article presents CREST, a novel domain-specific language for the modelling of cyber-physical systems. CREST is designed for the simple and clear modelling, simulation and verification of small-scale systems such as home and office automation, smart gardening systems and similar. The language is designed to model the flow of resources throughout the system. It features synchronous system evolution and reactive behaviour. CREST's formal semantics allow real-valued time advances and the modelling of timed system evolution. The continuous time concept permits the precise simulation of future system behaviour by automatically calculating next transition times. We present CREST in a practical manner, and elaborate on the Python-based DSL implementation and simulator.

1 Introduction

Cyber-physical systems (CPS) are combinations of software components, that perform computation, and hardware interfaces, such as sensors and actuators, which connect the system to the physical world. Enabled by inexpensive hardware, applications such as home and building automation, or more generally the Internet-of-Things (IoT), are recent and popular manifestations of CPS which offer the possibility to digitally control large parts of our lives. This recent proliferation requires more trust in CPS' correctness.

Classical CPS domains such as aviation and transport, heavy industry as well as large-scale and complex systems using dedicated formalisms, languages and tools to control, simulate and verify their systems. While these solutions are commonly used by financially potent institutions, creators of small and custom systems often lack the knowledge and resources to use such tools. The goal of our project is to give these people the means to easily model and check their CPS.

This project is supported by: FNRS STRATOS: Strategy based Term Rewriting for Analysis and Testing Of Software, the Hasler Foundation, 1604 CPS-Move, and COST IC1404: MPM4CPS

© Springer Nature Switzerland AG 2018
F. Khendek and R. Gotzhein (Eds.): SAM 2018, LNCS 11150, pp. 29–45, 2018.
https://doi.org/10.1007/978-3-030-01042-3_3

In this article we present the Continuous REactive SysTems (CREST) language. CREST is a domain-specific language (DSL) created for the modelling of small-scale CPS such as home, office and building automation, automated gardening systems and similar. The language particularly emphasises the simple representation of three CPS aspects: 1. the continuous flow of physical resources (e.g. light, heat, electricity) and data signals (e.g. on/off switches, control commands) within a system; 2. the state-based behaviour of CPS components; and 3. the evolution of a system over time.

CREST's strictly hierarchical system view encourages composition and system-of-systems designs. The formal language semantics guarantee a synchronous representation and evolution of the model, while still preserving dynamic behaviour. It features arbitrary time granularity, as opposed to fixed time steps, and hence avoids the need for *ticks* commonly used in other languages. CREST is implemented as an *internal DSL* in Python,[1] which means that it uses Python's execution environment and language as a foundation.

The rest of the paper is structured as follows: Sect. 2 provides related work and the reasoning behind the choice of designing a new DSL, instead of using existing solutions. Sect. 3 introduces the CREST language, its graphical syntax and semantics. Sect. 4 outlines the CREST's Python-based implementation, the interactive modelling environment and simulation capabilities. Sect. 5 concludes and discusses future work.

2   Motivation and Related Works

Over the years, a large number of formalisms, languages and tools have been developed to aid the modelling and verification of systems. Even though each one of them has its own, clear strengths, oftentimes the choice of one is not trivial and requires trade-offs. In order to find the most appropriate candidate for the modelling and simulation of CPS such as the ones described above, we performed a requirements analysis, collecting the properties of the target systems and comparing them to the available solutions.

For this evaluation we assumed three different case studies that should be modelled. The first one, a smart home system includes solar panels, a battery and an standard electricity mains for power supply, a water boiler, shower and various home appliances (e.g. IoT vacuum cleaner, TV, dishwasher). Next, an office system that features automated light and temperature regulation based on presence sensors, environmental sensors and work schedules. The third system is an automated gardening systems that uses a relay to control growing lamps and a water pump to automatically grow plants inside a home. Measurements are performed using light, temperature and soil moisture sensors.

Such systems require a modelling language/tool that is capable of representing the flow of physical influences (e.g. light, water, electricity) between components, additional to expressing the component's state and evolution over time.

---

[1] https://www.python.org/.

Next to structural considerations, an analysis of the systems' behaviour was performed. This exploration led to the discovery of six key aspects that should be supported by the chosen language/tool:

1. *Locality.* Despite the exchange of data and resources, system components usually have states and data that should remain local. As an example we can think of a lamp. Its state, life-time and power consumption are local attributes, independent of other components. Interaction occurs through a well-defined interface, i.e. the power plug and switch.
2. *Continuous Time.* Most CPS deal in some way with timing aspects. Plants require a certain amount of light per day, water consumption is measured per minute, etc. Ideally, the chosen formalism will allow arbitrary (real-valued) time steps so that all points in time can be analysed (not just the ones that coincide with *ticks*). The time concept has to support continuous influences between components (e.g. a pump filling a water tank).
3. *Synchronism.* While some changes happen over time, most effects are immediate. For example, a room is (virtually) immediately illuminated by a lamp. The actual time delay is negligible for our target applications. Even for energy saving lamps, whose luminosity increases over time, the transition to the on-state and dissipation of light starts immediately. The synchronism concept requires that as soon as a value changes, the entire system is synchronised and checked for possible changed influences between components.
4. *Reactivity.* The goal of CPS is to model components and systems that react to changes in their environment. When the sun sets, a home automation system should adapt and provide another light source.
5. *Parallelism and Concurrency.* While synchronism and reactivity prescribe each individual subsystem's behaviour, CPSs consists of many components acting in parallel. A tripped fuse shut down all electrical appliances at the same time.
6. *Non-determinism.* When it comes to real-world applications the evolution of a system is not always predictable. For example, the communication between wireless components can temporarily fail. It should be possible to model these scenarios.

This list served as a reference guide for the search of a suitable language. Additionally to the above properties we took properties such as simplicity, expressiveness and availability of formal semantics into account. Lastly, we are interested in the usability and suitability for our target domain, i.e. how it allows the expression of the data types and concepts required by our systems, as well as the complexity of the created solutions. The rest of this section presents the tools and languages that were evaluated before choosing to develop CREST.

2.1   Evaluation of Existing Tools and Languages

The modelling of software systems has been dominated by languages such as UML 2 and SysML [19]. Despite their versatility in the software world, their support for physical systems is rather limited. They lack important embedded systems concepts such as real-time behaviour and timing constraints. Extensions, such as the MARTE UML profile [18] aim to provide those missing features, at the cost of added complexity. MARTE for example provides a very complex web of languages, which makes the modelling of simple systems (e.g. home automation) complicated and time consuming. UML also entails an often-criticised architectural focus, which is necessary for efficient CPS modelling.

Architecture Description Languages (ADLs) such as AADL [9] are designed to overcome this problem by modelling systems using architectural component and connector views. However, in most cases they focus on pure architectural concepts and do not support behavioural concepts. CREST in contrast aims to merge the behavioural and architectural side. Extensions to ADLs have been proposed to overcome this shortcoming. AADL's Behavioural Annex [11] and MontiArcAutomaton (MAA) [22] extend the capabilities of AADL and MontiArc [12], respectively, and allow modelling of CPS using automata. While these extension do add the missing behavioural features, AADL's extension lacks a formal basis and MAA only supports the time-synchronous or cycle-based (*tick*) evolution and lacks support of clocks and similar time concepts. Further, MAA uses MontiArc's asynchronous message passing system and hence contradicts our synchronism requirement.

Hardware Description Languages (HDLs) such as VHDL [1] and Verilog [23] have been successfully used to model System-on-Chip designs and embedded systems from a functionality level down to the Transaction-Level Modeling and Register-Transfer Level. The C++-based and IEEE standardised SystemC [3] language is a valuable addition to the HDL domain. All three languages offer design as modules, events and message passing between ports, and allow for the storage of data. Aptly named, HDLs mostly target low-level systems and provide built-in support for embedded concepts (e.g. mutex, semaphores, four-valued logic) and measure time in sub-second granularity (e.g. picosecond). Most tooling and verification support only focuses on the generation and verification of TLM and RTL level designs, which is too low-level for our purposes. Another caveat is, that the language's semantics are not formally defined.

The Specification and Description Language (SDL) [10] is a strong candidate for the modelling of the systems such as ours. It provides hierarchical composition of entities (called *agents*) and behaviour using extended finite state machines. Its design is reactive, agents can perform their processing upon input signal receipt. Timing constraints can be modelled using *timers* that also trigger a signal upon expiration. SDL's rigorous formal basis is a compelling advantage that allows formal verification (e.g. [24]) and tool-independent simulation. SDL's weak point with respect to our requirements, is that all SDL signals are asynchronous. This goes against our view of CPS, where influences and signals are synchronous.

The family of synchronous languages, such as Lustre [13] or Esterel [2], is commonly employed in the field of reactive systems. A synchronous module waits for input signals acts upon them instantaneously and produces output signals. It is assumed that the reaction (i.e. computation) of a module is infinitely fast and hence no time passes during execution. One caveat however is, classical synchronous systems do no have a notion of time. In order to introduce this concept an external clock has to be defined as signal input. Recently as a Lustre-based extension, Zélus [4] overcomes this limitation by adding support for ordinary differential equations that model continuous behaviour. However, just as Lustre, Zélus' suffers from a steep learning curve and difficult syntax.

The CPS in our case studies consist in several components with state-based behaviour, where the component behaviour can change as time passes. This definition is close to the hybrid automata (HA) formalism [21]. HA contain a finite state automaton and model continuous evolution via variables that evolve according to ordinary differential equations (ODE). Transitions are executed according to state invariants and transition conditions. The popularity of HA and hybrid systems (HS) resulted in the development of many languages and tools, such as Simulink/Stateflow [7], HyVisual [5], Modelica, etc. Simulink is the de-facto industry standard of CPS modelling. It is possible to hierarchically design nonlinear, dynamic systems, using different time concepts (e.g. nonlinear, discrete, continuous). Stateflow adds a reactive finite state machine concept to Simulink. Neither Simulink nor Stateflow have formal semantics defined, although proposals exist (e.g. [14]). HyVisual is based on Ptolemy II [20] and allows the definition of hybrid systems with causal influences. It has, contrary to Simulink, a formal operational semantics that can be leveraged for simulation. However, HyVisual's only features a graphical syntax that can become complex to interact with.

A thorough study of HS tools and languages is given in [6] where Carloni et al. use two well-known case studies for their evaluation. The authors also compare tools for the verification of HS, which is a complex task in general where many properties are undecidable [15]. The drawback of HS is their complexity and required familiarity with the formalism. HS however, serve as a possible transpilation target of CREST models so they are used for verification and validation.

The knowledge gathered from these evaluations led us to the conclusion that the modelling of small CPS cannot conveniently be done by using the previous formalisms. The analysed languages and tools either target other domains (UML, HDL, ADL) or lack vital concepts (e.g. time in MontiArcAutomaton). The most promising candidates, the hybrid systems applications either lack formal semantics for verification purposes (Simulink, Modelica) or lack usability (e.g. HyVisual's graphical modelling environment, as pointed out in [6]). A subset of evaluation results is compared in Table 1.

3   CREST Language

The decision to develop CREST is based on the recognition that none of the evaluated candidates fills the need of a formal language meeting our requirements. CREST is the result of combining the most useful concepts of other systems languages, adapted to increase simplicity and usability. This section introduces

Table 1. Evaluation of a selection of candidates for modelling of small-scale CPS. Symbol meaning: ✓ (*Yes*), ✗ (*No*), ~ (*to a certain extent*), ? (*not fully known*)

Formalism/Tool	Locality	Cont. Time	Synchronism	Reactivity	Parallelism	Non-determ.	Formal basis	Simplicity	Expressiveness	Usab. & Suitab.
UML (MARTE)	✓	✓	✓	✓	✓	✓	✓	✗	✓	✗
AADL + Beh.Ann	✓	✓	✓	✓	✗	✓	✗	~	✓	✗
MontiArcAutomaton	✓	✗	✗	✓	✓	✓	✓	~	✓	✓
SystemC	✓	✗	~	✓	✗	~	✗	~	✓	✗
SDL	✓	✓	✗	✓	✓	✓	✓	✓	✓	✓
Esterel	✓	✗	✓	✓	✓	✗	✓	~	~	~
Zélus	?	~	✓	✓	?	?	✓	✗	~	~
Simulink/Stateflow	✓	✓	✗	✓	✓	✓	✗	~	✓	✓
HyVisual	✓	✓	✓	✓	✓	✓	✓	~	✓	✓
Modelica	✓	✓	~	✓	✓	✓	✗	✗	✓	~
CREST	✓	✓	✓	✓	✓	✓	✓	✓	~	✓

CREST's graphical syntax and outlines its semantics. For spatial reasons we cannot provide the formal definition and semantics, but refer the interested reader to the detailed technical report [17].

We will use the concrete example of a growing lamp to introduce the individual CREST concepts. Our growing lamp is a device that is used for growing plants indoors. When turned on, it consumes electricity and produces light. There is also a function where the lamp converts electricity into heat. This feature is controlled by an additional switch.

3.1 CREST Syntax

CREST's graphical syntax, called *CREST diagram*, was developed to facilitate the legibility of architecture and behaviour within the system. Figure 1 displays the complete CREST diagram of the growing lamp.

In CREST, each component clearly defines its scope. Visually this is represented by a black border, showing the scope's limits. The component's communication interface is drawn on the edge of this scope, while the internal structure and behaviour are placed on the inside.

System Structure. CREST enforces the view that all CPS are defined as hierarchical compositions. This concept is by expressed by defining components ("**entities**") in a nested tree-structure. A CREST system contains one, sole *root* entity. This entity can define arbitrarily many subentities, which can also

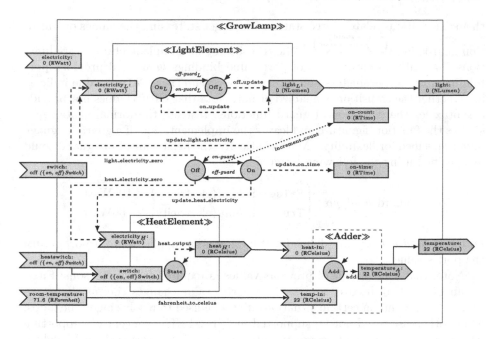

Fig. 1. A growing lamp entity with subentities

contain children, etc. The growing lamp for example, consists of two separate modules, one for light (`LightElement`), one for heating (`HeatElement`). Both are embedded within the `GrowLamp` entity.

The strict hierarchy concept asserts a simplified, localised view on an entity level. Each entity encapsulates its internal structure and allows us to treat it as a *black box*. This black box view facilitates composition, as the entity's *parent* can treat it as coherent instance, disregarding the inside.

The black box view is completed by the definition of an entity's communication interface, which consists of **input** ⊃⊐ and **output** ⊂⊐ ports. Ports are required for the modelling of the flow of resources through the system.

CREST specifies a third kind of port: **locals** ⊏⊐. This port type is not part of the interface, but rather serves as internal storage of data. In the example we see `on-time` and `on-count` as internal ports. All three types of port are associated with a particular resource.

In CREST, **resources** are value types consisting of a value *domain* and a *unit* (formally *Domain* × *Unit*). The growing lamp specifies units such as Watt or Lumen. Domains are sets of values, e.g. the natural numbers $\mathbb{N}$, rationals $\mathbb{R}$ or a set of discrete values such as {on, off} (for `Switch` in the example). Next to resources, each port specifies a value from its resource as its current value.

Entity Behaviour. CREST uses finite state machines (FSMs) to specify behaviour. Each entity defines a set of **states** and guarded **transitions** between them. Transitions relate source states with target states and the names of transition guards (e.g.). The transition guard implementations are functions that take an entity's set of port value bindings *bind* (and previous port bindings *pre*) as parameters and returns a Boolean (`True`, `False`) value indicating whether the transition is enabled or not. Note that CREST does not provide a syntax for the definition of guard functions. Instead, the formal syntax prescribes the function signature and leaves the implementation of a guard language under-specified for flexibility.[2] Mathematically, the behaviour of `on-guard` could be specified using the following formula:

$$\text{on-guard}(bind, pre) \begin{cases} \texttt{False} & \text{if } bind(\text{electricity}) < 100\text{Watt} \\ \texttt{True} & \text{if } bind(\text{electricity}) \geqslant 100\text{Watt} \end{cases}$$

Formally *bind* and *pre* are defined as functions that applied onto a port return the port's value.

Note, that the concept of previous values is required for two reasons: First, it can be used to discover and analyse ports' value changes (i.e. *bind(port)* $\neq$ *pre(port)*). Second, in certain situations it can be used to resolve algebraic loops, which otherwise could not be supported in CREST. The concept of supporting previous values is present as *pre* operator in other languages such as Modelica, Lustre and Esterel. In CREST's implementation *pre* is automatically managed for the user and in certain cases automatically used when necessary.

Resource Flow. Resource transfers between ports can be modelled using updates (- ➤). Updates are defined using a state, a target port and an update function name. If the automaton is in the specified state, the update function (identified by its name) is executed, modelling continuous changes. The function itself returns the target port's new value binding. Self-evidently the returned value has to be in the domain of the target port. Conceptually, updates are continuously executed so that the system's ports always hold the latest values. Practically, CREST's simulator asserts that the evaluations are performed when necessary, as explained below. The growing lamp defines several updates, such as `update_on_time`, `update_light_electricity` (both in GrowLamp) or `heat_output` (in HeatElement). Updates enforce CREST's *synchronism* principle. Provided the automaton is in the update's matching state, the continuous evaluation of update functions guarantees that the target port's value is the result of the update function execution, without delay or explicit message passing.

Similar to transition guards, the update functions' syntax is under-specified but constrained by a required signature. Update functions are executed with the current and previous port bindings *bind* and *pre* and additionally have access to another parameter δt. It is a value of the system's time-base $\mathbb{T}$ and holds

---

[2] Section 4 shows how Python is used as a host language for implementing transition guards and other parts of CREST.

the information about the amount of time that has passed since entering the associated FSM state. Hence, update functions can be used to model continuous behaviour and value updates. In the growing lamp's example the time-base is rational (i.e. $\mathbb{T} = \mathbb{R}$). As an example we provide the mathematical definition of update_on_time, which continuously accumulates the amount of time the automaton spent in time on:

$$\text{update\_on\_time}(bind, pre, \delta t) = pre(on\text{-}time) + \delta t$$

In CPS, resources are often continuously transferred from one port to another, independent of entity state or the time that has passed. In the example above, the growing lamp's heatswitch port value is transferred to the HeatElement's switch input, disregarding whether the lamp is on or off. In order to avoid the specification of the same update function for every state in the system, CREST offers **influences** ($\longrightarrow$) as a syntactic shortcut. Influences relate a source-port to a target-port and an update function name. The behaviour of influences is similar to updates, with the difference that only the source's value is considered for calculation of the target port value. Neither δt nor any other port values are considered for the calculation. In the growing lamp the influence fahrenheit_to_celsius is defined as follows:

$$\text{fahrenheit\_to\_celsius}(bind, pre, \delta t) = (bind(room\text{-}temperature) - 32) * 5/9$$

Lastly, a third type of resource flow is offered by CREST: **actions** ($\cdots\blacktriangleright$). Actions define update functions that are executed during the triggering of transitions. Similar to influences, actions are not allowed to access the δt parameter of the related update functions. The growing lamp scenario defines one action (increment_count) that is executed when the transition from Off to On is triggered. It is used to count the number of times the lamp has been switched on.

3.2   CREST Semantics

Note that for spatial reasons this section only contains a short description of the semantics. The full, formal semantics that are based on SOS rules are provided in the technical report on CREST's formalisation [17].

CREST's semantics allow two basic ways of interaction with the system: Setting of the root entity's input values and advancing time. After either one of these is performed, the system might be in an "unstable" state. The term unstable refers to a system where, due to the interaction a transition might become enabled or an influence or update target port value outdated. To correct this situation, the system has to be *stabilised*. Stabilisation is therefore the process of bringing a system into a state where all influences and updates have been executed, and no transitions are enabled.

In the following, we describe the stabilisation process after changing port values and advancing time. Figure 2 shows a diagram that is inspired by call-multigraphs [16]. Instead of procedure calls however, the arrows represent the triggering of other semantic procedures.

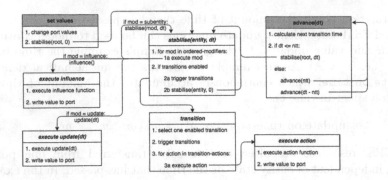

Fig. 2. An informal, schematic diagram of the semantic (sub-)processes for the `set-values` and `advance time` actions. Arcs represent the triggering of sub-procedures. Arc annotations represent conditional sub-procedure calls

Setting Values. As stated, any external modification of input port values requires a subsequent stabilisation. This means that all value modifications have to be relayed to dependant ports through updates and influences. In the `GrowLamp` example, a modification of the `electricity` value has to be propagated to the corresponding inputs of the light and heat modules' input ports. These modules will in turn modify their respective output port values, which will then trigger further propagation. We see that a simple value change has to be recursively propagated throughout the entire entity hierarchy, starting at the root entity, whose inputs have been modified.

In an entity it is possible that influence and updates are "chained", meaning that one *modifier* (influence, update or subentity) changes a port which is then read by another modifier to modify a different port. Such dependencies have to be taken into account when performing stabilisation to avoid delayed or erroneous value propagation. Therefore, the entity will sort the *modifiers* so that modifiers which read one port, in the sorting appear after a modifier writing to that port. The modifiers are then executed in this order, based on their type. If the modifier is an influence or update, the specified function is executed. If it is a subentity whose input bindings changed, the stabilisation is performed inside that subentity. As a result of the sorting, the subentity's inputs will have necessarily already received their updated values (provided there are any). The testing for changed input values, and recalculation only upon their change, enforces the *reactivity* principle that we specified as a requirement. Note, that circular dependencies are not allowed within CREST systems. If there are any interdependencies between values, they cannot refer to the current time period and instead have to be expressed using a port's *pre* value to break circularity. This solution is used extensively in other languages, see Simulink's *Unit Delay* blocks and Modelica's *pre* operator.

After triggering all influences and updates, one of the enabled FSM transitions is executed, provided there is one. CREST does not prescribe a selection procedure in case of multiple enabled transitions, meaning that *non-determinism* may occur. If a transition was enabled and executed (including the corresponding *actions*), another stabilisation is started to execute all updates that are related to the new FSM state. This stabilisation phase will, again, look for enabled transitions and trigger one if applicable.

The stabilisation process operates recursively. That means that if an entity triggers a subentity stabilisation, the subentity's modifiers are executed in order and any transitions within that subentity are triggered (followed by stabilisations) until no transitions are enabled. Only then, the control is returned back to the parent entity to continue. If there are several subentities that are independent (i.e. don't have dependencies between their inputs and outputs), they can be safely executed in *parallel*, as a result of the *locality* principle.

Note that no time passes between the update of port values and the end of the stabilisation process, whereas some other languages (e.g. Simulink) introduce a small time delay at every modification. CREST's *synchronism* can be found in languages such as Esterel. CREST differs from Esterel however, in that the entire system is stabilised instead of just the affected subset.

Advancing Time. The prior part of this section states that updates allow the modification of a system over time using a δt parameter. In fact, the semantics of advancing of time triggers the same stabilisation process as `set-values`, except that while `set-values` uses a $\delta t = 0$, `advance` specifies a $\delta t \geqslant 0$ as parameter. Further, all subentities perform the updates, independent of whether their input values change. This asserts that the update functions are executed correctly (i.e. according to the time parameter).

There is one particularity of time advances that has to be considered though: CREST implements eager transition triggering. This means that a transition has to be fired as soon as it is enabled. When advancing time however, it can occur that the `advance` routine is called with a δt that is bigger than the minimum time required to enable a transition. CREST implements a *continuous time* concept, that does not foresee "ticks" as system synchronisation points at which transition guards are evaluated. In order not to "miss" the precise moment when a transition becomes enabled, CREST makes use of a function that attempts to calculate the precise amount of time ntt that has to pass until any transition will be enabled. ntt is in the range $[0, \ldots, \infty)$, where 0 states that a transition is currently enabled (and that the system is not stabilised) and ∞ means that no transition can become enabled by just advancing time. Note, that the next-transition-time function depends on the implementation of updates, influences and guards and involves complex tasks such as the creation of inverse functions or the expression of the functions as sets of constraints. We will further discuss this function in the next section, with the Python implementation of CREST.

The information of the next transition time ntt creates two possible scenarios:

1. $ntt \geqslant \delta t$ (i.e. the time we plan to advance). CREST advances δt and the stabilisation task will execute updates and transitions until reaching a fixpoint.
2. $ntt < \delta t$. CREST divides the advance into two steps: First, *advance ntt*, advances until a transition is enabled. Updates and transitions are triggered, followed by stabilisation. Next, CREST recurses on the remainder ($advance(\delta t - ntt)$).

CREST's time semantics allow the simulation and verification based on real-valued clocks with arbitrary time advances. This is essential for the precise simulation of cyber-physical systems without the need for an artificial base-clock. The time-based enabling of transitions extends the language and adds a *continuous behaviour* to the otherwise purely reactive system. Other synchronous languages such as Lustre need external clocks to provide timing signals.

4 CREST Implementation and Simulation

While the graphical view is convenient for analysis and discussion of a system, the creation of larger systems is more efficient when using textual representations. We therefore implemented CREST as an internal DSL in the Python language. The concept of using a general purpose programming language as host for another DSL is famously used by SystemC, which is implemented in C++.

We chose Python as a target language for three reasons:

1. Distribution and package installation allow easy installation and extension. It also comes pre-installed on various operating systems.
2. It is easy to learn, flexible, has many useful libraries, and a large community.
3. Python's internals let us alter class instantiations and hide CREST specifics from users, while still enabling the use of the default execution engine.

4.1 PyCREST Implementation

PyCREST is developed as a set of Python libraries. This means the functionality can be imported and used in any standard Python program. PyCREST is developed to make use of Project Jupyter[3] notebooks as an interactive development and execution environment. Since PyCREST also features integrated plotting utilities, it is possible to create PyCREST systems and visualise them as CREST diagrams. In the following we provide a small excerpt that showcases the use of PyCREST and the definition of an entity, as displayed in Listing 3. A more complete example is provided online as an introduction to CREST[4].

Entities are defined as a regular Python class that inherits from PyCREST's `Entity`. PyCREST further provides a class for each model concept (Input, State, Update, etc.) as well as additional decorators (e.g. @influence, @transition).

---

[3] https://jupyter.org/.
[4] https://mybinder.org/v2/gh/stklik/CREST/sam-demo/.

Entity ports, transitions and updates are defined as class attributes or decorated methods as shown in the example. PyCREST also supports many other classic Python concepts such as constructors, sub-classing, etc.

4.2   Simulation

The previous section briefly outlines the use of next-transition-time calculation. The calculation of the exact time of system changes is vital for the correct simulation of CREST systems, as CREST does not rely on artificial base clocks to identify the points for recalculation of data. Instead PyCREST's *simulator* uses Microsoft Research' Z3 [8] theorem prover to create a set of constraints that represents the transition's guard and searches for the minimal δt that will solve the constraints. CREST also searches all influences and updates ("modifiers") that either directly or indirectly modify the transition guard, and translates them to Z3 constraints. The creation of constraints is based on transpilation of the modifiers' source code. After the translation, Z3 is instructed to find the minimum value of δt that will enable a transition. The process is repeated for all outgoing transitions of the individual entities' current states. Finding the minimum of these results yields the next transition time.

```
1   class LightElement(Entity):
2       # port definitions with resouces and an initial value
3       electricity = Input(resource=Resources.electricity, value=0)
4       light = Output(resource=Resources.light, value=0)
5
6       # automaton states - specify one as the current (initial) state
7       on = State()
8       off = current = State()
9
10      # transitions and guards (as lambdas)
11      off_to_on = Transition(source=off, target=on,
12          guard=(lambda self: self.electricity.value >= 100))
13      on_to_off = Transition(source=on, target=off, \
14          guard=(lambda self: self.electricity.value < 100))
15
16      # updates are annotations
17      @update(state=on, target=light)
18      def set_light_on(self, dt=0):
19          return 800
20
21      @update(state=off, target=light)
22      def set_light_off(self, dt=0):
23          return 0
```

Fig. 3. The PyCREST definition of the LightElement entity

Z3 turned out to be powerful and efficient enough for most of the CPS that we defined. However, this strong dependency also imposes limitations. Z3 can quickly find solutions to most linear constraint sets. However, some systems define non-linear constraints. An example is the ThreeMasses problem [6], where three masses are placed on a surface. One of the masses has an initial velocity and bumps into the second one, which in turn bumps into the third one, shortly after. The third mass falls off the edge of a surface and accelerates towards the ground, off which it keeps bouncing, thus repeatedly switching from upwards to downwards motion. The difficulty lies in the consideration of acceleration, velocity and position of the masses in two dimensions, as well as the repeated reduction thereof using a restitution factor.

In the presence of non-linear constraints, Z3 can only provides *a* solution to the constraint set, but cannot guarantee that it is optimized (i.e. minimal or maximal) δt value. We found, however, that the simulation is precise enough for our purposes. The ThreeMasses system is implemented in PyCREST as a benchmark,[5] displaying the capabilities of the simulator. In general, the modelling of CREST systems with non-linear constraints is discouraged until an alternative constraint solver, that adds non-linear optimisation capabilities is introduced. Further, at the time of writing, PyCREST has no special treatment of zero-crossings. In fact, all changes in behaviour, including zero crossings, are executed as usual. Zeno behaviour is discouraged and usually leads to exceptions thrown by the Python interpreter. PyCREST catches this exception and informs the user, but does not put in place any recovery procedures.

4.3   Function Approximation

It is evident that not all functions can be translated to Z3 constraints. In fact, only a subset of Python, consisting of variable assignments, unary and binary operators, and conditional statements and expressions is currently supported. Loops, recursions and function calls are not allowed in CREST.

Instead, such functions can be defined through execution traces and then interpolated. The domains of interpolation, splines and function fitting have been extensively studied in mathematical fields, and there exist many tools and libraries for the creation of interpolations and splines. CREST uses Python libraries such as SciPy and NumPy[6] for these purposes.

CREST distinguishes between influence and update approximation. Influences only depend on one particular port and are assumed to be linear in the form $A * source\text{-}val + B$, where A and B are the parameters to be found. The function can be piecewise defined, e.g. as step function or as shown in Fig. 4.

The approximation of update functions is more complex, as updates can calculate a port's new value based on all of its entity's ports' current and previous bindings additionally to the δt time parameter. Despite the increased number of parameters, CREST tries to extract a δt-linear spline from the data provided. This is achieved by first creating an approximation of the multidimensional data and then selecting the slice of data that represents the current port values, as visualised by the dark slice of the multidimensional surface in Fig. 5.

---

[5] https://mybinder.org/v2/gh/stklik/CREST/sam-demo.
[6] https://scipy.org/ http://www.numpy.org/.

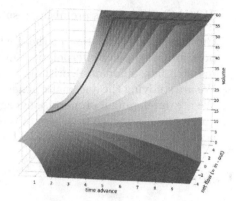

$$heat\_output = \begin{cases} 0 & \text{if } electricity_H \leq 0 \\ 60 & \text{if } 1500 < electricity_H \\ \frac{electricity_H * 0.9}{25} & \text{otherwise} \end{cases}$$

Fig. 4. Piecewise interpolation

Fig. 5. Multi-variable interpolation

4.4 Verification

CREST's simulation revolves around the change of a root entity's input ports (i.e. external input), the advance of time (i.e. internal state changes) and output produced by these system changes. Verification on the other hand requires the creation of the state space of the CREST system's evolution and analysis of execution traces. Due to the unbounded number of values of real-valued clocks, state spaces of timed systems are unbounded or even infinitely large. A full discussion of CREST's verification exceeds the scope of this paper. CREST's approach however is closely related to hybrid systems verification [6].

5   Conclusion and Future Works

This article introduces CREST, a domain-specific language for the definition of continuous reactive systems. CREST's target domain is the modelling of cyber-physical systems' architecture and continuous timely behaviour. The design, syntax and semantics serve the six core concepts locality, continuous time and behaviour, synchronism, reactivity, parallelism and concurrency and non-determinism. CREST achieves this by evading the base-clock concept, while still preserving synchronism and choosing synchronisation points based on system behaviour. This trait permits continuous value changes, arbitrarily fine time advances and convenient modelling on largely different time scales within the same model. It also allows for the efficient simulation of behaviour and time. CREST ensures a hierarchical structure that facilitates composition. The language supports concurrency and parallelism, as they are a omnipresent in both software and physical worlds. The automaton-based behaviour of CREST entities enables to easily capture the non-determinism and complexity of CPS.

While CREST shows promising results, we see several areas of improvement:

- Currently the calculation of the next transition time has rudimentary support for one type of interpolation and approximation. We aim to extend our research into different algorithms to provide better results.
- We are studying the automatic generation of controllers from CREST models.
- We are developing a property language that allows non-expert users to define queries in a language that part of their systems. This facilitates removes the need to know language such as LTL or CTL temporal logics.

References

1. Ashenden, P.J.: The Designer's Guide to VHDL, 3rd edn. Morgan Kaufmann Publishers Inc., San Francisco, CA, USA (2008)
2. Berry, G., Gonthier, G.: The Esterel synchronous programming language: design, semantics, implementation. Sci. Comput. Program. **19**, 87–152 (1992)
3. Black, D.C., Donovan, J., Bunton, B., Keist, A.: SystemC: From the Ground Up. Springer, New York Inc, Secaucus, NJ, USA (2010)
4. Bourke, T., Pouzet, M.: Zélus: a synchronous language with ODEs. In: 16th International Conference on Hybrid Systems: Computation and Control (2013)
5. Brooks, C., Cataldo, A., Lee, E.A., Liu, J., Liu, X., Neuendorffer, S., Zheng, H.: Hyvisual: a hybrid system visual modeler. Technical Report UCB/ERL M05/24, EECS Department, University of California, Berkeley (2005)
6. Carloni, L.P., Passerone, R., Pinto, A., Angiovanni-Vincentelli, A.L.: Languages and tools for hybrid systems design. Found. Trends Electron. Des. Autom. **1**, 1–193 (2006)
7. Colgren, R.: Basic Matlab, Simulink And Stateflow. AIAA (American Institute of Aeronautics & Ast (2006)
8. De Moura, L., Bjørner, N.: Z3: an efficient SMT solver. In: Proceedings 14th International Conference Tools and Algorithms f.t. Construction and Analysis of Systems (2008)
9. Feiler, P., Gluch, D., Hudak, J.: The architecture analysis & design language (AADL): an introduction. Technical Report CMU/SEI-2006-TN-011, Software Engineering Institute, Carnegie Mellon University (2006)
10. Fischer, J., Holz, E., Löwis, M., Prinz, A.: SDL-2000: a language with a formal semantics. in: Rigorous Object-Oriented Methods 2000 (2000)
11. Franca, R.B., Bodeveix, J.P., Filali, M., Rolland, J.F., Chemouil, D., Thomas, D.: The AADL behaviour annex – experiments and roadmap. In: 12th IEEE International Conference on Engineering Complex Computer Systems (2007)
12. Haber, A., Ringert, J.O., Rumpe, B.: Montiarc - architectural modeling of interactive distributed and cyber-physical systems (2014)
13. Halbwachs, N., Caspi, P., Raymond, P., Pilaud, D.: The synchronous dataflow programming language LUSTRE. In: Proceedings of the IEEE (1991)
14. Hamon, G., Rushby, J.: An operational semantics for stateflow. In: Wermelinger, M., Margaria-Steffen, T. (eds.) FASE 2004. LNCS, vol. 2984, pp. 229–243. Springer, Heidelberg (2004). https://doi.org/10.1007/978-3-540-24721-0_17
15. Henzinger, T.A., Kopke, P.W., Puri, A., Varaiya, P.: What's decidable about hybrid automata? J. Comput. Syst. Sci. **57**(1), 94–124 (1998)

16. Khedker, U.P., Sanyal, A., Sathe, B.: Data Flow Analysis - Theory and Practice. CRC Press (2009). http://www.crcpress.com/product/isbn/9780849328800
17. Klikovits, S., Linard, A., Buchs, D.: CREST formalization. Technical report, Software Modeling and Verification Group, University of Geneva (2018). https://doi.org/10.5281/zenodo.1284561
18. Object Management Group: UML Profile for MARTE: Modeling and Analysis of Real-Time Embedded Systems (OMG MARTE) Version 1.1 (2011). https://www.omg.org/spec/MARTE/1.1/PDF, OMG Document Number: formal-2011-06-02
19. Object Management Group: OMG Systems Modeling Language (OMG SysML) Version 1.5 (2017). https://www.omg.org/spec/SysML/1.5/PDF, OMG Document Number: formal-2017-05-01
20. Ptolemaeus, C. (ed.): System Design, Modeling, and Simulation using Ptolemy II. Ptolemy.org (2014)
21. Raskin, J.: An introduction to hybrid automata. In: Hristu-Varsakelis D., Levine W.S. (eds.) Handbook of Networked and Embedded Control Systems (2005)
22. Ringert, J.O., Rumpe, B., Wortmann, A.: Architecture and Behavior Modeling of Cyber-Physical Systems with MontiArcAutomaton (2015)
23. Thomas, D., Moorby, P.: The Verilog Hardware Description Language. The Verilog Hardware Description Language. Kluwer Academic Publishers, San Francisco (1996)
24. Vlaovič, B., Vreže, A., Brezočnik, Z., Kapus, T.: Verification of an SDL Specification — a Case Study. Elektrotehniški vestnik (Electrotechnical Review) (2005)

On the Ontological Expressiveness of the High-Level Constraint Language for Product Line Specification

Angela Villota[1,2]([✉]) [iD], Raúl Mazo[1,3] [iD], and Camille Salinesi[1] [iD]

[1] Université Paris 1 Panthéon Sorbonne, 75013 Paris, France
angela-patricia.villota-gomez@etu.univ-paris1.fr,
{raul.mazo,camille.salinesi}@univ-paris1.fr
[2] Universidad Icesi, Calle 18 No. 122–135, Cali, Colombia
[3] Universidad EAFIT, GIDITIC, Medellín, Colombia

Abstract. The High-Level Constraint Language (HLCL) consolidates the constraints scattered in several product line notations in an abstract and technologically independent language. Previous research has demonstrated that HLCL is suitable to represent most product line constraints from a practical point of view. However, the question about to what extent the HLCL is able to represent product line variability is still open. In this study, we refer to the ontological expressiveness theory to answer this question and to evaluate how well HLCL can represent the state of affairs for which it is proposed. Therefore, this evaluation considers HLCL's ontological expressiveness regarding its completeness and clarity. Our results show that (1) HLCL closely represents the concepts in the ontological framework. However, some variability concepts should be integrated for obtaining a 100% level of completeness. (2) HLCL's high level of abstraction impacts its clarity. The discussion of the research presented in this paper opens the perspectives to build a constraint-based language for product line engineering.

Keywords: Product line engineering · Constraint language
Ontological analysis

1 Introduction

The High-Level Constraint Language (HLCL) is an abstract constraint-based language that was developed for representing product line variability [8]. Product line variability relates to the common and optional characteristics of products in a product line and is the key cross-cutting concern in product line engineering. HLCL can be used (1) as a specification language to create Product Line Models (PLMs); or (2) as an intermediate representation of other product line notations [17,23]. HLCL is intended to provide a unified view of many product line languages because it gathers the constraints that are met in many product line notations, i.e., feature-based notations [17,23]; variation point notations;

© Springer Nature Switzerland AG 2018
F. Khendek and R. Gotzhein (Eds.): SAM 2018, LNCS 11150, pp. 46–66, 2018.
https://doi.org/10.1007/978-3-030-01042-3_4

Dopler models [17]; and goal-oriented notations [18,25], among others. Additionally, variability models represented in HLCL have been used to perform different tasks in product lines such as configuration [8], specification [17,23], analysis & verification [22], and simulation [16]. In this sense, it is right to state that HLCL is a reflection of the state of the art of constraint programming in product line engineering because it gathers the variability relations in several product line languages and has been used in different stages of the development of product lines. However, there is still an unanswered question: Is HLCL expressive enough to encompass any product line model? This study addresses this challenge by evaluating HLCL's completeness and clarity from the perspective of the expressiveness in the context of ontological analysis. The theory of ontological expressiveness is based on the observation that models of information systems are essentially models of real-world systems. We build our study on the theory of ontological expressiveness introduced by Wand and Weber [27] and revised/extended by other authors [6,9] because it provides a well-founded evaluation framework. Additionally, the theory of ontological expressiveness has already been used to evaluate the expressiveness of conceptual modeling languages such as the entity-relation model [26]; UML [5], the i^* language [11]; and BPMN [20]. In the product line context, theoretical analysis of variability modeling languages concerning their ability to represent variability in real-world domain models has been considered in Reinhartz-Berger et al. [21] and Asadi et al. [1]. More particularly, Asadi et al. [1] proposed a theoretical framework for variability and applied their framework evaluating the expressiveness of Feature Models (FM) and the Orthogonal Variability Model (OVM) [1]. Our study uses the proposals of Asadi et al. to evaluate the HLCL's ontological expressiveness. Four criteria were precisely measured to evaluate ontological expressiveness through completion and clarity: (1) degree of deficit, (2) degree of excess, (3) degree of redundancy, and (4) degree of overlap [20]. The results of the evaluation are twofold: on the one hand, HLCL closely represents the general principles of variability defined in the reference model. However, some variability concepts should be integrated for obtaining a 100% level of completeness. On the other hand, the metrics related to clarity show that ontological clarity is affected by HLCL's high level of abstraction. We compared our results regarding completeness with the ones presented by Asadi et al. From this comparison, and considering that HLCL consolidates the constraints scattered in several product line languages, we concluded that the gap in the HLCL's completeness reflects a gap in the state of the art of the product line languages. This gap moves our research towards a discussion of what changes should be considered to provide the product line community with a constraint-based language for product line engineering. The remainder of this paper is organized in the following way. Section 2 presents the HLCL while Sect. 3 describes the background concepts related to the theory of ontological expressiveness. Section 4 outlines the design and execution of the ontological analysis. Section 5 presents the discussion and some challenges for variability languages. Finally, Sects. 6 and 7 present related work and conclusions.

2   The High-Level Constraint Language

The High-Level Constraint Language (HLCL) is an abstract constraint-based language where constraints are presented as primary concepts. The idea of a constraint language that consolidates product line notations is not a novelty. In their work, Djebbi and Salinesi [8] exposed the need for a product line language characterized for being *concise* but comprehensive in scope and *abstract* enough for representing different notations. The constraint programming paradigm [24] was the first choice candidate to propose HLCL for many reasons. First, most product line notations emphasize the specification of constraints to define acceptable configurations (e.g., requires, excludes in FODA models [12]). Second, several product line languages have been transformed into constraint programs to perform tasks such as analysis, verification, configuration, testing, and simulation among others [3]. Third, written in a common language, constraints from different PLMs can be integrated into a unique program and solved in an integrated way. Finally, PLMs expressed as constraint programs can be directly executed and analyzed by off-the-shelf solvers.

The first formalization of HLCL was presented by Salinesi et al. in [23] then it was further developed by Mazo et al. in [17]. These works switched the focus of PLMs specification from the concepts of feature, variation points or dependencies to the concept of constraints that apply to variables. This constraint-based approach enabled product line designers to enhance variability descriptions with complex constraints (i.e., encourages, discourages [14]) that cannot be specified with the constructs offered by current languages. Many publications demonstrate that HLCL is able to represent most of the product line notations such as feature-based, variation point-based, decision-based, goal-based and UML related notations [17,23]. This ability for representing several product line languages supports the claim that HLCL is an image of the state of the art of the product line modeling languages.

HLCL is a solver agnostic language. Thus, HLCL can be used as an intermediate representation of other product line notations in a solver-independent way. Once represented in HLCL, product line constraints can be compiled in any solver's language. This feature is exploited within the VariaMos software tool [16]. Currently, VariaMos supports the specification of product line models using notations such as FODA [12], REFAS [18], among others.

The core constructs of HLCL are **variables**, **domains**, **values**, and **constraints** as presented in Table 1. Variables in HLCL have a domain, and at a given moment in time, a value. Variables represent elements in a model (e.g., features, requirements, design fragments, components, or any other reused artifact). The domain of variables can be Boolean, integer, interval, enumeration or string. To indicate that an element can be either included or excluded in a product can be done by representing such element as a variable with a Boolean domain. Constraints are used to specify variability relations in product lines; Table 2 presents a summary of the variability relations supported by the HLCL. There are four types of constraints in HLCL: Boolean, arithmetic, global and reified. Boolean and arithmetic constraints are expressions using Boolean

Table 1. Core constructs of the high-level constraint language.

Construct	Definition
Variable	Represent product line elements. A variable has a domain, and it is paired with a value at a given time
Domain	The domain of variables can be Boolean, integer, interval, enumeration or string
Values	Represent the elements in the domains
Constraint	Constraints are relations over a set of variables $C(x_1, x_2, \ldots, x_n)$ producing sets of values $\{v_1, v_2, \ldots, v_n\}$ where v_i is assigned to each variable x_i

$(\wedge, \vee, \neg, \Rightarrow,$ etc.) and arithmetic $(+, -, \times, \div,$ etc.) operators. Global constraints are applied on a set of variables at a time using well-known predicates such as `all_different`, `all_equal`, `abs_value`, among others. A reified constraint is a constraint whose truth value can be captured with a Boolean variable, which can itself be part of another constraint. Reified constraints make possible to reason on the realization of constraints.

Table 2. Variability relations supported by HLCL.

Notation	Variability relations	Publications
Feature based	Optional, mandatory, requires, exclusion, alternative/XOR decomposition, OR relation, group cardinality, feature cardinality, attribute, complex constraints	[17, 23]
Variation point based	Dependency decomposition: All of, optional, mandatory, requires, exclusion, alternative/XOR, OR relation, group cardinality, individual cardinality, attribute, complex constraints	[17, 23]
Dopler/ decision	Root/visibility condition, requires/decision effects/ inclusion conditions, validity condition, asset dependencies, group cardinality, complex constraints	[15, 17]
Goals	Elements of constraints, operators allowing the intentional definition of a constraint (e.g., using a function or an arithmetic expression)	[18, 25]
UML	Optional, mandatory, requires, group cardinality	[17]

3   Ontological Expressiveness in Modeling Languages

The ontological expressiveness theory is a framework to analyze the expressiveness of conceptual modeling languages [27]. This theory is based on the observation that conceptual models of information systems are, essentially, models of real-world systems. The evaluation of a conceptual modeling language requires a mapping of the language's constructs with respect to a foundational ontology [9,27]. In conceptual modeling, a foundational ontology is understood as a formally and philosophically well-founded model of categories that can be used to articulate conceptualizations in specific engineering models [11]. The mapping between ontological constructs and language constructs should focus on two sets: the set of ontological constructs and the set of language constructs, as presented in Fig. 1. This mapping, considers two steps: the representation mapping and the interpretation mapping [27]. On the one hand, representation mapping serves to determine whether and how an ontological construct is represented using the language constructs. On the other hand, interpretation mapping describes whether and how a language construct stands for a real-world construct. To conclude about the expressiveness of the examined language, it is decisive to determine the presence or absence of any of the four observable defects in conceptual modeling languages: construct deficit, construct excess, construct redundancy and construct overload.

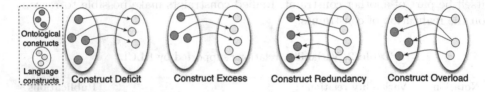

Fig. 1. Defects in a conceptual modeling language, taken from [27].

Figure 1 shows the defects in conceptual modeling languages. If a language has construct deficit, then the language is ontologically incomplete. The ontological clarity of the language is undermined If a language has either construct excess, construct redundancy, or construct overload. The presence or absence of these defects can be measured with the metrics of potential ontological deficiencies proposed by Recker et al. [20] and described in Sect. 4.

3.1 Ontology for Variability Modeling Languages

Three criteria were taken into account to select an ontology for evaluating the HLCL. The first criterion is the type of the language to be analyzed. As suggested by Guizzardi et al. in [9], the type of the language (i.e., domain-independent, domain-specific) is the most important criterion for selecting the reference model in an ontological analysis. Domain-independent languages are compared to domain-independent foundational ontologies such as BWW [27] or UFO [10]. Instead, domain-specific languages should be compared using domain-specific ontologies. HLCL has a duality with respect to this first criterion given that variability languages should be domain-independent but also have particular characteristics regarding variability. Therefore, the selected ontology should include domain-independent constructs along with variability related constructs. Thus, the second criterion is the ability to represent different variability relations. To the best of our knowledge, there exist two ontologies with concepts from a domain-independent ontology (BWW) that also include variability concepts: Reinhartz-Berger et al. [21] and Asadi et al. [1]. However, Reinhartz-Berger et al.'s variability is oriented to the behavior of the system, and the variability concepts in Asadi et al. are of general purpose. The third criterion is the use of the ontology in similar studies. To the best of our knowledge, the ontology of Asadi et al. is the only one used to evaluate ontological expressiveness in variability languages (i.e., FODA and OVM). For the aforementioned reasons, we chose the ontology proposed by Asadi et al. for the ontological analysis of the HLCL.

3.2 Ontology

Asadi et al.'s ontology groups concepts into variability sources and variability patterns. A *variability source* is an element in which variability may happen. The concepts considered as variability sources correspond to things, properties, lawful state space, lawful event space, and history in the BWW ontology [27]. Table 3 presents the concepts and their definitions. In this table, we included the definition of concepts *state*, *state law*, and *event* because they are relevant for the understanding and mapping of the *lawful state space* and *lawful event space*. Also, the definitions of *lawful state space* and *lawful event space* are highlighted in the table to denote that the next highlighted rows contain concepts and definitions subjacent to each concept.

A *variability pattern* represents the different types of variability that can be observed in different products in a particular product line. Variability patterns are derived from a series of similarity classes regarding the variability sources. Here we describe the variability patterns included in the ontology (Table 3), a more detailed description is available in [1]. First, we introduce the definitions of similarity and equivalence, and then we explain the four variability patterns. Let $S = \{s_1, s_2, \ldots, s_m\}$ be a set of elements belonging to a product P_1 and $T = \{t_1, t_2, \ldots, t_n\}$ be a set of elements in product P_2.

Definition 1. *Equivalence. S is equivalent to T ($S \equiv T$) iff there is a mapping between S and T.*

Definition 2. *Similarity. S is similar to T with respect to an equivalence subset p, denoted as $S \cong_p T$, iff there exists S', T' such as $S' \subset S$ and $T' \subset T$, then $S' \equiv T'$. In other words, the concept of similarity refers to elements that are common to products in a product line.*

Full Similarity One-Side. Two products are full similarly one-side when they satisfy the similarity relation and an equivalence can be established w.r.t. subsets of S or T. Let S', T' be two subsets, $S' \subset S$ and $T' \subset T$, then either $S' \equiv T$ or $T' \equiv S$.

Partial Similarity. Two products are similar when they satisfy the similarity relation.

Dissimilarity. Two products are completely dissimilar if no similarity relation can be established.

Ordering. Variability regarding ordering appears when two products S, T have a similarity relation but they are dissimilar with respect to an ordering relation. Thus, there exists the ordered sets S', T' such as $S' \subset S$ and $T' \subset T$ and $S' \equiv T'$ but S' and T' are dissimilar with respect to their order.

Table 3. Summary of the ontology [1]

		Concepts	Definition
Variability source	Structure	Things	A thing is an elementary unit. The real-world is made up of things. A composite thing may be made up of other things (composite or primitive).
		Properties	Things possess properties. A property is modeled via a function that maps the thing to some value.
		Lawful state space	The lawful state space is the set of **states** of a thing that comply with the **state laws** of the thing.
		State	The state of a thing is the vector of values for all attribute functions of a thing.
		State law	A state law restricts the values of the properties of a thing to a subset that is deemed lawful because of natural laws or human laws. A law is considered a property.
	Process	Lawful event space	The lawful event space is the set of all **events** in a thing that are lawful
		Event	An event is a change in state of a thing.
		History	It is the chronologically-ordered states that a thing traverses in time.
Variability pattern		Full similarity one-side	Two products S, T are full similarly one-side when they satisfy the similarity relation, and an equivalence relation can be established w.r.t. subsets of S or T.
		Partial similarity	Two products are similar when they satisfy the similarity relation.
		Dissimilarity	Occurs when no similarity relation can be established.
		Ordering variability	Occurs when two products differ by an order relation.

4 Ontological Analysis of the Expressiveness of HLCL

As a first step in the evaluation of the HLCL expressiveness, we established the specific goal, questions, and associated metrics to answer the research questions by using the Goal-Question-Metric (GQM) approach [2]. The refinement of the stated questions relies on the analysis of three hypotheses (each one with null and alternative forms) related to the defined metrics, as synthesized in Table 4. The metrics in this experiment are the four measures of potential ontological deficiencies proposed by Recker et al. [20]: the degree of deficit, the degree of excess, the degree of redundancy, and the degree of overload.

Goal. Evaluate the HLCL with respect to its completeness and clarity from the point of view of the expressiveness in the context of an ontological analysis.

Q1. Does HLCL map all the constructs in the ontological model? With this question, we will determine the completeness or incompleteness (construct deficit) of the HLCL using the degree of deficit. $DoD = \frac{\#not\ mapped\ ontological\ constructs}{\#ontological\ constructs}$

Q2. Are there any HLCL constructs that cannot be mapped into ontological constructs? This question is related to determine if the HLCL has construct excess using the degree of excess. ($DoE = \frac{\#notmappedlanguageconstructs}{\#languageconstructs}$)

Q3. Is the mapping a one-to-one relation? With this question, we can determine if the HLCL has construct redundancy and construct overload using the degree of redundancy and degree of overload (DoR, DoO). Thus, together with Q2, Q3 leads to conclude about the clarity of the language. DoR and DoO are calculated as follow: $DoR = \frac{\#lang.const.mappingthesameont.const.}{\#languageconstructs}$, $DoO = \frac{\#lang.const.mappingmanyont.const.}{\#languageconstructs}$

Table 4. Hypotheses

Question	Null hypothesis	Alternative hypothesis
Q1	$H1_0$: All ontological constructs were mapped to HLCL constructs	$H1_1$: One or more ont. construct cannot be mapped to HLCL constructs
	$H1_0 : DoD = 0\%$	$H1_1 : DoD > 0\%$
Q2	$H2_0$: All the HLCL constructs were mapped	$H2_1$: One or more HLCL const. cannot be mapped to ont. constructs
	$H2_0 : DoE = 0\%$	$H2_1 : DoE > 0\%$
Q3	$H3_0$: The map is one-to-one	$H3_1$: The map is NOT one-to-one
	$H3_0 : DoR = 0\% \wedge DoO = 0\%$	$H3_1 : DoR > 0\% \vee DoO > 0\%$

4.1 Mapping HLCL Constructs to Ontological Constructs

The mapping between the language constructs in Table 1 and the ontological constructs in Table 3 was performed in two steps. First, we performed a representation mapping to determine whether and how ontological constructs are represented via a language construct. Then, we performed the interpretation mapping to determine whether and how a grammatical construct stands for a real-world construct and answer the research questions. Table 6 presents a summary of this mapping. Also, we illustrate the representation mapping using a small example of a hypothetical case of a Movement Control System (MCS) of a car. This example is a simplified extract of the model in [23]. First, we present the description of the example and give some examples of valid products. Then, we present the specification of the MCS using HLCL (Table 5) and the products as solutions of the constraint program in Table 7.

Example. A Movement Control System (MCS) assists drivers to park, helping them to detect obstacles and controlling the speed and correct the trajectory. The MCS can be composed of a processor, an internal memory slot, some sensors, and some feedback devices. Sensors are used to measure the speed and position of a car through speed sensors and position sensors. An MCS may contain a speed sensor and zero to two position sensors. Feedback can be visual, audio or vibration, and a single product can have at most two kinds of feedback. To compute the location of a car, the MCS uses the processor that can have one to seven cores. The size of the internal memory can have one of the values in the set {2 GB, 4 GB, 8 GB, 16 GB, 32 GB}. Additionally, the size of the memory depends on the number of cores in a processor, the pair ⟨cores; internal memory⟩ can have the following values ⟨0;0⟩, ⟨1;2⟩, ⟨2;4⟩, ⟨3;8⟩, ⟨4;16⟩, ⟨5;32⟩.

Table 5 contains the variables and constraints used to represent the MCS product line using HLCL. The resulting constraint satisfaction problem has 839 solutions or representations of valid products. Each solution is a set of pairs *variable, value* (x_i, v_i). In a solution, a pair (x_i, v_i) where v_i is equal to one represents the inclusion of the component associated with variable x_i in the product. The MCS example includes non-Boolean variables for those cases when additional information related to components should be considered, as in the case of the cores of a processor and the size of the memory. Thus, this additional

Table 5. HLCL specification for the running example

Variables and domains
[MCS, SpeedSensor, PosSensor, PosSensor1, PosSensor2, Processor, Feedback, Visual, Audio, Vibration, Memory] ∈ $\{0,1\}$ ∧ Size ∈ $\{0,2,4,8,16,32\}$ ∧ Cores ∈ $\{0..7\}$

Constraints

C_1 : (MCS $\Rightarrow$ SpeedSensor ≥ 0) ∧ (SpeedSensor $\Rightarrow$ MCS),

C_2 : (MCS $\Rightarrow$ Processor ≥ 0) ∧ (Processor $\Rightarrow$ MCS),

C_3 : (MCS $\Rightarrow$ Memory ≥ 0) ∧ (Memory $\Rightarrow$ MCS),

C_4 : (MCS $\Rightarrow$ PosSensor ≥ 0) ∧ (PosSensor $\Rightarrow$ MCS),

C_5 : (MCS $\Rightarrow$ Feedback ≥ 0) ∧ (Feedback $\Rightarrow$ MCS),

C_6 : PosSensor $\Rightarrow$ ($0 \leq$ PosSensor1 + PosSensor2 ≤ 2),

C_7 : Feedback $\Rightarrow$ ($1 \leq$ Visual + Audio+ Vibration ≤ 2),

C_8 : Relation (Core, Size) [(0,0), (1,2), (2,4), (3,8), (4,16), (5,32)],

C_9 : Memory $\Leftrightarrow$ (Size > 0), C_{10} : Processor $\Leftrightarrow$ (Cores > 0),

C_{11} : PosSensor1 $\Rightarrow$ *PosSensor*, C_{12} : PosSensor2 $\Rightarrow$ *PosSensor*,

C_{13} : Audio $\Rightarrow$ Feedback, C_{14} : Visual $\Rightarrow$ Feedback, C_{15} : Vibration $\Rightarrow$ Feedback,

Examples of products

P_1 :{SpeedSensor, Processor, Feedback, Audio, Memory, Cores=1, Size=2}

P_2 : {PosSensor, PosSensor1, PosSensor2}

information is represented using integer variables with domains ranging in the set of values presented in the description of the MCS. The domains of `Cores` and `Size` contain a zero to represent those products with no processor, nor memory. Products in Table 5 do not contain the variables assigned to zero in the corresponding solution (components not selected). For instance, in product P_2, the components `Processor, Feedback, Audio, Cores` were selected, the rest of the components are no part of the product.

4.2   Representation Mapping

Mapping the Sources of Variability. Things and **properties** were mapped to variables in HLCL. The ontological model defines things as elementary units that have properties. Those properties represent a particular characteristic of a thing. In HLCL, elements in a product line (e.g., feature, requirement, design fragment, component or any other reusable artifact) are represented by variables associated with Boolean domains. The information related to structural elements (things) are the attributes. These attributes are represented using variables with domains of different types, regarding the possible values of the attribute (attributes, values [3]). In our example, each component in the MCS is mapped to Boolean variables ranging in $\{0, 1\}$ and the attribute Size representing the size of the internal memory is mapped to a variable with domain $\{0, 2, 4, 8, 16, 32\}$. For each attribute, a constraint in the form $element \Leftrightarrow (attribute > 0)$ should be introduced. Therefore, when an element is selected, all its attributes are entailed and vice versa (e.g., C_4 and C_7 in Table 5).

In the ontological model, the **lawful state space** is an ontological construct defining the set of states of a thing complying with the state laws of the thing. First, we map the **state** of a thing representing the possible values of its attributes. In HLCL, the **domain** of a variable represents the set of possible values for such variable. Thus, we map the state of a thing to the set containing the domains of the variable(s) used for representing a thing and its attributes. Second, we map a **state law** that is a rule that restricts the values of the attributes of a thing. In HLCL, **constraints** are expressions that represent rules restricting the domains of variables. Hence, the state laws are mapped to the constraints over the variables representing the state of a particular thing. Finally, we conclude that the **lawful state space** can be mapped to the set of values (in the domain) agreeing with the constraints in the model. For instance, consider the attribute core in the example in Table 5 its domain (state) is defined as the integers in the interval $[0, 7]$. However, considering C_8 and the domain of the attribute Size, the lawful state space for Core is the set $\{0, 1, 2, 3, 4\}$.

The **lawful event space** is the set of all events in a thing that are lawful (with respect to the state laws). In this mapping, we consider that (1) an **event** is defined as a change in the state of a thing that can be internal or external, (2) states were mapped to HLCL domains in previous mappings. Thus, events are mapped to **constraints** because they are the HLCL constructs that continually produce changes in the domain of variables. More particularly, the mapping considers constraints that trigger other constraints like C_6 in the example in

Table 5. In C_6, the selection of a position sensor (`PosSensor = 1`) triggers another constraint that will change the domain of variables `PosSensor1` and `PosSensor2`. Now, considering that the lawful state space is represented by sets of values satisfying the constraints, we map the **lawful event space** to the constraints in the HLCL model. Note that for this mapping we treat constraints not just as the rules in the domain of a system but also as in the computational model of the Concurrent Constraints Programming [24] where constraints reside in a store and act as agents consulting the values in the domains and modifying the domains to preserve consistency.

The mapping determined a lack of representation for the ontological construct **history**. Asadi et al. ontology defines history as the chronologically-ordered states that a thing traverses in time. In HLCL as in other constraint languages based in CCP [24] there exist two moments: first, when the problem is specified and all the possible values in the domain of a variable are defined; second, when the solver determines which values satisfy all the constraints in the problem. Then, a value associated with a variable does not change in time. Therefore, HLCL does not have constructs to specify the sequence of changes in the values assigned to variables.

Table 6. Representation mapping between ontological constructs and HLCL constructs.

Concepts			Mapping - Rationale
Variability source	Structure	Things	**Boolean Variables** - Elements in a product line (e.g., feature, requirement, design fragment, component or any other reusable artifact) are represented by variables associated with Boolean domains.
		Properties	**Variables** - The information related to things (e.g., attribute) are represented using variables with domains ranging in the possible values of the attribute. An element is linked to its attributes by a constraint in the form $element \Leftrightarrow (attribute > 0)$.
		Lawful state space	**Values** (in the domain) that respect the constraints in the model.
		State	**Domains** of variables representing attributes. This mapping considers that the state is the set of values for an attribute.
		State law	**Constraints** - State laws as the rule that restricts the values of the attributes of a thing are mapped to the constraints over the variables representing the attributes of a particular thing.
	Process	Lawful event space	**Constraints** over the variables to representing the state of a thing.
		Event	**Constraints** - Considering that event are changes in the state of a thing and states were mapped to domains, events are mapped to constraints that trigger other constraints and produces changes in the domains of elements and attributes.
		History	**No HLCL construct can map this ontological construct.**

Mapping the Variability Patterns. The variability patterns are observable characteristics of the products in a product line. In this mapping, we show how the constraints in the HLCL can be used to specify variability relations that generate products where the variability patterns are observable. This mapping included constraints representing variability in previous publications [17,23] and listed in Table 2. To illustrate this mapping, we use a subset of the 831 valid products in the MCS example (Table 7). Additionally, particular instances of constraints mapping variability patterns are described in Table 8.

Table 7. Examples of valid products in the Movement Control System (MCS) product line.

P_1 : {SpeedSensor, Processor, Feedback, Audio, Memory, Cores = 1, Size = 2 }
P_2 : {PosSensor, PosSensor1, PosSensor2}
P_3 : {SpeedSensor, Feedback, Audio, Vibration, Memory, Processor, Cores = 2, Size = 4}
P_4 : {SpeedSensor, Processor, Memory, Cores = 1, Size = 2}
P_5 : {SpeedSensor, Feedback, Audio, Vibration, Visual, Memory, Processor, Cores = 2, Size = 4}

Table 8. Constraints mapping variability patterns.

Variability pattern	Constraint	HLCL constructs	Semantics
Full similarity one-side	(1) $C \Rightarrow P$	**Constraints** with Boolean domains, and logical operators	If P is selected then C may be selected, but if C is present, then P is present too
	(2) $C \leq P$	**Constraints** with integer domains, arithmetic operators	
Partial similarity	(1) $P \Leftrightarrow C_1 \vee \cdots \vee C_n$	**Constraints** with Boolean domains, and logical operators	If P is selected then one or more C_i are selected
	(2) $(C_1 \Rightarrow P) \wedge \cdots \wedge (C_n \Rightarrow P) \wedge P \geq 1 \Rightarrow C_1 + \cdots + C_n \geq m \wedge P \geq 1 \Rightarrow C_1 + \cdots + C_n \leq n$	**Constraints** with integer domains, and Boolean, arithmetic operators	If P is selected then at least m and at most n C_i are selected
Dissimilarity	$(C_1 \Rightarrow P) \wedge \ldots \wedge (C_n \Rightarrow P) \wedge P \geq 1 \Rightarrow C_1 + \cdots + C_n \geq 1 \wedge P \geq 1 \Rightarrow C_1 + \cdots + C_n \leq 1$	**Constraints** with integer domains, and logical, arithmetic operators	If P is selected then, one or zero C_i are also selected
Ordering variability	No HLCL construct can map this ontological construct		

Full Similarity One-Side. This pattern can be mapped to constraints in HLCL used for representing optional relations [12]. Within an optional relation, it is possible to find products including an element, or not. Then, the use of optional relations causes the inclusion of two or more products with the full similarity one-side property in the set of solutions. For example, consider products P_1 and P_3 in Table 7. Optional relations can be represented with boolean and integer constraints. For instance, in the MCS example, C_1 to C_5 are optional relations. Other examples of constraints used to represent optional relations in HLCL tare in Table 8.

Partial Similarity. This pattern can be mapped to constraints in HLCL used for representing variability relations that produce products sharing common elements. The most common variability relations with this characteristic are OR-relations [12], and group cardinality $\langle m, n \rangle$ relations [7]. For instance consider C_7, that represents a group cardinality $\langle 0, 2 \rangle$. This constraint produces valid products such as P_1, P_3 and P_5 exhibiting partial similarity. Table 8 shows how to represent OR and group cardinality in HLCL.

Dissimilarity. This pattern can be mapped to constraints in HLCL used for representing variability relations such as alternative (XOR) [12], or group cardinality $\langle 1, 1 \rangle$ [7]. These relations produce products without common elements. For instance, products P_2 and P_4 do not have common elements. Table 8 shows how to represent alternative and group cardinality $\langle 1, 1 \rangle$ in HLCL.

Ordering This variability pattern cannot be mapped in HLCL because there are no constraints to determine the order of the selection of values for variables. In addition, under the concurrent constraint programming model, it is not possible to establish an ordering for the application of constraints [24].

4.3   Results

To answer the research questions, we performed an interpretation mapping to determine whether and how a grammatical construct stands for a real-world construct. Accordingly, Table 9 presents the interpretation mapping. Rows in Table 9 represent the HLCL constructs, and columns represent the ontological constructs. A bullet is depicted when the HLCL construct in the row maps the ontological construct in the column.

Q1: Does HLCL Map all the Constructs in the Ontological Model? Both the representation and interpretation mapping showed a construct deficit for representing the ontological constructs: history and ordering (highlighted columns in Table 9). Moreover, HLCL does not support the design of product line models where explicit consideration is given to sequence and order in the product line. Accordingly, we expect that HLCL users will encounter difficulties in meeting the potential need for explicit represent constraints such as: "element E_1 must be selected before E_2", or "start reconfiguration after five time units". Regarding the results of Asadi et al. in [1], a similar deficiency was also found to exist in FMs and OVM. Consequently, neither HLCL, FMs nor OVM can represent history and ordering.

Q2: Are There any HLCL Constructs that Cannot be Mapped into Ontological Constructs? All constructs in HLCL were mapped to the elements in the ontology proposed by Asadi et al. [1]. Hence, HLCL does not present construct excess.

Q3: Is the Set of Mapped Constructs a One-to-One Relation? The mapping of ontological constructs to language constructs is not one-to-one. Table 9 shows that it is not possible to have a one-to-one mapping considering the difference in the number of constructs (HLCL has four constructs, the ontology has nine constructs). In consequence, the absence of a one-to-one mapping causes two defects: (1) there is one ontological construct mapping to more than one HLCL constructs (construct redundancy), and (2) there are HLCL constructs mapped to different ontological constructs (construct overload). These two defects are also observable in Table 9. First, columns in Table 9 serve to identify which ontological constructs are mapped to more than one HLCL construct. Thus, columns with more than one bullet are instances of construct redundancy. In the table, one instance of construct redundancy is observable, the mapping (lawful state space → domains, values). Second, rows in Table 9 are used to find which HLCL constructs are mapped to more than one ontological construct. Therefore, rows with more than one bullet are instances of construct overload. As seen in the table, two of the four HLCL constructs are involved in more than one mapping: variables and constraints.

Table 9. Interpretation mapping between ontological constructs and HLCL constructs.

Constructs	Ontology								
	Variability Sources					Variability Patterns			
	Things	Properties	Lawful state space	Lawful event space	History	Full similarity one-side	Partial similarity	Dissimilarity	Ordering variability
Variables	•	•							
Domains			•						
Values			•						
Constraints				•			•	•	•

Ontological Completeness and Clarity. The Recker et al. Degree of Deficit (DoD), is the measure usually used to conclude about the level of ontological completeness in a conceptual modeling language. Under this idea, the lower the DoD, the higher level of ontological completeness. HLCL exhibits a 22% of degree of deficit. Therefore, HLCL completeness level is 78%. We interpret this result as HLCL closely represents the general principles of variability under the Asadi et al. ontological framework. To evaluate the ontological clarity of HLCL, we calculate the Degrees of Excess (DoE), Redundancy (DoR) and Overlap (DoO). HLCL exhibits a low degree of excess (DoE 0%), and medium degrees of redundancy and overload (DoR, DoO 50%). On the one hand, a low DoE is a desirable situation as it prevents user confusion due to the need to ascribe meaning to constructs that do not appear to have real-world meaning. On the other hand, the levels of redundancy and overload indicate that HLCL might be unclear and will produce potentially ambiguous representations of real-world domains.

5   Analysis and Discussion

The analysis of the results obtained in this evaluation of the HLCL under the theory of ontological expressiveness contributes to taking forward the discussion of HLCL's expressiveness. The results of the evaluation should be analyzed from two different perspectives: completeness and clarity. HLCL presents a medium level of clarity due to its levels of redundancy and overload. This redundancy and overload levels depend on the number of constructs in HLCL and especially in the repeated use of constraints for mapping variability patterns. The *constraint* construct is a generic construct that represents a set of expressions. The mapping presented in Sect. 4.2 includes particular instances of constraints to explicitly demonstrate how HLCL constructs represent variability patterns in the ontology. To enhance the clarity of HLCL, we propose to extend the set of HLCL constructs to include constraint expressions mapping frequently used variability relations. These new constructs would be considered syntactic sugar as they can be removed without any effect on the expressive power of HLCL.

Ontological incompleteness arises because it is not possible to map any HLCL construct with the ontological constructs related to time: history and ordering. A similar observation was reported by Asadi et al. after analyzing FMs and OVMs [1]. In their study, Asadi et al. concluded that both languages lack variability completeness as they do not have any construct for representing order. This conclusion is not surprising given that the formalisms associated with these variability languages (e.g., first-order logic and concurrent constraint programming [3]) does not model time. Indeed, the lack of expressiveness concerning the notion of time is not inherent only to these three languages. To the best of our knowledge, there is no product line notation including constructs for modeling time in product lines. Therefore, the gap in the HLCL's expressiveness demonstrated in this study, reflects a gap in the state of the art of the product line notations. Consequently, we consider that the inclusion of time as a native concept in variability languages should be considered as a challenge in the design of variability languages.

The notion of time in computational models represents the sequence of changes in the state of a system. Time can be used in product line notations to specify variability in process or behavior and also variation between product releases. To address these, notations require sophisticated elements able to represent temporal constraints aiming to (1) enhance variability, (2) schedule changes, and (3) sequence constraints. Temporal constraints *enhance variability*

languages by allowing to represent preferences regarding the time of activation
of an element in a product line including constraints such as "element A is activated before/after the activation of element B", "in the next time unit, element
A is activated", or "element A is activated after three units of time". These
temporal and scheduling constraints are particularly relevant to Dynamic Software Product Lines (DSPLs). The goal of the DSPL is to build systems that
dynamically adapts itself to fluctuations in user needs, environmental conditions, and resource constraints at runtime. In this context, temporal constraints
might be useful for including rules to schedule reconfigurations (adaptations).
The inclusion of temporal constraints might enable the use of constraints such as:
"the reconfiguration starts at time x", "the reconfiguration occurs during event
E", "a reconfiguration will occur eventually". *Sequence constraints* are useful to
perform staged configuration where it is necessary to produce a series of intermediate configurations compelling to a collection of requirements. For instance,
Burdek et al. in [4] include temporal constraints to perform staged configuration to determine an order relation between configuration stages. In their work,
Burdek et al. include time constraints in a feature-based notation.

5.1   Towards a Product Line Engineering Constraint Language: PLEC

This section introduces the Product Line Engineering Constraint Language
(PLEC), a domain specific language for product line specification. This language aims to overcome the limitations of HLCL previously discussed. PLEC
is a CP-based language that can be used (1) as an intermediate representation
of other product line notations and (2) as a specification language to create
PLMs. Therefore, in the design of PLEC, we separate the concerns regarding
the *representation* of PLMs as constraint programs from the concerns regarding
the *specification* of PLMs. To this end, PLEC provides a collection of constructs
based on variability relations to specify PLMs. At the same time, the semantics
of the models specified in PLEC are represented using constraint programs in
HLCL. Table 10 presents an extract of the PLEC syntax. The complete syntax
and semantics are out of the scope of this paper. This paper focuses on report-
ing the results of the evaluation of HLCL and on highlighting the strengths and
weaknesses of this language to justify its evolution.

As presented in Table 10, PLEC includes the constructs to represent
⟨*PL_constraints*⟩ and ⟨*time_constraints*⟩. On the one hand, ⟨*PL_constraints*⟩
provide the user with variability specific constructs with the objective of improving the clarity of the language. To provide the semantics of these constructs we
use the transformation rules proposed in previous works [17,18,23,25]. As an
example, the specification of the MCS using PLEC is presented in Table 11. On
the other hand, ⟨*time_constraints*⟩ provide the user with time constructs, such
as `always`, `next`, `eventually`, `until`, and `unless-next` inspired by Linear Temporal Logic (LTL) [19]. These new constructs enable the user to use expressions
such as "`eventually` A is selected", "`unless` A is selected `next` B is selected"
to represent temporal relations between constraints in PLMs.

Table 10. Extract of the syntax of PLEC.

⟨*model*⟩	::=	⟨*identifier*⟩ ⟨*variable*⟩$^+$ ⟨*constraints*⟩$^+$
⟨*variable*⟩	::=	{'**instantiable**' '[' ⟨*int*⟩ ',' ⟨*int*⟩'] '}*
		⟨*type*⟩ ⟨*identifier*⟩ '**values:**' ⟨*values*⟩
⟨*values*⟩	::=	⟨*interval*⟩ | ⟨*enumeration*⟩
⟨*constraints*⟩	::=	⟨*PL_constraints*⟩ | ⟨*time_constraints*⟩
⟨*PL_constraints*⟩	::=	⟨*structural*⟩ | ⟨*hierarchical*⟩ | ⟨*traversal*⟩ | ⟨*refinement*⟩
		| ⟨*rule*⟩
⟨*time_constraints*⟩	::=	**always**⟨*PL_constraint*⟩ | **next**⟨*PL_constraint*⟩ |
		eventually⟨*PL_constraint*⟩ |
		⟨*PL_constraint*⟩ **until**⟨*PL_constraint*⟩ |
		unless ⟨*PL_constraint*⟩ **next**⟨*PL_constraint*⟩

Table 11. The MCS product line specified using PLEC.

model MCS
boolean SpeedSensor, Processor, Feedback, Visual, Audio, Vibration, Memory
instantiable [0,2] **boolean** PosSensor
integer Cores **values:** 0..7
integer Size **values:** [0,2,4,8,16,32]
C_1 : **structural:** MCS **variants:** [SpeedSensor,PosSensor,Processor,Memory,Feedback]
C_2 : SpeedSensor **is optional**
C_3 : PosSensor **is optional**
C_4: Processor **is optional**
C_5: Memory **is optional**
C_6: Feedback **is optional**
C_7: **attributes:** [Size] **of** Memory
C_8: **attributes:** [Cores] **of** Processor
C_9: **structural:** Feedback **variants:** [Visual,Audio,Vibration] **card:** [1,2]
C_{10}: **vars:** (Cores,Memory) **variants:** [(1,2),(2,4), (3,8),(4,16), (5,32)]

5.2   Threats to Validity

To discuss the limitations of our study, we elaborate the threats to validity of our work and the strategies used to minimize their effects [13]. The validity of our results may be affected by the selection of the ontology and the mapping between the language and the ontology. To mitigate the bias in selecting the ontology, we first performed a literature review searching for foundational ontologies containing domain-independent and variability-related constructs. Next, we studied the concepts in the selected ontologies as well as the purpose and application of the ontology. As a result, we selected the Asadi's et al. ontology. Though this ontology may not be complete as it contains a subset of the constructs from BWW [27], we agree with Asadi et al. that the variability patterns describe the possible cases of variability in a product line [1]. Moreover, we believe that we will obtain similar results evaluating the HLCL expressiveness using other foundational ontologies along with Asadi et al.'s variability patterns. In this conclusion we considered that the results regarding HLCL's completeness are the product of the difficulties of HLCL to represent ontological constructs related to the sequence of events and temporal constraints. In the case of the HLCL's clarity, overlapping and overload will be present as long as the generic construct *constraints* is used to map all variability constructs in the ontology.

To decrease the threats regarding the mapping between the language and the ontology the analysis was conducted in three steps. First, one researcher separately mapped the HLCL constructs against ontological constructs to create a first mapping draft. Second, two researchers met to discuss and define a second draft. Third, all the researchers discussed and produced a third version of the mapping. By reaching a consensus at the end of this process, we procured to increase the reliability and validity of the mapping.

6   Related Work

Many works have applied the theory of ontological expressiveness to evaluate conceptual modeling languages such as the entity-relation model [26]; UML [5]; the i^* language [11]; and BPMN [20] to mention a few. In the domain of product lines, there are two well-known works [1,21] using the theory of ontological expressiveness both using the BWW ontology [27] as a basis and extending it to accomplish their purposes. First, Reinhartz-Berger et al. [21] included a set of constructs to analyze process variability and later to determine variability in terms of software behavior. This framework was used to perform a feasibility analysis. Second, Asadi et al. [1] included a collection of variability patterns aiming to provide a framework for evaluating the ontological expressiveness of variability modeling languages. In their work, Asadi et al. use their framework to evaluate two variability languages: FMs and OVM. Our work applies the theory of ontological expressiveness to provide a theoretical analysis of HLCL as a variability modeling language in order to determine its ability to represent variability in real-world domain models. To the best of our knowledge, there is no evaluation of the expressiveness of a language that abstracts product line constraints as HLCL does. In addition, this paper considers the results of Asadi et al. to conclude about the state of the variability languages and the challenges that future research should consider.

7   Conclusions and Future Work

This paper presents the design, conduction, and results of an evaluation of the expressiveness of the HLCL as a conceptual modeling language under the light of the ontological expressiveness theory. The results of the evaluation were analyzed from two perspectives: ontological completeness and ontological clarity.

Firstly, the results showed that HLCL has a high level of completeness (78%). However, some variability concepts should be integrated for obtaining a 100% level of completeness. More precisely, we consider that the inclusion of temporal constraints will make HLCL complete. These temporal constraints can be used with the purpose of (1) enhancing variability, (2) scheduling changes, and (3) introducing events as sequence constraints. Secondly, from the metrics related to clarity, we can conclude that HLCL is a concise language without excess (0%). Nevertheless, it seems that HLCL's high level of abstraction impacts its clarity because there exist significant levels of redundancy and overload (50%). Therefore, potential users may face difficulties to use the constraints for specifying variability in PLMs. To solve this issue, we propose to include variability relations as constructs of the language. Additionally, we compared our results regarding completeness with the ones presented by Asadi et al. in their ontological analysis of FMs and OVMs [1]. The analysis of our results along with this comparison let us conclude that the gap in the HLCL's expressiveness is also a gap in the state of the art of the product line notations. Our results point to new challenges in future research for product line specification and new directions on our objective to provide a constraint-based language for the product lines domain. In future work, we will answer the questions risen by the results of this study. Is it appropriate to pursue the development of a generic constraint-based language' or should we better separate the constraint programming concerns from the product lines concerns? We are more inclined to continue our work in the second direction, where we aim to develop PLEC, a constraint-based domain specific language for product line specification. In the design of PLEC, we separated the concerns regarding the specification of product lines from the formalization of product line models. With these concerns separated, PLEC can still be used (1) as an intermediate representation of other product line notations using the several transformation rules in literature [17,18,23,25]; and (2) as a specification language to create more expressive PLMs with a collection of product line constraints that will include time constraints to overcome the limitations of HLCL.

References

1. Asadi, M., Gasevic, D., Wand, Y., Hatala, M.: Deriving variability patterns in software product lines by ontological considerations. In: Atzeni, P., Cheung, D., Ram, S. (eds.) ER 2012. LNCS, vol. 7532, pp. 397–408. Springer, Heidelberg (2012). https://doi.org/10.1007/978-3-642-34002-4_31
2. Basili, V.R., Caldiera, G., Rombach, H.D.: The goal question metric approach. In: Encyclopedia of Software Engineering. Wiley, New York (1994)
3. Benavides, D., Segura, S., Ruiz-Cortés, A.: Automated analysis of feature models 20 years later: a literature review. Inf. Syst. **35**(6), 615–636 (2010). https://doi.org/10.1016/j.is.2010.01.001
4. Bürdek, J., Lity, S., Lochau, M., Berens, M., Goltz, U., Schürr, A.: Staged configuration of dynamic software product lines with complex binding time constraints. In: Proceedings of the Eighth International Workshop on Variability Modelling of

Software-Intensive Systems - VaMoS 2014, pp. 1–8. ACM Press, New York (2013). https://doi.org/10.1145/2556624.2556627

5. Burton-Jones, A., Meso, P.: The effects of decomposition quality and multiple forms of information on novices' understanding of a domain from a conceptual model. J. Assoc. Inf. Syst. **9**(12), 1 (2008)

6. Burton-Jones, A., Wand, Y., Weber, R.: Guidelines for empirical evaluations of conceptual modeling grammars. J. Assoc. Inf. Syst. **10**(6), 495–532 (2009). https://doi.org/10.17705/1jais.00201

7. Czarnecki, K., Helsen, S., Eisenecker, U.: Formalizing cardinality-based feature models and their specialization. Softw. Process. Improv. Pract. **10**(1), 7–29 (2005). https://doi.org/10.1002/spip.213

8. Djebbi, O., Salinesi, C.: Towards an automatic PL requirements configuration through constraints reasoning. In: Second International Workshop on Variability Modelling of Software-Intensive Systems (VaMoS), pp. 17–23 (2008)

9. Guizzardi, G.: Ontology-based evaluation and design of visual conceptual modeling languages. In: Reinhartz-Berger, I., Sturm, A., Clark, T., Cohen, S., Bettin, J. (eds.) Domain Engineering, pp. 317–347. Springer, Heidelberg (2013). https://doi.org/10.1007/978-3-642-36654-3_13

10. Guizzardi, G., Falbo, R., Guizzardi, R.: Grounding software domain ontologies in the unified foundational ontology (UFO): the case of the ODE software process ontology. In: Memorias de la XI Conferencia Iberoamericana de Software Engineering (CIbSE 2008), Recife, Pernambuco, Brasil, 13–17 February 2008, pp. 127–140 (2008)

11. Guizzardi, R., Franch, X., Guizzardi, G.: Applying a foundational ontology to analyze means-end links in the i^* framework. In: 2012 Sixth International Conference on Research Challenges in Information Science (RCIS), pp. 1–11. IEEE, May 2012.https://doi.org/10.1109/RCIS.2012.6240425

12. Kang, K., Cohen, S., Hess, J., Novak, W., Peterson, A.: Feature-oriented domain analysis (FODA) Feasibility study. Technical Report Software Engineering Institute, Carnegie Mellon University (1990)

13. Kitchenham, B., et al.: Preliminary guidelines for empirical research in software engineering. IEEE Trans. Softw. Eng. **28**(8), 721–734 (2002). https://doi.org/10.1109/TSE.2002.1027796

14. Martinez, J., Ziadi, T., Mazo, R., Bissyande, T.F., Klein, J., Traon, Y.L.: Feature relations graphs: a visualisation paradigm for feature constraints in software product lines. In: Second IEEE Working Conference on Software Visualization, September 2014, pp. 50–59. IEEE (2014). https://doi.org/10.1109/VISSOFT.2014.18

15. Mazo, R., Grünbacher, P., Heider, W., Rabiser, R., Salinesi, C., Diaz, D.: Using constraint programming to verify DOPLER variability models. In: Proceedings of the 5th Workshop on Variability Modeling of Software-Intensive Systems - VaMoS 2011, pp. 97–103. ACM Press, New York (2011). https://doi.org/10.1145/1944892.1944904

16. Mazo, R., Muñoz-Fernández, J.C., Rincón, L., Salinesi, C., Tamura, G.: VariaMos: an extensible tool for engineering (dynamic) product lines. In: Proceedings of the 19th International Conference on Software Product Line - SPLC 2015. pp. 374–379. ACM Press, New York (2015). https://doi.org/10.1145/2791060.2791103

17. Mazo, R., Salinesi, C., Diaz, D., Djebbi, O., Lora-Michiels, A.: Constraints: the heart of domain and application engineering in the product lines engineering strategy. Int. J. Inf. Syst. Model. Des. **3**(2), 33–68 (2012). https://doi.org/10.4018/jismd.2012040102

18. Muñoz-Fernández, J.C., Tamura, G., Raicu, I., Mazo, R., Salinesi, C.: REFAS: a PLE approach for simulation of self-adaptive systems requirements. In: Proceedings of the 19th International Conference on Software Product Line - SPLC 2015, pp. 121–125. ACM Press, New York (2015). https://doi.org/10.1145/2791060.2791102
19. Pnueli, A.: The temporal logic of programs. In: 18th Annual Symposium on Foundations of Computer Science (SFCS 1977), September 1977, pp. 46–57. IEEE, Washington, DC, USA (1977). https://doi.org/10.1109/SFCS.1977.32
20. Recker, J., Rosemann, M., Indulska, M., Green, P.: Business process modeling a comparative analysis. J. Assoc. Inf. Syst. **10**(4), 1 (2009)
21. Reinhartz-Berger, I., Sturm, A., Wand, Y.: External variability of software: classification and ontological foundations. In: Jeusfeld, M., Delcambre, L., Ling, T.-W. (eds.) ER 2011. LNCS, vol. 6998, pp. 275–289. Springer, Heidelberg (2011). https://doi.org/10.1007/978-3-642-24606-7_21
22. Salinesi, C., Mazo, R.: Defects in product line models and how to identify them. In: Software Product Line - Advanced Topics, chap. 5, p. 50. InTech (2012). https://doi.org/10.5772/35662
23. Salinesi, C., Mazo, R., Djebbi, O., Diaz, D., Lora-Michiels, A.: Constraints: the core of product line engineering. In: Fifth International Conference on Research Challenges in Information Science (RCIS), pp. 1–10 (2011). https://doi.org/10.1109/RCIS.2011.6006825
24. Saraswat, V.A., Rinard, M.: Concurrent constraint programming. In: Proceedings of the 17th ACM SIGPLAN-SIGACT Symposium on Principles of Programming Languages - POPL 1990, pp. 232–245. ACM Press, New York (1990). https://doi.org/10.1145/96709.96733
25. Sawyer, P., Mazo, R., Diaz, D., Salinesi, C., Hughes, D.: Using constraint programming to manage configurations in self-adaptive systems. Computer **45**(10), 56–63 (2012). https://doi.org/10.1109/MC.2012.286
26. Shanks, G., Moody, D., Nuredini, J., Tobin, D., Weber, R.: Representing classes of things and properties in general in conceptual modelling. J. Database Manag. **21**(2), 1–25 (2010). https://doi.org/10.4018/jdm.2010040101
27. Wand, Y., Weber, R.: On the ontological expressiveness of information systems analysis and design grammars. Inf. Syst. J. **3**(4), 217–237 (1993). https://doi.org/10.1111/j.1365-2575.1993.tb00127.x

Distributed Computing on Distributed Memory

Andreas Prinz$^{(\boxtimes)}$

Department of ICT, University of Agder, Agder, Norway
andreas.prinz@uia.no

Abstract. Distributed computation is formalized in several description
languages for computation, as e.g. Unified Modeling Language (UML),
Specification and Description Language (SDL), and Concurrent Abstract
State Machines (CASM). All these languages focus on the distribution of
computation, which is somewhat the same as concurrent computation.
In addition, there is also the aspect of distribution of state, which is often
neglected. Distribution of state is most commonly represented by communication between active agents. This paper argues that it is desirable
to abstract from the communication and to consider abstract distributed
state. This includes semantic handling of conflict resolution, e.g. in connection with data replication. The need for abstract distribution of state
is discussed and a novel semantics for concurrency based on an abstract
distributed state is presented. This semantics uses runs over so-called
multistates, and hides the internal communication for replica handling.
This way, distributed computation is described over an abstract memory
model.

1 Introduction

There are several ways to formalize *sequential* computation. Abstract State
Machines (ASMs) [5] faithfully model such computations as proven with the
sequential ASM thesis [10] showing that every sequential algorithm is captured
by sequential ASMs. A similar result for (synchronous) *parallel* algorithms is
reported in [6].

For *concurrent* systems a similar result is achieved with concurrent ASMs
(CASM) in [3]. It improves over earlier work of partially ordered runs in [9]
and generalizes the notion of sequential consistency as defined in [13]. CASMs
define a concurrent algorithm as a family of agents interacting using the following
concurrency postulate, thus defining *concurrent ASM runs*.

A concurrent process or algorithm is given by a finite set $\mathcal{A}$ of pairs
$(a, alg(a))$ of agents a, which are equipped each with a (sequential) algorithm $alg(a)$ to execute. In a concurrent $\mathcal{A}$-run started in some initial state
S_0, each interaction state S_n $(n \geq 0)$ where some agents (say those of some
finite set A_n of agents) interact with each other yields a next state S_{n+1}

© Springer Nature Switzerland AG 2018
F. Khendek and R. Gotzhein (Eds.): SAM 2018, LNCS 11150, pp. 67–84, 2018.
https://doi.org/10.1007/978-3-030-01042-3_5

by the moves of all agents $a \in A_n$ which happen to simultaneously complete the execution of their current $alg(a)$-step they had started in some preceding state S_j ($j \leq n$ depending on a).

But what about *distributed* computation? Distributed computation refers to sequential agents that are distributed in space. They have their own computation capability, such that computation is distributed. In order to work together, they need some sharing of data, i.e. some joint state. There are two main ways to handle state.

The first way to handle distributed state is called *local state*. It means there is no shared state at all, and each agent has its own local state. A joint computation is achieved using message exchange. The Specification and Description Language (SDL) [12] is an example of this approach.

In local state, each memory location is only accessible by one agent. When agents need to share data, this is done using signal exchange. All currently existing distributed systems use at their core local state with signal exchange. For example, a distributed database will have local data at several nodes, where the data is synchronized using signal exchange. In local state, access to shared data is done by sending and receiving signals.

This way, access primitives for shared data are send and receive, while local data is accessed with read and write. However, local state is a low-level concept, and often algorithms want to speak about shared data directly.

The second, more high-level way to handle distributed state is called *global state*, meaning that the state is in principle accessible for all agents with different agents having different views on the state in terms of visibility. This approach is prominently used in CASM.

Typically, high-level global state is implemented using some lower-level protocols based on local state and signal exchange. These protocols translate data access by read and write into data access by send and receive[1]. In global state, the access primitives for the agents are read and write for all types of data, local and shared.

We call the handling that is done to manage the global state for *memory model*. It includes the translation of memory access into signal exchange. For the user, the memory model implementation details are not of concern, but the properties of the memory model are essential.

In this paper, we consider two main types of memory models: *centralized* and *distributed*. In the centralized case, there is conceptually only one copy of the data, which is used to answer all read and write requests. In the distributed case, there are several copies of the data for use in read and write requests.

Typically, centralized state is *consistent* in the sense that all agents have the same view on the data. The consistency in the distributed case is dependent on the used protocol. In fact, this area is the main focus of this paper, because we will see that all specification methods favour a centralized memory model.

---

[1] As communicating ASMs [4] show, it is also possible to implement local state on top of global state.

Partially ordered runs from [9] use a strong form of centralized state, where concurrent runs are only valid when they can be sequentialized. Sequential consistency [13] has a weaker promise and only insist on sequential order for each agent and causality, i.e. a value v read needs a previous write of v. CASM is again more general than sequential consistency. There are several more models of consistency, but in this paper, the main focus is on *inconsistency*.

Known distributed algorithms (see e.g. [2,24,25]) are normally described based on local state or global centralized state. Does this mean that this covers all distributed computation, even inconsistent ones?

We already noted that all distributed state is message-based on a low level. On an even lower level, real hardware lives in the realm of physics and can be considered on a conceptual global centralized state (see also [3]). This indicates, that on low level CASM runs as defined in [3,4] capture all distributed computation. So the answer to the question is "Yes" on a low abstraction level.

However, modern web applications often provide a higher-level distributed state. This distributed state is not always well defined, since local copies are allowed to differ, as already observed in [22]. This may lead to inconsistent views and lost updates. On this higher level, the answer to the question is "No".

Inconsistency may occur in case of data replication. CASM illustrates such behaviour using an independent read - independent write (IRIW) algorithm A [3] with four agents $a_1, \ldots, a_4$ as follows.

$a_1: \quad x := 1$
$a_2: \quad y := 1$
$a_3: \quad Read(x); Read(y)$
$a_4: \quad Read(y); Read(x)$
initially $x = y = 0$

There is no sequentially consistent run (see [13]) where (1) each agent stops after having finished its program and (2) eventually a_3 reads $x = 1, y = 0$ and a_4 reads $x = 0, y = 1$. To see this, lets assume that a_3 reads $x = 1$ and $y = 0$. Looking at a_4, it can $Read(y)$ before or after a_3 does its $Read(y)$. If a_4 reads y after a_3, then it will also read its x after a_3 reads its x. This implies that it must read $x = 1$. If, alternatively, a_4 reads y earlier or at the same time as a_3, then it will read the value $y = 0$.

However, if x and y are replicated with two copies each, and an update by the programs a_1 or a_2 first affects only a single copy, while the update propagation to the other copy can happen later, such a behaviour will indeed be enabled.

This example can even be simplified using just two (or even one) agents with an own read - own write (OROW) algorithm as follows.

$a_1: \quad x := 1; Read(x)$
$a_2: \quad x := 2; Read(x)$
initially $x = 0$

With sequential consistency, it is impossible to achieve x = 0 in any of the reads. Furthermore, it is impossible that a_1 reads 2 and a_2 reads 1. This is because for a_1 reading 2, $x := 2$ has to be before $x := 1$, while for a_2 reading 1, it has to be the other way around. Both of them are not possible together.

Still, if x is replicated with two copies, and only one of them is used for writing and the other one for reading, it is possible to have $x = 0$. In the same style, a_1 can read 2 and a_2 can read 1 when a_1 writes to the first copy and reads from the second, while a_2 writes to the second copy and reads from the first.

These examples show that the properties of the memory model are essential in the analysis of distributed algorithms. Please remember that the memory model is the protocol used to implement global state. Then the algorithm behaviour is dependent on two parts:

1. the algorithms of the agents (distribution of computation), and
2. the memory model used (distribution of state).

With these two parts it is possible to check whether the resulting behaviour of the algorithm is acceptable. Here, the memory model can be thought of as a parameter of the distributed semantics. In real situations, it would amount to the configuration of the database storing the values. Different memory models (configurations) might lead to different behaviours. We will call concurrent algorithms on top of a memory model as *distributed algorithms* in this paper.

This paper is dedicated to understanding distributed algorithms that are based on distribution of state. We will (1) provide evidence of the need to consider distributed state and (2) define distributed runs over distributed state.

We will first shortly recap local state and global centralized state in Sects. 2 and 3. Then we will look into examples of global distributed state in Sect. 4 showing that distributed state is real. In Sect. 5, we introduce distributed runs over distributed state, and compare them with global centralized state in Sect. 6. Finally, we conclude in Sect. 7.

2   Local State

In this section, we shortly introduce local state. The idea behind local state is that the state is local to the agents and data sharing happens with message exchange. We assume that the reader is familiar with local state and we use SDL and process calculi as examples.

2.1   SDL

Specification and Description Language (SDL) [12] is an ITU standardized language that was developed for the specification of telecommunication protocols and systems. Later, it was also used for distributed systems in general. The main entity in SDL is an agent (process, block, or system), which is an active entity having local state. This local state is not visible to other agents. In order to work together, agents can send messages between each other thereby exchanging information.

SDL also introduces derived concepts of remote procedure calls, remote variables, and some form of shared data within the agent hierarchies, which are based on signal exchange.

2.2 Process Calculi

Process calculi [16] provide an abstraction for distributed computation. They feature sequential processes with the possibility to send and receive messages. The processing power of the processes is often very limited and the local state is often not modelled directly.

The main component of a system description is its signal exchange, i.e. which messages are sent and received. CCS [15] and CSP [11] are examples of such languages. Based on their strong mathematical foundation, they have been used to define the semantics of higher level languages like SDL.

2.3 Summary

Local state uses communication to provide shared state. This is general, but for some algorithms too low abstraction level. Therefore, often more high-level concepts are also provided.

3 Global Centralized State

In this section, we discuss global centralized state, which behaves as if there was just one copy of each shared memory location for write and read. Conflicts in access are solved in some way. This model is related to the ACID properties as known from databases.

First, we recap the ACID properties, and then we look at how global centralized state manifests for Abstract State Machines (ASM) and UML.

3.1 ACID

ACID is a set of properties that many distributed database systems adhere to. Basically, it is an extension of the sequential world into the distributed world. The underlying idea is to create distributed database systems in a way as if the reality was not distributed. ACID stands for the four properties **A**tomicity, **C**onsistency, **I**solation, and **D**urability.

The constituent operations of an *atomic* transaction either occur all, or none. *Consistency* is a property of the database states, saying that each database state must fulfill all rules for the state. The *isolation* property means that intermediate results are not visible. *Durability* ensures that changes made by finished transactions will become available.

3.2 Concurrent Abstract State Machines

Concurrent Abstract State Machines (CASM) are given by a finite set of agents $a \in \mathcal{A}$ with an associated (sequential) ASM $alg(a)$ each, composed in the usual way using the following constructs (see [5] for more details).

assignment	$f(t_1, \ldots, t_{ar_f}) := t_0$ (with terms t_i built over Σ),
parallel composition	$r_1\ r_2,$
sequential composition	$r_1\ ;\ r_2,$
branching	IF φ THEN r_+ ELSE $r_-,$
forall	FORALL x WITH $\varphi(x)$ DO $r(x),$
choice	CHOOSE x WITH $\varphi(x)$ IN $r(x)$, and
let	LET $x = t$ IN $r(x).$

The ASMs are defined over a global signature Σ of function symbols f, each with an arity ar_f. Functions that are used by several agents are called shared, and functions that are updated are called dynamic. In this paper, we are interested in such dynamic, shared functions.

From the signature Σ, we can define a global state S with partial functions f_S of arity ar_f over some fixed base set B. We call a function symbol f and its arguments $v_i \in B$ a *location*—often simply written as $f(v_1, \ldots, v_{ar_f})$—, and $val_S(f, (v_1, \ldots, v_{ar_f})) = f_S(val_S(v_1), \ldots, val_S(v_{ar_f}))$ the value at this location in state S. For formal reasons, the partial function f is completed such that all handling is done on total functions with the special value $undef \in B$.

In each state, $alg(a)$ defines an update set for agent a (see again [5] for more details). A next state is defined from the current state by applying a clash-free update set, thus ensuring that the state is always well-defined.

This general prerequisite is preserved in *concurrent ASM runs* [3]. Here the successor state of a (global) state S_i is obtained by applying a clash-free update set Δ that results from the union of update sets Δ_a for some subset of agents, $a \in \mathcal{A}' \subseteq \mathcal{A}$, each of which was built in some state $S_{j(a)}$ with $j(a) \leq i$.

3.3 UML

The Unified Modeling Language (UML) [20] does not speak a lot about distributed computation. UML features objects that are connected. There are also objects containing objects, and this would lead to the cases we discuss here.

Data in UML is stored with structural features. They have a semantics of just one value each time (see [20]): "Within an execution scope, the *StructuralFeature* has a separate and independent value or collection of values for its owning Classifier and for each Classifier that inherits it." Access to the value is given by a *StructuralFeatureAction*, which includes read and write. There is no indication of concurrency in this context.

However, in the UML standard [20] there is a concurrency property of type *CallConcurrencyKind* associated with each behavioural feature. It would be natural to think of structural feature actions as behavioural features, thus using a similar concurrency handling as for them as well. There are three possible values for *CallConcurrencyKind* and [20] includes the following table.

The first two values relate to sequentialized access in order to resolve conflicts. This is in essence global centralized state: only one access at a time. The responsibility for sequential access can be at the caller ('sequential') or at the callee ('guarded').

Sequential	No concurrency management mechanism is associated with the *BehavioralFeature* and, therefore, concurrency conflicts may occur. Instances that invoke a *BehavioralFeature* need to coordinate so that only one invocation to a target on any *BehavioralFeature* occurs at once
Guarded	Multiple invocations of a *BehavioralFeature* that overlap in time may occur to one instance, but only one is allowed to commence. The others are blocked until the performance of the currently executing *BehavioralFeature* is complete. It is the responsibility of the system designer to ensure that deadlocks do not occur due to simultaneous blocking
Concurrent	Multiple invocations of a *BehavioralFeature* that overlap in time may occur to one instance and all of them may proceed concurrently

For the value 'concurrent', the general understanding of users is that the object is responsible for integrity, but that this is done without enforcing sequentiality. This makes sense when the server object has full control over all its subobjects, because then the critical part is the behaviour of the clients. However, when the server object itself is distributed, the situation is different, and integrity might be a problem.

In the specification of foundational UML (fUML) [21] and Action Language for Foundational UML (Alf) [19], CallConcurrencyKind is not mentioned. However, as in UML itself, access to a structural feature is defined as reading or writing its current value - with the understanding that there is just one such value. This does not allow for replicas of the value.

The fUML semantics is loose and only specifies the essential sequentiality constraints needed in each implementation, thus allowing maximal concurrency. Concrete implementations may add more sequentiality. Even in the maximal concurrent case, state is considered global as each location has just one place of storage. We can conclude that UML has not considered distributed state and the specification is mostly written from the client point of view. However, the description of the value 'concurrent' would also allow other (inconsistent) ways of handling. Then UML would need a mechanism to describe the different levels of inconsistency, as we do in Sect. 5.

3.4 Summary

Global centralized state provides an abstract access to shared state. Distributed databases fall into this category, because they intend to provide a user experience of a global centralized state, even though there might be an underlying distribution of storage nodes. ACID provides a nice characterization of this idea.

If distributed state is consistent and works for the user as if it was centralized, then there is no point in looking at the distributed copies from the user point of view. However, when the distribution influences the execution of the algorithm, then it is important to be aware of it, as we will see in the next section.

4 Global Distributed State

Centralized state comes at a cost. A lot of communication is needed in order to make a distributed set of locations appear as one, which conflicts with the general desire of availability of the state. Therefore, the non-centralized BASE properties are considered. The relation between ACID and BASE is captured in the CAP theorem. In this section we look first at BASE and CAP and show then how inconsistent (non-centralized) distributed runs appear in the noSQL database system Cassandra, in Java and in Blockchain.

4.1 BASE and CAP

Massively distributed databases as in Internet distribution services have high rates of changes which leads to problems to ensure the ACID properties. These services often rely on the BASE properties, which is an abbreviation for **B**asically **A**vailable, **S**oft state, and **E**ventual consistency.

The main focus of BASE is *basic availability*, i.e. it is possible to access the database whenever needed. It is not guaranteed that the access leads to the latest value, but there will be an answer. This leads naturally to a *soft state*, which means the state is changing even during times without input.

The previous two properties can lead to inconsistency. In order to save the situation, *eventual consistency* provides consistency in the limit. Once the system does not get more data, it will stabilize in a consistent state. As the system is continuously active, this situation only arises for parts of the state.

The CAP theorem (Brewer's theorem) claims that there is a larger design space for distributed computation than given by ACID and BASE, and that ACID alone is too restricted to capture all distributed computation.

In its simplest formulation the CAP theorem states that it is impossible for a distributed computer system to simultaneously fulfill all three of the following requirements [7].

Consistency: All users/nodes see the same data at the same time.
Availability: It is guaranteed that every request receives a response.
Partition tolerance: The system continues to operate despite partitioning.

In this paper, partitions relate to distribution of state. Partitions are a normal situation in distributed computations due to smaller and larger network failures. Even a connected network might have too long latency and be considered disconnected. For distributed state, ACID amounts to a focus on consistency, while BASE focuses on availability with a spectrum of possibilities in between.

4.2 Cassandra

In the noSQL database system Cassandra [1,23] data is replicated using a fixed *replication factor* onto several *nodes* that are used for data storage and relate to physical machines. The nodes do also have behaviour, as they are responsible for data consistency. Agents communicate with Cassandra via their home node using requests and responses. Internally, the home node communicates with the other nodes in the system, but this is invisible to the agent. In Cassandra, nodes are grouped into clusters and data centres, which is not important here.

Cassandra relies on totally ordered timestamps to disambiguate different values v in different replicas of a function f. From two different values, the one with the later timestamp is used. Conceptually, timestamps are based on a global clock that always advances[2]. Cassandra assumes that timestamps fulfil the following requirements.

1. All timestamps are different from each other. When there are equal time-stamps, Cassandra uses lexical sorting of the values in order to determine the last timestamp.
2. Timestamps respect read/write causality. In other words, it is impossible to read a value from the future, i.e. all received timestamps are in the past. In the presence of clock drift, this means that the clock drift between nodes is less than their communication delay.

Cassandra allows to adapt the level of consistency using so-called read and write policies. Essentially, a policy tells how many replicas one needs to contact in order to read or write a value. In practice, *all* replicas are contacted for each request, and the policy tells how many replies one needs. When reading, the receiver takes the value with the latest timestamp of all incoming values.

In this paper, we consider the following Cassandra policies.

ONE   It is enough with one received answer.
QUORUM   We need answers from more than half of the replicas.
LOCAL_QUORUM QUORUM on the local data center.
ALL   We need answers from all replicas.

Using policy ONE for reading and writing gives us all the behaviour described in the introduction for IRIW and OROW. With the policy LOCAL_QUORUM, the inconsistencies in OROW disappear and with ALL, also IRIW is consistent. This way, choosing the policy amounts to choosing the consistency level of Cassandra.

4.3   Java Memory Model

The Java memory model [8] describes how Java programs interact with memory (see also [14]). More specifically, it details the interaction of Java threads on shared memory. The basic idea of the Java memory model is that each thread in itself follows a sequential model, and that all events that the individual thread cannot observe can happen in whatever order, i.e. reordering of code is allowed as long as it does not invalidate the sequential case.

Of course, as soon as threads are put together in concurrent runs, also events in other threads may become observable, and thus strange runs are possible.

---

[2] In reality, a global clock means perfect clock synchronization, which is impossible.

When looking at IRIW, the order of reading x and y in a_3 and a_4 is not relevant for the sequential case. Thus, also the inconsistent case given in the introduction is possible with the Java memory model.

In Java, the inconsistency can be blamed conceptually to the existence of several cached copies of the memory location, which essentially brings us to distributed state. IRIW can be fixed in Java making variables x and y volatile, which disables local cache copies and brings us back to consistent runs.

In the case of OROW, the written value of x can already be observed in the $Read(x)$ in the sequential case. This way, OROW will be consistent as is with respect to the Java memory model.

The important point here is that the semantics of Java is given with two parts: one detailing the processing, and one detailing the memory management. The memory management itself is dependent on flags in the code detailing which consistency level to apply (volatile = sequentially consistent).

4.4 Blockchain

Blockchain [18] implements a distributed protocol for bookkeeping with a growing linked list of records (blocks). Each block contains a sequence of records and a pointer to the previous block. For the electronic currency bitcoin [17], records are coin transactions.

For this article it is not important how the details of blockchain work, in particular the security part of the protocol. For us the distributed algorithm used is relevant.

In blockchain, several agents have to agree on the sequence of transactions. The general idea is that the agents collect records and translate them into blocks. The sequence of blocks then implies the sequence of records.

Each agent collects the records it can find and wraps them into a next block. As the agents run concurrently, there are several possible situations.

1. The agent finishes the work first and sends out the result. Then this new block is the starting point for the next block.
2. The agent finds a new block before finishing its own work. In this case, it drops its own work and starts with a next block. It will drop all its pending records that are already in the new block and include the remaining ones in the next block.
3. The agent finishes the work after another agent, but does not realize this due to the distributed nature of the system. This way, there can be several "current" blocks available in the network. These conflicts are solved by length of the chain. As long as there are two chains with the same number of blocks, the situation is undecided. If one of the chains gets a new block, it is the one to continue with. In this case, all the records missing in the longest protocol are collected and put into the next block.

This protocol is very dynamic and does not guarantee inclusion of records even when they appear in a block. The dynamic nature of the protocol allows large parts of the network to be disconnected and that may change the picture when they get accessible again. In principle, this can happen quite late from the current point of time, which means that consistency and durability (and therefore ACID) are spoiled.

4.5 Summary

We see that there is a considerable design space of distributed algorithms which are not consistent in terms of state, i.e. they are not ACID. This is triggered by the CAP theorem, which claims that one has to reduce consistency in order to keep availability.

This need is met with concrete implementations of noSQL databases that provide eventual consistency instead of strong consistency (e.g. Cassandra). Java was faced with a similar challenge to explain the behaviour of its concurrent code and came up with a distributed memory model.

Blockchain comes from a completely different area of algorithms, but it is still based on the idea of global state that different agents view differently. This way Blockchain provides some kind of BASE.

This means that when we talk about distributed computations, we have to take into account algorithms that work on top of inconsistent state. This inconsistent state typically arises out of the existence of several distributed copies of the same location, which are not (yet) synchronized. This is true for Cassandra, for Java and for Blockchain. In the remainder of the paper we will focus on Cassandra, because it has most options to adapt the state handling.

5 Semantics with Multistates

As we have seen, the formal models of distribution either support local memory with signal exchange or they are based on global centralized memory. It is possible to describe local based on centralized or the other way around.

The distributed memory model as described in Sect. 4 can be captured by detailed low-level description of the corresponding memory model (MM), see Fig. 1. Such a specification has been written to ensure that the translation is possible. It defines one system for the memory model and one for the algorithm, and connects them using signal exchange. Whenever the algorithm wants to read some data, it sends a read request to the memory model, and receives a message with the value read. In the same way, for each write it will send a write request and receive a confirmation of the write.

This means the original algorithms of the agents are changed by inserting signal send and receive actions for each read and write request, as shown in Fig. 1. The left-hand side of Fig. 1 will execute $alg(a)$ over global centralized memory locations, while the right-hand side will execute the adapted $alg(a)$ over global distributed memory as given by the memory model.

However, when we want to analyze the algorithm of the agents, we need to dig down into the details of the memory model. This is not what we want.

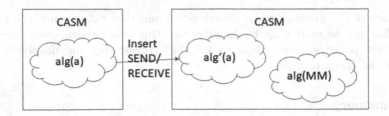

Fig. 1. Defining distributed algorithms over Cassandra

Instead, we would like to have an abstract description of the underlying memory model, i.e. how distributed copies of locations are handled. This is depicted in Fig. 2.

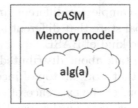

Fig. 2. Defining distributed algorithms with memory management

Such an abstract, high-level description will be provided in this section. For the sake of presentation, CASM is used as base method, but a similar approach would be possible in other languages.

CASM can model distribution of state in terms of the underlying communication, but not on the level of memory management. Therefore, we define a high-level description of memory management with multistates as a formalization of distributed state and distributed runs on top of multistates.

5.1 Multistates

We extend the definition of CASM such that it includes the memory model as shown in Fig. 2. The intention is to provide the behaviour of the right-hand side of Fig. 1 with several configuration options similar to Cassandra. One natural configuration option is of course global centralized memory.

This is done by defining a conceptual global state with several replicas that are handled in the underlying abstract memory model. The agents only configure the memory model, specifying it descriptively. This way, the semantics of the distributed algorithm is parametrized with the memory model.

First, we define a distributed global state by introducing multiple values per shared location.

Definition 1 (multivalue). *A multivalue M is a multiset that contains pairs $(v_1, t_1), \ldots, (v_x, t_x)$. The v_i are values from B, with undef as a possible value. The t_i are abstract integer timestamps, where larger means later.*

We write $time(p)$ and $value(p)$ to access the timestamp and value of a pair p, respectively.

Definition 2 (multistate). *A multistate S is a mapping of all shared locations[3] to multivalues, similar to CASM states. The size of the multiset $val_S(\ell)$ is constant for the location ℓ and reflects the number of replicas maintained by the memory model for ℓ, denoted $replicas(\ell)$.*

5.2 Policies

A policy is a way to select subsets of multivalues. They are used to provide different memory models. In this paper, we consider only three basic policies as already described in Sect. 4.2.

$$policy_{\text{ONE}}(M) = \{M' \subseteq M \bullet |M'| \geq 1\}$$
$$policy_{\text{QUORUM}}(M) = \{M' \subseteq M \bullet 2 * |M'| > |M|\}$$
$$policy_{\text{ALL}}(M) = \{M\}$$

Each policy provides a set of allowed subsets of the multivalue M. The policies are totally ordered with respect to the multivalue sets they provide.

$$\text{ALL} \subseteq \text{QUORUM} \subseteq \text{ONE}.$$

Policies are used for reading and writing of locations. A read access to location ℓ corresponds to the value of one of the elements in the multivalue associated with ℓ. From a possible subset of the multivalue according to the policy, we find the latest element, and extract the value of it.

$\text{Read}(\ell, policy^{read}) =$
$\qquad \text{CHOOSE } values \in policy^{read}(val_S(\ell)) \text{ IN } value(max_{\leq_{time}}(values))$

Similarly, a write access to ℓ with new value val replaces some elements in the multivalue given by the policy by the same number of elements with the new value val and the timestamp now.

$\text{Write}(\ell, policy^{write}) =$
$\qquad \text{CHOOSE } values \in policy^{write}(val_S(\ell)) \text{ IN}$
$\qquad\qquad val_S(\ell) := val_S(\ell) \setminus values \uplus \langle (val, now)^{|values|} \rangle$

---

[3] The non-shared locations are not relevant here.

5.3   Multistate ASM Semantics

Now we use multistates and policies to define distributed ASM runs similar to CASM runs.

Definition 3 (distributed run). *A distributed ASM (DASM) is given by a finite set of agents $a \in \mathcal{A}$ with an associated sequential ASM $alg(a)$ each (see also [3]), and a number of replicas as well as a read and a write policy for each location.*

A distributed run of $\mathcal{A}$ is a sequence of multistates together with a sequence $A_0, A_1, \ldots$ of subsets of A such that each state S_{n+1} is obtained from S_n by applying to it the updates computed by the agents $a \in A_n$ by using the Write *routine with the corresponding policy as defined above. Each of the agents started its current (internal) step by reading its input and shared locations in some preceding state S_j depending on a, using the* Read *as defined above with the corresponding policy. The updates of all agents in the same step have to be consistent.*

The initial multistate of a DASM run is based on the corresponding initial state of a CASM run. Instead of a value v for location ℓ, we use the multiset $\langle v^{replicas(\ell)} \rangle$.

Given a multistate S, the read policy rp defines a multistate S_{rp} that can be selected by agent a, and the rule of $alg(a)$ defines an update set Δ, which according to the write policy defines a new successor multistate S'. As the read- and write policies permit several states to be selected and different ways to update the multistate assigned to a location ℓ, there are several possible successor multistates. All of these possibilities form valid multistate runs.

The ordering of the policies extends to the valid runs, i.e.

$$runs(\text{ALL}) \subseteq runs(\text{QUORUM}) \subseteq runs(\text{ONE}).$$

We add a background activity related to the soft state update of Cassandra to propagate all updates to all replicas of a location ℓ as follows. This activity provides the eventual consistency and helps to finally make the states consistent.

```
Propagate=
    CHOOSE ℓ ∈ Locations IN
        CHOOSE val₁, val₂ ∈ valₛ(ℓ) WITH time(val₁) > time(val₂) IN
            valₛ(ℓ) := valₛ(ℓ) \ {val₂} ⊎ {val₁}
```

With this definition of (distributed) multistate runs of a DASM $\mathcal{A}$ we achieve the following properties.

1. The multistate runs of the DASM $\{(a, alg(a)\}_{a \in \mathcal{A}}$ define the behaviour of the agents. The memory model is a parameter for the semantics given by different policies and replication factors.
2. Using a replication factor of 1 in DASM runs brings us back to CASM runs (independent of the policy).
3. In general, DASM runs allow more behaviour than CASM runs.

For the last point, let us look again into the IRIW example from the introduction with two replicas for both x and y.

We start with an initial multistate $\{x \mapsto \langle(0,0),(0,0)\rangle, y \mapsto \langle(0,0),(0,0)\rangle\}$ When we consider a read- and write-policy ONE, then a_1 and a_2 can make a joint step leading to the multistate $\{x \mapsto \langle(0,0),(1,1)\rangle, y \mapsto \langle(0,0),(1,1)\rangle\}$. This allows the value read by a_3 to be $x = 1$ and $y = 0$, while still the value read by a_4 can be $x = 0$ and $y = 1$. This DASM run is not possible with CASM.

However, when the write policy is ALL, then all replicas will always have the same values, which is the same as if there was just one replica. This is of course possible with CASM, see the second item above. Finally, read- and write policies of QUORUM are the same as ALL in case of two replicas.

Looking into OROW with three replicas, the initial multivalue for x is $\langle$ (0,0), (0,0), (0,0) $\rangle$. When we use policies ONE, then a_1 and a_2 can make a step each leading to the new multivalue $\langle(0,0),(1,1),(2,2)\rangle$. After that, any combination of values read is possible.

When using a write policy of ALL, then again only the same results as with CASM runs are possible.

6   Centralized State and Multistate

In this section we want to see in which sense global centralized state is a special case of global distributed state (multistate). This means we compare distributed runs of the system in Fig. 2 with CASM runs of the system to the left in Fig. 1. More precisely, we want to see which read and write policies lead to CASM runs.

In order to compare CASM runs with distributed runs, we need to compare CASM states with multistates, i.e. single replicas with multiple replicas. We define an abstraction function from multistates to CASM states as a point-wise abstraction from multivalues to values based on a read policy rp as follows.

$$abstract(M, rp) = value(min_{\leq time}(\{max_{\leq time}(values) \mid values \in rp(M)\}))$$

First, we select all possible sets of values given by the policy ($values \in rp(M)$) and find the latest element in each of these sets ($max_{\leq time}$). Then we select the earliest element from all these latest elements ($min_{\leq time}$) and extract its value. This reduces the multivalue to just one value, but which value is used by CASM? As CASM favours consistency, it uses the latest value available, thus for a match with CASM, the abstraction function has to provide the latest element in M.

Lets look at an example to make the definition more understandable. Let $M = \langle$ (0,1), (1,2), (2,3) $\rangle$. We use the policy ONE, which gives $policy_{ONE}(M) = \{\langle$ (0,1) $\rangle, \langle$ (1,2) $\rangle, \langle$ (2,3) $\rangle, \langle$ (0,1), (1,2) $\rangle, \langle$ (0,1), (2,3) $\rangle, \langle$ (1,2), (2,3) $\rangle, \langle$ (0,1), (1,2), (2,3) $\rangle$ $\}$. The latest elements of these multisets are (0,1), (1,2), (2,3), (1,2), (2,3), (2,3), and (2,3). The earliest element of them is of course (0, 1), which gives us the result value of 0.

We can also use the policy QUORUM, which gives $policy_{QUORUM}(M) = \{\langle$ (0,1), (1,2) $\rangle, \langle$ (0,1), (2,3) $\rangle, \langle$ (1,2), (2,3) $\rangle, \langle$ (0,1), (1,2), (2,3) $\rangle\}$. The latest elements of the multisets are now $(1,2), (2,3), (2,3),$ and $(2,3)$. The earliest element of them is $(1,2)$, which gives us the result value of 1.

Using the policy ALL, we have $policy_{\text{ALL}}(M) = \{\langle\ (0,1),\ (1,2),\ (2,3)\ \rangle\}$, which has the only latest element $(2,3)$ and gives the final result value of 2.

Using the defined abstraction function *abstract* we can translate multistate runs into CASM runs by replacing the multistates with their abstractions. The moves of the agents stay the same. We will call the property that all abstracted multistate runs of a system coincide with CASM runs for *centralized*.

Definition 4 (centralized). *A DASM with agents $a \in \mathcal{A}$ and ASMs $alg(a)$ is called centralized iff all its abstracted runs using the function abstract are valid CASM runs of the CASM with the same agents $a \in \mathcal{A}$ and the same $alg(a)$.*

We have already seen that a write policy of ALL leads to centralized runs. The following result is a generalization of this observation.

Proposition 1. *Let $\{(a, alg(a))\}_{a \in \mathcal{A}}$ be a DASM.*

- *If the write policy is ALL, then the DASM is centralized (independent of the used read policy).*
- *If the read policy is ALL, then the DASM is centralized (independent of the used write policy).*
- *If the write policy is QUORUM and the read-policy is QUORUM, then the DASM is centralized.*

Proof. First, we observe that the abstraction of the initial states always leads to a valid CASM state, as they only include one value. This way, the abstracted initial state of the DASM matches an initial state of the CASM.

If the write policy is ALL, then in each write for a location ℓ, all values in the multivalue $val_S(\ell)$ are replaced by the new value. This means that for each location ℓ in each state only the latest value is stored with multiplicity $replicas(\ell)$. That again means that the *abstract* function provides exactly this value, making the first statement obvious.

If the read policy is ALL, then only the latest value from the complete multivalue is selected in the *abstract* function. As any write policy writes a new value at least once, the latest value for any location ℓ will be present as the latest value in $val_S(\ell)$. Therefore, exactly this latest value is provided by the *abstract* function making also the second statement obvious.

If the write policy is QUORUM, then for each location ℓ the multiplicity of the latest value in $val_S(\ell)$ is at least $\lceil \frac{replicas_\ell + 1}{2} \rceil$. Consequently, in the *abstract* function with read policy QUORUM, each set will contain at least once this value and use it for the maximum. Then again, the minimum is taken from a set with just one element. This means that in every multistate for each location ℓ, $val_S(\ell)$ is abstracted to the corresponding value for ℓ in the CASM state, which makes the run centralized. $\qquad\square$

7   Conclusion

In this paper, we have looked into different views on distributed computation, in particular with respect to distributed state. A low-level way of describing distribution of state is local state with message exchange. On top of that, one can define global centralized (ACID) state. There are real cases (Cassandra, Java MM) that go beyond ACID, and a more general formulation of state can use a memory model as a parameter to the run.

We extended the notion of distributed run with distribution of state based on the ideas of the distributed database system Cassandra. This way, distribution is given by a *distribution of computation* (agents having their threads of computation) and *distribution of state* (multistates).

Distributed runs are parametrized with a memory model given by a replication factor and a read and a write policy, such that a user can specify the expectations towards the memory management system for her algorithm. This way, the runs abstract from the underlying message exchange.

These multistate runs are more general than CASM runs, and can capture also runs over modern distributed database management systems or over the Java memory model. Using specific policies, it is possible to restrict the available runs to CASM runs.

Future work would include formal descriptions of the concepts 'availability' and 'eventual consistency'.

Acknowledgements. This work benefited from many discussions with Egon Börger and Klaus-Dieter Schewe. In particular, the modelling of Cassandra in CASM is joint work with them. I am grateful for the helpful comments of the anonymous reviewers.

References

1. Apache Software Foundation: Apache Cassandra 2.0—Documentation. http:// cassandra.apache.org/ (2016)
2. Best, E.: Semantics of Sequential and Parallel Programs. Prentice Hall, Upper Saddle River (1996)
3. Börger, E., Schewe, K.D.: Concurrent abstract state machines. Acta Inf. **53**(5), 469–492 (2016)
4. Börger, E., Schewe, K.D.: Communication in abstract state machines. J. Univ. Comp. Sci. **23**(2), 129–145 (2017)
5. Börger, E., Stärk, R.F.: Abstract State Machines: A Method for High-Level System Design and Analysis. Springer (2003)
6. Ferrarotti, F., Schewe, K.D., Tec, L., Wang, Q.: A new thesis concerning synchronised parallel computing—simplified parallel ASM thesis. Theor. Comp. Sci. **649**, 25–53 (2016)
7. Gilbert, S., Lynch, N.: Brewer's conjecture and the feasibility of consistent, available, partition-tolerant web services. SIGACT News **33**(2), 51–59 (2002). https:// doi.org/10.1145/564585.564601
8. Gosling, J., Joy, B., Steele, G.L., Bracha, G., Buckley, A.: The Java Language Specification, Java SE 8 Edition. Addison-Wesley Professional, 1st edn. (2014)
9. Gurevich, Y.: Evolving algebras 1993: lipari guide. In: Börger, E. (ed.) Specification and Validation Methods. Oxford University Press (1995)
10. Gurevich, Y.: Sequential abstract-state machines capture sequential algorithms. ACM Trans. Comp. Logic **1**(1), 77–111 (2000)

11. Hoare, C.A.R.: Communicating sequential processes. Commun. ACM **21**(8), 666–677 (1978). https://doi.org/10.1145/359576.359585
12. ITU: Z.100 series, specification and description language SDL. Technical Report, International Telecommunication Union (2011)
13. Lamport, L., Lynch, N.: Distributed computing: models and methods. In: Handbook of Theoretical Computer Science, pp. 1157–1199. Elsevier (1990)
14. Manson, J., Pugh, W., Adve, S.V.: The java memory model. SIGPLAN Not. **40**(1), 378–391 (2005). https://doi.org/10.1145/1047659.1040336
15. Milner, R.: A Calculus of Communicating Systems. Springer, New York (1982)
16. Mironov, A.M.: Theory of processes CoRR abs/1009.2259 (2010)
17. Nakamoto, S.: Bitcoin: A peer-to-peer electronic cash system. http://bitcoin.org/bitcoin.pdf
18. Narayanan, A., Bonneau, J., Felten, E., Miller, A., Goldfeder, S.: Bitcoin and Cryptocurrency Technologies: A Comprehensive Introduction. Princeton University Press, Princeton (2016)
19. Object Management Group (OMG): Action Language for Foundational UML (Alf), Version 1.1. OMG Document Number formal, 04 July 2017 (2017). http://www.omg.org/spec/ALF/1.1/
20. Object Management Group (OMG): OMG® Unified Modeling Language® (OMG UML®), Version 2.5.1. OMG Document Number formal, 05 December 2017. http://www.omg.org/spec/UML/2.5.1
21. Object Management Group (OMG): Semantics of a Foundational Subset for Executable UML Models (fUML), Version 1.3. OMG Document Number formal, 02 July 2017. http://www.omg.org/spec/FUML/1.3
22. Prinz, A., Sherratt, E.: Distributed ASM - pitfalls and solutions. In: Aït-Ameur, Y., Schewe, K.D. (eds.) Abstract State Machines, Alloy, B, TLA, VDM and Z - Proceedings of the 4th International Conference (ABZ 2014). Lecture Notes in Computer Science, vol. 8477, pp. 210–215. Springer, Heidelberg (2014)
23. Rabl, T., Sadoghi, M., Jacobsen, H.A., Gómez-Villamor, S., Muntés-Mulero, V., Mankowskii, S.: Solving big data challenges for enterprise application performance management. PVLDB **5**(12), 1724–1735 (2012)
24. Tanenbaum, A.S., Van Steen, M.: Distributed Systems. Prentice-Hall (2007)
25. Winskel, G., Nielsen, M.: Models for concurrency. In: Abramsky, S., Gabbay, D., Maibaum, T.S.E. (eds.) Handbook of Logic and the Foundations of Computer Science: Semantic Modelling, vol. 4, pp. 1–148. Oxford University Press (1995)

Pattern Libraries Guiding the Model-Based Reuse of Automotive Solutions

Maged Khalil[✉]

Continental Teves AG & Co. oHG – Chassis & Safety
Division/Systems & Technology, Guerickestr. 7,
60488 Frankfurt am Main, Germany
maged.khalil@continental-corporation.com

Abstract. The reuse of proven solutions (e.g., Safety Mechanisms or architecture designs) for safety-critical applications is considered a good practice for increasing confidence in the system design and cutting development cost and time, and is widely-spread in practice. However, reuse in safety-critical applications is mostly ad-hoc, with lack of process maturity or adequate tool support. Moreover, it is difficult to assess the quality or completeness of a reuse process, if there is no "definition of done". In previously published works, we defined a structured "Pattern Library "approach for the reuse of Safety Mechanisms (fault avoidance/error detection and handling) in the automotive domain, elaborating a prototypical tool implementation for the Pattern *User* role. This paper expands this definition and elaborates the usage workflow of the Pattern Library approach for the Pattern *Developer* role, demonstrating how the approach can be used to guide reuse, but also – via a summary of multiple evaluations – identify tool gaps and help guide and prioritize tool extension and selection.

Keywords: Reuse · Design patterns · Safety · Safety Mechanisms
Model-based tool requirements · System design

1 Introduction

1.1 Background

In practice, the reuse of architectural designs, development artifacts and entire code sequences is widely-spread, especially in well-understood domains. This trend holds true for the development of safety-critical products, with well-established architectural measures and Safety Mechanisms in wide reuse, as is reusing the corresponding safety-cases aiming to document and prove the fulfillment of the underlying safety goals. A Safety Mechanism is defined by the ISO26262 International Automotive Safety Standard [1]. as a "technical solution implemented by E/E functions or elements, or by other technologies (mechanical etc.), to detect faults or control failures in order to achieve or maintain a safe state". Safety Mechanisms are concrete instances of a category of implementation-independent solution descriptions targeting safety. The solutions used in a "Safety Mechanism" are in fact not limited to safety but may also be useful for all manner of dependability or RAMSS – Reliability, Availability, Maintainability, Safety and Security – issues. Wu und Kelly described a very similar

© Springer Nature Switzerland AG 2018
F. Khendek and R. Gotzhein (Eds.): SAM 2018, LNCS 11150, pp. 85–104, 2018.
https://doi.org/10.1007/978-3-030-01042-3_6

grouping of architectural designs or "Tactics" in [3]. and proceeded to describe a design pattern and template for capturing them. Tactics capture the abstract principles or primitives of a design pattern.

The primary aim of the approach presented here is make Safety Mechanism reuse within an organization better (more systematic, repeatable, effective) by approaching Safety Mechanisms as if they were Design Patterns. We understand that Safety Mechanisms are strictly not design patterns, and are not aiming at capturing a new kind of Design Pattern. We wish to use the structure provided by the design pattern template and general rigor of defining a design pattern to improve solution component capturing for reuse in a practical setting.

Wu and Kelly used a graphical notation of safety cases to capture the rationale attribute of their tactics template. We will be using the same notation in our example. A safety case is "a documented body of evidence that provides a convincing and valid argument that a system is adequately safe for a given application in a given environment", where an argument is "a connected series of claims intended to establish an overall claim." A safety case should communicate a clear, comprehensive and defensible argument that a system is acceptably safe to operate in a particular context [2].

The use of patterns in safety-critical software development in conjunction with model-based development techniques is documented and well suited for these needs, for instance [5]. Patterns of safety cases for well-known problems have been suggested in academic literature as well, e.g., for using COTS (Commercial-Off-The-Shelf) Components [43]. The reuse of safety-cases – and Safety Mechanisms in general – is mostly ad-hoc, with the practitioners focusing on the central artifact – a piece of code, an algorithm or a design model – and forgetting that this does not tell the entire story needed for proper reuse. Loss of critical knowledge and traceability, lack of consistency and/or process maturity and inappropriate artifact reuse being the most widely spread and cited drawbacks [4].

1.2 Motivation

Yet be it the design pattern or the development artifact, the single item does not tell the entire story. For example, to correctly deploy homogenous redundancy, shown in Fig. 1, many other aspects have to be covered:

- one has to define the requirements the pattern fulfills,
- refine the requirements and draw up a specification,
- detail a (logical) component architecture,
- optimize a deployment strategy that guarantees the duplicate components will not run on the same hardware resource,
- and finally, show how the usage of this Safety Mechanism contributes to System Safety, i.e., the safety case.

Doing this in a structured, repeatable and assessable manner is a further problem. To begin with, it is difficult to assess the quality or completeness of a reuse process, if there is no "definition of done". Providing this structure was our first step. But merely defining yet another design pattern attribute catalog is not the answer to the challenges

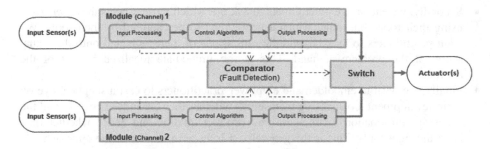

Fig. 1. Homogenous duplex (hardware) redundancy pattern [12]

surrounding the reuse of Safety Mechanisms in practice. The new definition needs to be a part of a more holistic approach, leveraging model-based capabilities to provide tool-supported reuse automation in a Systems Engineering context, e.g., as provided by the Systems Engineering Lifecycle Processes standard ISO15288 [30]. While Safety Mechanisms are not limited to software only, the development of complex Systems has become a software-intensive endeavor in and of itself. Thus to achieve our goals, our approach leverages a combination of software engineering paradigms; chief among them Model-Driven Engineering (MDE) [41] – treating models as first class citizens, component-based software engineering (CBSE) [42], and reuse repositories as presented in [36, 43].

The next aspect we focused on was the usability and adequacy of the modeling approach for the task at hand. The author has considerable hands-on industrial experience, and has observed first-hand, as well as received plenty of anecdotal evidence to the pervasiveness of the golden hammer syndrome, in industry as well as academia. Practitioners who are long accustomed to a tool or programming language will often see problems and solutions through the prism of their tool of choice, in this case blurring the lines between what is generally describable, and what is describable in their tool/language of choice. There is a noted tendency to bend the language or tool and contort it to address the problem at hand, and view the resultant solution in satisfactory light. Case in point; one only has to observe the sheer number of UML profiles in literature, used to cover every possible activity and purpose, regardless of whether UML is the right tool for the job. In essence, the limits of the tool's expressiveness become the limits of knowledge documented – and eventually *perceived* – by the user, creating a vicious circle.

We aim to break that circle, in a three-pronged approach.

- First and foremost, we do not wish to limit ourselves to, nor do we indeed have any preference for, any particular modeling language, framework, or development environment. We do, however, encourage the use of domain-adequate context-rich models, as these will – as our results have demonstrated – allow the capturing of more information. Our approach's basis is the capturing of solutions (with all information) in the exact artifacts which will be (re)used.

- Secondly, we encourage practitioners to ask not which reuse aspects they *can* cover using their tools, but rather which aspects *need* to be captured by their tools. We want practitioners to look beyond the limitations of their tools and onto the actual scope of the problem at hand. This is the immediate localized impact of the approach.
- Finally, we wish to embolden and empower practitioners to cast a skeptical eye on their development tools; asking themselves whether they are indeed covering all the necessary information for their desired product quality, and hence whether they have the right tools. This is the generalized long-term impact of the approach.

These 3 points form the basis of the approach presented in this paper. We focus on capturing all the necessary information we *have to* capture for the reuse, as defined by the pattern catalog; instead of focusing on the aspects we *can* capture using one tool-chain or another.

1.3 Previous Work

The reuse of Safety Mechanisms can be made both simpler and more robust through the encapsulation of all information into a consistent structured package, which can then be stored as a library element, along with the corresponding safety case to support it, as we demonstrated in previously published works [11]. In them we defined a structured approach for the reuse of Safety Mechanisms (fault avoidance/error detection and handling) in the automotive domain, capturing them in a "pattern library", based on Design Pattern literature. This library uses a simplified description of Safety Mechanisms, covering established solution algorithms and architectural measures/constraints in a seamless model-based approach with corresponding tool support.

The classical approach to capturing Design Pattern - as found in literature - focuses on capturing useful solutions in a generic fashion (via structured prose and diagrams), which is understandable across organization or even domain boundaries. In contrast, our approach focuses on the in situ capturing of the information necessary for the reuse within the artifacts actually used during development used within an organization. The approach provides guidance for the reuse in practice, based on a meta-model covering both development artifacts and safety case elements, which can be instantiated into any existing development environment. At the foundation of the approach, an attribute catalogue was defined, identifying the aspects of a safety mechanism that have to be captured for the reuse to be successful. The structure and usage of this reusable library element concept in a seamless model-based development tool is the focus of another previous publication [12]. The use-cases given here are discussed in detail in [33].

1.4 Contribution

In this work, we expand on previous definitions of the Safety Mechanism pattern attribute catalogue and corresponding Pattern Library approach. We will give previously unpublished detailed descriptions of how a Pattern Developer can use the approach in practice to capture Safety Mechanisms. We demonstrate the primary benefits of the pattern library approach for solution reuse via a primary instantiation in a domain-independent research CASE tool (AutoFOCUS3 – AF3). Deeply rooted in the user-centric nature of Design Patterns, our contribution can be summarized as:

1. An expanded definition of the usage workflow of the Pattern Library approach for the Pattern *Developer* role – capturing Safety Mechanisms for reuse.
2. With the Safety Mechanism Pattern Library at its heart; a systematic, repeatable and assessable approach – for reusing Safety Mechanisms, which can be instantiated into any development environment.

We also provide a summary of use-case demonstrators (published in detail in [33]) showing: the feasibility of the reuse approach in multiple frameworks; a generalization of the approach for application to the systematization of the reuse of technical solutions (in the automotive domain) – demonstrating the general usefulness of the Pattern Library approach – beyond Safety Mechanisms; and finally demonstrations of the usefulness of the approach not only for improving direct reuse, but also as a gauge of the adequacy of the employed development environment/tool suite for the reuse, as well as its usefulness of the approach as a guide for tool extensions/selection.

The structure of this paper is as follows. Section 2 details our approach and gives expanded definitions and details of the usage workflow for the Pattern *Developer* role. We discuss related work in Sect. 3 before concluding this paper in Sect. 4 with observations and lessons learned from applying our approach.

2 Design Pattern Based Approach

The reuse of safety-critical automotive solutions is wide-spread, but is marred, however, by several problems [12]:

- Safety-cases in the automotive domain are not well integrated into architectural models and as such
- they do not provide comprehensible and reproducible argumentation
- nor any evidence for the correctness of the used arguments.
- Most safety analyses (STAMP, FMEA, FTA, etc.) have to be performed at system level, yet the components/measures/Safety Mechanisms themselves need to be reused locally/independently,
- and are not tied in any structured manner to other elements needed to provide the relevant context.

2.1 Pattern Library Approach

Using a simplified description of Safety Mechanisms s according to the most common subtypes (avoidance/detection/handling) we define a pattern library covering known solution algorithms and architectural measures/constraints in a seamless holistic model-based approach with corresponding tool support. The pattern library comprises the minimum set of elements needed for correct reuse, i.e. the requirement the pattern covers, the specification of how one plans to implement it and the architecture elements/measures/constraints required as well as the supporting safety case template, based on the established structure notation known as GSN [17], and may include deployment or scheduling strategies, which would then be integrated into existing development environments. This enables an early analysis of hazards and risks, as well as the frontloading of many design aspects, which is recommended by most safety standards. Subsequently, fault types can be matched both to probable hazards, but more importantly to the problem categories they fall into or are most similar to, from a system architecture design viewpoint. Combining this with known architectural constraints and patterns for solving them, we can thus reason about which types of architectural patterns are relevant for the system under analysis. The fault types, along with their requirements, are bundled with solution arguments, comprising components, their (sub-)architectures, deployment plans and schedules, and other relevant information, into pattern libraries, which are rounded up by the corresponding safety-case templates (or skeletons) to provide argumentation for achieving the goals.

Underlying the approach is the consistent use of patterns as a user-centric aide to practitioners: from the categorization of hazard types, over the abstract modeling of the respective safety concepts, and down to their implementation in the system architecture description, with a focus on providing argument chains in a seamless model-based environment.

To structure the capturing of the Safety Mechanisms, we defined an attribute catalogue, shown in the next table (Table 1). The selection of attributes is based on an extensive literature survey of Design Pattern attribute catalogues, but most influenced by the works of the Gang of Four [31], Kelly [4], Douglas [20] and Armoush [29].

Table 1. Safety mechanism attribute catalogue [12].

Attribute	Meaning
Name	Name of the Safety Mechanism
Intent	Immediate purpose of the Safety Mechanism
Motivation	Rationale behind using the Safety Mechanism
Applicability	Situation and conditions to which the Safety Mechanism can be applied, as well as counterexamples
Structure	Representation of the elements of a pattern and their relationship (preferably in graphical form)
Participants	Complementary to the *Structure* attribute; provides a description of each of the Safety Mechanism pattern elements, including potential instantiation information
Collaborations	Shows how the pattern's various elements (e.g., sources of contextual information, argument structure, requirements, logical components) collaborate to achieve the stated goal of the pattern. Moreover, this attribute focuses on capturing any links between the pattern elements that could not be captured clearly and explicitly or were not the focus of the Structure attribute, e.g., dynamic behavior
Consequences	Captures information pertaining to the instantiation and deployment of the pattern, as well as to the impact it may have on the system

(continued)

Table 1. (*continued*)

Attribute	Meaning
Implementation	Describes the implementation and should include its possible failure modes or dysfunctional behavior as well as any constraints or possible pitfalls
Implications	This characteristic covers the impact of applying the pattern on the non-functional aspects of the system. This may include traits such as reliability, modifiability, cost, and execution time
Usage classification	Categorizes the Safety Mechanisms according to their usage (fault avoidance/error detection and handling)
Example	Exemplary (preferably graphical) representations of the Safety Mechanisms are especially useful if the previous attributes were not captured graphically, or are very complex. Otherwise optional
Related patterns	Provides a listing of Safety Mechanism related to the pattern being documented. This may, for instance, include patterns that are derived from this pattern

2.2 Safety Mechanism Pattern Library

The attribute catalogue is the first step towards a systematic capturing of Safety Mechanisms for reuse. We identified the types of development artifacts most likely to contain the information required for each attribute and then proceeded to provide a guide for instantiating the approach into various development environments. The approach provides guidance for the reuse in practice, based on a meta-model covering both development artifacts and safety case elements, which can be instantiated into any existing development environment.

At its essence, the approach can be divided into 5 simple steps for the practitioner:

1. Identify the information necessary for a systematic reuse of the solution in practice, and structure this information into an attribute catalogue. E.g., name, applicability, implications.
2. Identify the types of development artifacts that should/could contain the necessary information. E.g., textual requirements, state charts, graphical safety cases, code...
3. Define a data-model (linking all the development artifacts, capturing the information necessary for reuse – as defined in the attribute catalogue), and use it to set up a "library" mechanism capturing the reusable solution and all its related artifacts.
4. Evaluate whether and to what degree the development environment/tool suite used by the practitioner can actually capture the necessary information.
5. Extend the development environment/tool suite as necessary, using the gaps identified in the evaluation step to both guide and prioritize the tool extension.

Applying this to the Safety Mechanism reuse problem, we used a simplified description of Safety Mechanisms according to the most common subtypes (avoidance/detection/handling) to define a pattern library covering known solution algorithms and architectural measures/constraints in a seamless holistic model-based approach with corresponding tool support. The pattern library comprises the minimum set of elements needed for correct reuse, i.e. the requirement the pattern covers, the specification of how one plans to implement it and the architecture elements/measures/constraints required as well as the supporting safety case template, based on the established structure notation known as GSN [17], and may include deployment or scheduling strategies, which would then be integrated into existing development environments. This enables an early analysis of hazards and risks, which is recommended by many safety standards. Subsequently, fault types can be matched both to probable hazards, but more importantly to the problem categories they fall into or are most similar to, from a system architecture design viewpoint. Combining this with known architectural constraints and patterns for solving them, we can thus reason about which types of architectural patterns are relevant for the system under analysis. The fault types, along with their requirements, are bundled with solution arguments, comprising components, their (sub-) architectures, deployment plans and schedules, into pattern libraries, which are rounded up by the corresponding safety-case templates to provide argumentation for achieving the goals.

Underlying the approach is the consistent use of patterns as a user-centric aide to practitioners: from the categorization of hazard types, over the abstract modeling of the respective safety concepts, and down to their implementation in the system architecture description, while providing argument chains in a seamless model-based environment.

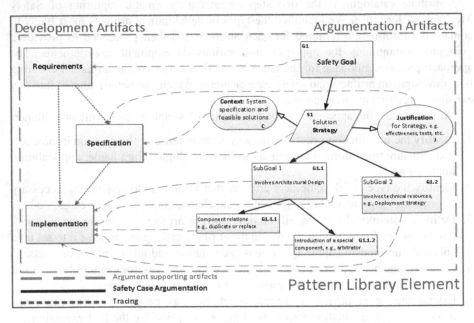

Fig. 2. Generic safety mechanism pattern library element [12]

Figure 2 gives a sketch of a generic library element comprising development artifact categories. The left part of the schematic gives possible development artifact elements– requirements, specification, and implementation description – of the reusable pattern, while the right part shows the corresponding argumentation artifacts comprising a safety case skeleton – shown exploded for clarity – with connections to the relevant development artifact categories. The argumentation artifacts based on a graphical safety argumentation notation, in this case the Goal Structuring Notation (GSN) introduced in [2, 17]. Both sides together comprise the pattern library element, the building blocks of which are the four artifact categories requirements, specification, implementation and argumentation.

While the left part of the schematic, comprising the various development artifacts necessary for reuse, as well as the right side safety case description, can entirely originate in one seamless tool – as will be shown in our first use case in Sect. 3 – this is not necessary. As long as the artifacts' relations are well-defined, the development artifacts may reside in multiple tools or repositories and be in varying formats; the binding element is the safety case shown on the right hand side, which gives the story and rationale behind the reusable pattern, supported in-tool by the pattern library mechanism. This specific aspect is particularly important for the practical reuse in a safety-critical development context, where each practitioner may have their own disparate tool landscape. This forms a cornerstone of our approach. Depending on the development environment used, the relation between artifact categories will differ according to the definitions provided for how the different category views (if available) interact. The pattern library mechanism can then be in general terms interpreted as a weaving model, which binds the pattern elements together and allows their reuse. Additional mechanisms for the instantiation, also depending on the development environment, may be necessary. More details about the approach, the attribute catalogue, and the structure of this reusable library element concept in a seamless model-based development tool are provided in [12]. The use-cases whose results are summarized in Sect. 4 are discussed in detail in [33].

2.3   Instantiation in AutoFOCUS3

Introduction to AutoFOCUS3

AutoFOCUS3 (AF3) is a research computer-aided software engineering (CASE) tool, which allows modeling and validating concurrent, reactive, distributed, timed systems on the basis of formal semantics [7]. Most importantly, AF3 provides a graphical user interface that facilitates the modeling of embedded systems in different layers of abstraction while supporting different views on the system model, including the requirements-, component- and platform- view essential for the description of complex systems. This support for views enables applying paradigms such as "separation-of-concerns" – different views for different stake-holders/concerns – as well as "divide-and-conquer" – different hierarchy layers allowing the decomposition of engineering problems to facilitate solution, as championed by the IEEE 42010 standard [8].

Introducing the Pattern Library Approach to AF3

An early attempt at reusing architectural patterns in AF3 was presented in [9]. In it, the authors demonstrated how Homogenous Duplex Redundancy (HDR), and Triple Modular Redundancy (TMR) could be integrated as patterns into AF3. Before this work, AF3 had no pattern capability. The approach was successful in demonstrating that design patterns for embedded-system Safety Mechanisms can be supported in AF3 and that they are useful. Practitioners who experimented with the feature gave positive feedback and voiced their interest in having the functionality expanded.

Using the Attribute Catalogue and evaluation scoring system introduced in the previous sections, the quality of the existing Safety Mechanism capturing in AF3 was evaluated, resulting in a sobering score of 42%. The shortcomings, described in detail in [33], were mostly due to the domain-independent nature and limitations of the tool itself, which had not been developed for our purpose.

Using the individual evaluation scores for each attribute to identify gaps in the tool as well as to guide and prioritize the extension of AF3, the tool suite was expanded in two steps. The first, presented in [10], added safety case expression capability to AF3. The second expansion, driven by the author and presented in [11], instantiated our Safety Mechanism Pattern Library approach, developing the detailed workflow description in this paper.

The practical applicability, along with an initial usage description – for the pattern *User* role – and description of the implementation (with screenshots), were presented in [12]. Detailed definitions of the data-model elements and relations shown in Fig. 3, were also given.

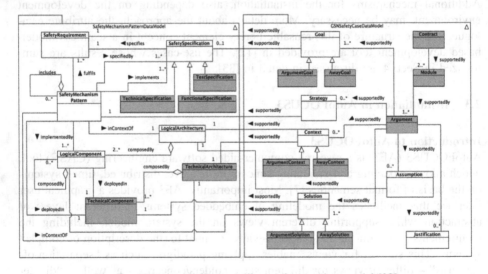

Fig. 3. AF3 extended pattern library element data model [32]

Safety Mechanism Pattern Developer

A comprehensive analysis of all the Safety Mechanisms found in our literature survey (approx. 40), led us to identify three archetypes of structures for capturing and instantiating Safety Mechanisms in AF3, detailed in [12]. To save a new Safety Mechanism, the *Developer* has to decide which of these archetypes best fits their need.

The *Developer* is aided in this task by a wizard, shown in Fig. 5, which also assures that library elements cannot be created without the mandatory information.

But first, Fig. 4 shows the steps a developer has to undertake to document a new Safety Mechanism Pattern in AF3, some of which are optional. The steps are explained in more detail next.

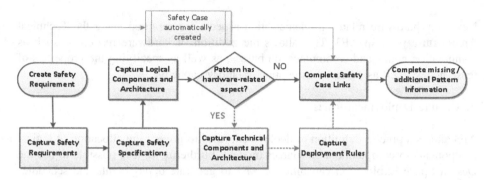

Fig. 4. Workflow steps for safety mechanism pattern *developer* role in AF3

1. Create Safety Requirement

By designating a requirement as safety-relevant, a corresponding Safety Case is automatically created.

2. Capture Safety Requirement

The Safety Requirement now has to be filled in with all relevant information. This is done using MIRA – the Model-Based Integrated Requirements Specification and Analysis Tool in AF3, which also allows to check requirements for consistency and completeness, as well as defining general maturity levels for requirements.

3. Capture Safety Specifications

Next, the *Developer* can specify the behavior of the Safety Mechanism formally, e.g., using tables or state automata. This allows for a formal verification of the implemented Safety Mechanism, as well as the automated generation of test-cases, which can then be used to check the system architecture specification against the requirements in a continuous manner.

4. Capture Logical Components and Architecture

The *Developer* can now begin with the actual implementation of the Safety Mechanism Pattern, by defining logical components and their relations in the Logical Architecture view in AF3. Referring to the description of AF3 provided in [7], this includes many aspects – such as typed directed ports – allowing for a detailed and precise documentation of the pattern implementation.

If the pattern is implemented entirely in software and has no hardware aspects, the Developer can skip to Step 7, otherwise we proceed to the next step.

5. Capture Technical Components and Architecture

Next, any hardware related implementation aspects are captured using the Technical Architecture view in AF3. This allows the addition of hardware resources, such as computation nodes and communication busses, as well as specifying the properties of these nodes, such as power consumption, memory capacity.

6. Capture Deployment Rules

AF3 allows a precise definition of deployment rules to govern the allocation of logical components to computational resources (nodes). Furthermore, it is possible to use the Design Space Exploration capability of AF3 to generate deployments and schedules optimized to fulfill multiple criteria, such as worst case execution time, memory constraints, bus loads or power consumption, but also safety constraints, such as ASIL-decomposition and random hardware failure probabilities, as seen in [34].

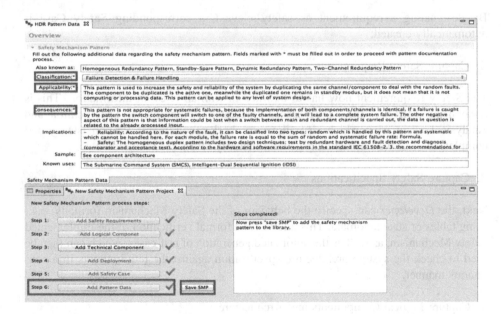

Fig. 5. AF3 Safety mechanism pattern *developer* wizard interface [32]

7. Complete Safety Case Links

In order to make use of the integrated argumentation capability in AF3, the *Developer* has to build the safety case – arguing the use and functionality of the Safety Mechanism Pattern he is developing – and link all its elements to the corresponding development artifacts in the other AF3 views (Requirements and Specification – Logical Architecture – Technical Architecture – Deployment).

8. Complete missing/additional Pattern Information

Finally, the wizard guides the Developer to provide additional pattern information, such as the pattern classification.

Throughout this process, the *Developer* is guided by the wizard, whose interface can be seen in Fig. 5, which makes sure that all mandatory information, necessary for the correct documentation of the Safety Mechanism Pattern attributes, is provided into the library element. The new Safety Mechanism Pattern can now be saved as an element of the pattern library, where it is accessible to other AF3 pattern *Users*.

As seen in the evaluations in [33] and the summary in Sect. 4, although the approach brought significant improvements to AF3's capability of capturing Safety Mechanism Patterns for reuse, some of the required pattern attributes are still nevertheless not satisfactorily captured in AF3's artifacts – especially *implications* and *consequences*. We appended the library mechanism with the capability to add some short textual information to enhance the documentation qualities of these attributes. This is meant as a stop-gap until AF3 capabilities improve enough to allow capturing the information solely in modeling artifacts. These shortcomings factored into our evaluations.

3 Related Work

A recent survey of patterns in safety-critical development provided in [19] demonstrates that patterns tend to focus on clear target types of problems; engineering step (requirements, design, implementation, ...), category (argumentation pattern, safety/security pattern, design pattern – like redundancy, ...), as well as abstraction (e.g. software, hardware, ...), and used these to organize the results. This is useful, yet somewhat too narrow or isolated an approach for an effective reuse of technical solutions in practice. This is because be it an architecture description or the software or hardware development artifact, the single item does not tell the entire story, as discussed in Sect. 1. A holistic Systems Engineering approach is needed.

The survey also observed wide-spread use of model-based techniques, with different modeling methods and languages used in accordance with the needs of safety engineers (mostly graphical notations like UML/SysML and GSN), but also textual patterns.

Combining the power of model-based techniques with the design pattern approach seems a logical step. In fact, Douglass himself documented his first patterns for real-time embedded systems using UML [20]. The examples are abundant – using UML to capture hardware design process patterns [21] or software product line patterns [22]; or using models to capture hardware design patterns [23] – yet the fact remains, that the focus was on leveraging the capabilities of model-based techniques for the documentation of the patterns, rather than capturing them for direct reuse in a practical setting.

The Assured Reliability and Resilience Level (ARRL) approach, presented in [24], provides a push in that direction, by leveraging Quality of Service (QoS) paradigms, arguing against Safety Integrity Levels (SIL) and seeking to supplant them with ARRLs. This is meant to transform components into a compositional framework, where "ARRL level components carry a contract and the evidence that they will meet this contract given a specific set of fault conditions". While the notion has its charm, there are several limitations to this approach: it assumes that the information is available in the models or components it is applying ARRL to, which is often not the case; it assumes that a transformation of the information, contracts and guarantees is possible into ARRL, without loss of information. In practical settings, this is not a trivial assumption, as each company will have its own artifacts; and finally, it requires the adoption of a new framework, which will undoubtedly meet very high resistance from industry, as well as substantial and not entirely drawback-free changes to existing and established safety standards and practices. Our approach works inside the practitioners' tools.

Denney and Pai [25] offer automation support for the generation of (partial) safety cases, by considering three inter-related tables – namely one each for hazards, system requirements, and functional requirements – as idealizations of the safety analysis and development processes. The argument structures are then automatically populated by predefined mappings from the tables. The approach is useful for structuring requirements and argumentation, is for the most part formalized, and has functioning tool support [26]. The approach does not, however, directly link design architectures or product artifacts in its function; or address patterns; or how the aspects needed for reuse are covered; nor does it show how the method may work in other fields.

Armengaud [27] proposed a conceptually similar approach for automating the assembly of safety cases. His approach is based on linking ISO 26262 activities and work products – for instance, design and test artifacts evidence – by means of information models. However, the approach does not address how these models structure the safety case argument; nor does he address the reuse of patterns or safety mechanisms in safety.

Hawkins et al. present a very pragmatic approach – quite similar to ours – in [28], based on the automatic generation of assurance cases from design artifacts. The approach uses model weaving to link various elements relevant for arguing the safety of architecture design and product information from AADL [35] with a meta-model of GSN, to generate a safety case argument structure. A main advantage of the approach is that the weaving models are bidirectional; allowing the generation of updated argument structures to match changes in product information, but also allowing the reflection of changes in the argument structure back to the product and architecture design. This facilitates the co-evolution of architecture design and product information with the assurance case. The approach targets development environments using (or based on) AADL, which is not widely adopted in the automotive domain; and it does not address implementation artifacts or issues. Furthermore, the approach does not address patterns or reuse exactly, but is focused on the generation of assurance cases. The approach can, however, be used to support safety patterns, by adapting it to maintain the co-evolution of the system design and product information side with the argumentation side of a safety pattern library element. In that capacity it is most useful when applied to abstract high-level patterns. For concrete solutions such as Safety Mechanisms, our focus, it would be much simpler and more precise to directly link the assurance case elements to the design and implementation artifacts supporting them. In that scope, the model-weaving approach mentioned above would be too general in its current form, and on the other hand, attempts to make it more precise would probably be over-kill and counter-productive. Its strengths simply lie elsewhere.

More closely related are the works of Hauge [37] and Hamid [36]. Hauge introduces a pattern language for safety design – called Safe Control Systems (SaCS) - with which he proceeds to capture known approaches towards a safe system design. These include both product-based as well as process-based safety concepts enabling a safe-design. Hauge's selection of what a "safety concept design" is builds on the work of Habli and Kelly in [39], in which they introduce safety case patterns for generic safety concepts – i.e., repeatable argument patterns – using GSN. The SaCS language provides good coverage of safety concept design, as demonstrated in the analysis given in [37], and expanded on in [38]. Hamid introduces a holistic approach for model repository-centric reuse of solutions for complex applications. His approach provides a methodology and tool-support for developing model repositories, supporting two categories of users: "reuse" producers and "reuse" consumers, and is demonstrated via a preliminary prototype that captures security and dependability pattern models. Hamid builds on his previous work in [40], in which he introduces so-called "SEMCO (System and software Engineering with Multi-Concerns support)", which is an integrated repository of modeling artifacts aiming at enabling the co-evolution of models covering various engineering concerns, e.g., safety, security.

Hauge's work targets basic "patterns" in safety concepts, such as "Hazard Analysis", "Risk Analysis", and "Establish System Safety Requirements" and how to combine them into composite "Safety Requirements" patterns. Our work focuses on the practical reuse of the category of technical solutions collected under the term "safety mechanisms", as well as the generalization of the concept for other types of model-based reuse. While Hamid's work offers a holistic and precise approach to building modeling repositories. Its reliance on model transformations, while supporting a more precise definition of his holistic model repositories, can be somewhat cumbersome and inflexible to a practitioner, and this reason made us opt for the relative flexibility of model-weaving. More importantly, both Hauge and Hamid have come up with their own modeling languages and tools. Similar to the ARRL and related approaches presented here, this assumes that practitioners are willing, or even capable, of completely abandoning their domain/industry-established tools in favor of an academic suite with little to no commercial support. In contrast our approach provides a blueprint for practitioners to tailor and instantiate it into their own tool suites for their own exact purposes, while enabling them to evaluate the adequacy of those tools for their individual purposes and providing a guide for eventual tool extensions/replacements.

4   Conclusions and Lessons Learned

The design of functional-safety systems is largely driven by best practices – like the use of fault monitors, safe states, or redundant paths. These best practices can often be presented in form of patterns – both to describe a possible solution but also to document an argumentation about their contribution to a safety case. Our approach provides for a library of such patterns, allowing the identification and reuse of suitable measures and their corresponding components along with their safety cases. It also guides practitioners into a systematic capturing – in the Pattern *Developer* role – and reuse of technical solutions such as Safety Mechanisms – in the Pattern *User* role.

4.1   Discipline vs. Design Freedom – the Pattern Library in Practice

Expanding the number of Safety Mechanisms considered in previous works to all found in literature, we evaluated approx. 40 and implemented 7 in the AF3 Case-Study, finding none that could not readily be captured using our approach, thus demonstrating that our Safety Mechanism attribute catalogue and Pattern Library approach apply to all categories of Safety Mechanisms.

Our observations with practitioners who tried out the tool led us to increase the rigor and discipline enforced by the tool itself, to both guide and reign in abuses by the users, who – without guidance – were inevitably attracted to "short-cuts", focusing on their central artifact of interest and trying to forego the onerous task of filling in all the other necessary information.

While the wizard shown in Sect. 2.3 has certainly increased this discipline, we feel that a certain sensitization, speaking to the mindset of the practitioners, is necessary and cannot be achieved by tool constraints alone, which when raised beyond a certain threshold led the practitioners to label the tool "unusable" and abandon it altogether.

4.2   Case Study Evaluation Results

This section gives a short summary of results presented in detail in [33]. We carried out case-studies instantiating the approach into 3 development environments: AF3, introduced in this paper – a domain-independent CASE tool; the SAFE Modeling Framework, described in [13, 14], an automotive safety-critical application software architecture description framework; and finally a generalization and instantiation of the approach into the COREPA Framework at Continental – a globally leading automotive Tier 1 supplier. COREPA is a library of reusable – functional and technical – solution components with a focus on automated driving and advanced driver assistance system applications, used to develop and tailor complex system designs as well as guide future component roadmaps. The results of the first evaluations of COREPA were used to guide tool expansions, introducing formal design space-exploration (DSE) capability [15]. The DSE was used to enable the synthesis of deployments from logical (platform-independent) system models to technical (platform-specific) system architecture models, including multi-criteria optimization. This enables a correct-by-design generation of preliminary architecture concepts for complex vehicle function application bundles for various customers with disparate and occasionally conflicting design constraints – and all at the push of a button. The capabilities were further extended to enable the synthesization of the technical architecture by optimized selection from a library of technical component models, as described in [16].

Using these case studies, we demonstrated the following benefits from using the approach:

- A guided capturing of reusable solutions. As an immediate benefit of the approach, practitioners no longer have to wonder if they have captured all the necessary information nor approach the problem in an ad-hoc fashion. Pre-defining the attributes necessary to capture a reusable solution guarantees that practitioners know which information needs to be captured.
- A gauge of if and how well the necessary information is being captured in the current tool-suite. Pre-defining the attributes necessary to capture the reusable solution also means that practitioners will no longer be limited by the current capabilities of their tools, or the way they currently use them, but will look into adapting and expanding their tool-suite to better suite this goal, as they now have a gauge to test against. This is a more abstract, longer-term benefit.
- An aide for selecting better tools. Knowing exactly which information needs to be captured means that practitioners can look beyond the limitations of their current tools, and onto adopting such tools as truly fit their needs. This is the most abstract, long-term benefit of the approach.

Our observations while evaluating the second and third case studies confirm an earlier hypothesis: the more detail-rich and context-adequate or domain-specific a modeling/tool framework, the higher the number of attributes one can capture in its models and the better the quality and degree of attribute capturing, thus increasing the quality of the final product. This hypothesis is supported by our observations while evaluating the second and third case studies. The shortcomings exposed by the first evaluation reflect limitations due to the domain-independent nature of AF3, with many of the missing features being very specific to tools specifically developed for safety-critical automotive embedded systems development.

We interpret the results of the case-studies as a validation of the approach's premise, based on predefining the information targeted for capture in the model-based development environment in a structured systematic approach – independently of the environment itself.

Importantly – and contrary to related work, our approach features an explicit model-based representation of the reusable solutions within the practical context of their usage and the problems they solve, which can be instantiated into any model-based development environment. This has several advantages, including (1) a better characterization of the problem space addressed by the pattern – better than the textual description otherwise used in pattern templates, (2) a more natural representation of the transformations embodied in the application of the pattern, and (3) a better handle on the selection, rationale and application of the patterns [18]. Our approach is not limited to one type or category of artifact, but targets the capturing of all information necessary for successful system design reuse.

Finally, and most importantly, the COREPA case study demonstrates how the underlying concept of our approach can generically be applied to a model-based reuse-in-practice problem in general, guiding both the systematic reuse as well as the corresponding tool development in a large-scale industrial setting with demonstrated positive impact.

Acknowledgement. The initial specification of this approach stems from and was carried out in the integrated development environment for the ITEA2 SAFE project and the EUROSTARS SAFE-E project, with proof-of-concept implementation in the research CASE tool AUTO-FOCUS3 (AF3). AF3 is the result of the hard work of many researchers and employees of the Software and Systems Engineering Department at the fortiss Institute in Munich, Germany.

References

1. International Standards Organization, ISO 26262 Standard, Road Vehicles Functional Safety (2011). www.iso.org
2. Kelly, T., Weaver, R.: The goal structuring notation. A safety argument notation. In: Proceedings DSN 2004 Workshop on Assurance Cases (2004)
3. Wu, W., Kelly, T.: Safety tactics for software architecture design. In: Proceedings of the 28th Annual International Computer Software and Applications Conference, (COMPSAC 2004), vol. 1, pp. 368–375. IEEE Computer Society, Washington, DC, USA (2004)
4. Kelly, T.P., McDermid, J.A.: Safety case construction and reuse using patterns. In: 16th International Conference on Computer Safety, Reliability and Security (SAFECOMP 1997) (1997)
5. Wagner, S., Schatz, B., Puchner, S., Kock, P.: A case study on safety cases in the automotive domain: modules, patterns, and models. In: Proceedings International Symposium on Software Reliability Engineering (ISSRE 2010), IEEE Computer Society (2010)
6. Khalil, M.: Pattern-based methods for model-based safety-critical software architecture design. In: ZeMoSS 2013 Workshop at the SE 2013 in Aachen, Germany (2013)
7. AutoFOCUS 3, research CASE tool, af3.fortiss.org, fortiss (2018)
8. ISO/IEC/IEEE 42010: Systems and software engineering—Architecture description (2011). www.iso.org
9. Carlan, C.: Implementierung unterschiedlicher Redundanzkonzepte zur automatischen Generierung entsprechender logischer Strukturen für ein sicheres Verhalten gemischt-kritischer Systeme im CASE-Tool AutoFocus3. Bachelor Thesis (German). Technische Universität München. Faculty of Informatics. Chair of Software and Systems Engineering (2012). http://download.fortiss.org/public/carlan/BA_Carmen_Carlan.pdf
10. Voss, S., Schatz, B., Khalil, M., Carlan, C.: A step towards Modular Certification using integrated model-based Safety Cases. VeriSure (2013)
11. Khalil, M., Schatz, B., Voss, S.: A pattern-based approach towards modular safety analysis and argumentation. In: Embedded Real Time Software and Systems Conference (ERTS2014) – Toulouse, France (2014)
12. Khalil, M., Prieto, A., Hölzl, F.: A pattern-based approach towards the guided reuse of safety mechanisms in the automotive domain. In: Ortmeier, F., Rauzy, A. (eds.) IMBSA 2014. LNCS, vol. 8822, pp. 137–151. Springer, Cham (2014). https://doi.org/10.1007/978-3-319-12214-4_11
13. The ITEA2 SAFE Project/The EUROSTARS SAFE-E Project. www.safe-project.eu
14. The SAFE Consortium. Deliverable D3.5c "SAFE Meta-Model: System, SW, HW reference meta-model definition. www.safe-project.eu ITEA2 (2014)

15. Eder, J., Zverlov, S., Voss, S., Khalil, M., Ipatiov, A.: Bringing DSE to life: exploring the design space of an industrial automotive use case. In: 2017 ACM/IEEE 20th International Conference on Model Driven Engineering Languages and Systems (MODELS) (2017). https://doi.org/10.1109/MODELS.2017.36

16. Eder, J., Zverlov, S., Voss, S., Ipatiov, A., Khalil, M.: From deployment to platform exploration: automatic synthesis of distributed automotive hardware architectures. In: 2018 ACM/IEEE 21st International Conference on Model Driven Engineering Languages and Systems (MODELS). Accepted (2018)

17. Kelly, T., Habli, I., et al.: Origin Consulting (York) Limited, on behalf of the Contributors. Goal Structuring Notation (GSN). GSN COMMUNITY STANDARD VERSION 1, November 2011

18. Mili, H., El-Boussaidi, G.: Representing and applying design patterns: what is the problem? In: Briand, L., Williams, C. (eds.) MODELS 2005. LNCS, vol. 3713, pp. 186–200. Springer, Heidelberg (2005). https://doi.org/10.1007/11557432_14

19. Gleirscher, M., Kugele, S.: A study of safety patterns: first results (2016). https://doi.org/10.13140/rg.2.2.23347.22562

20. Douglass, B.P.: Doing Hard Time: Developing Real-Time System with UML, Objects, Frameworks, and Pattern. Addison-Wesley, New York (1999)

21. Damaševicius, R., Štuikys, V.: Application of UML for hardware design based on design process model. In: ASP-DAC '04: Proceedings of the 2004 Asia and South Pacific Design Automation Conference, pp. 244–249. IEEE Press, Piscataway, NJ, USA (2004)

22. Rincon, F., Moya, F., Barba, J., Lopez, J.C.: Model reuse through hardware design patterns. In: DATE '05: Proceedings of the conference on Design, Automation and Test in Europe, pp. 324–329. IEEE Computer Society, Washington, DC, USA (2005)

23. Gomaa, H., Hussein, M.: Model-based software design and adaptation. In: Proceedings of the 2007 International Workshop on Software Engineering for Adaptive and Self-Managing Systems, p. 7. IEEE Computer Society (2007)

24. Verhulst, E., Sputh, B.H.C.: ARRL: a criterion for composable safety and systems engineering. In: Workshop SASSUR (Next Generation of System Assurance Approaches for Safety-Critical Systems) of the 32nd International Conference on Computer Safety, Reliability and Security SAFECOMP (2013)

25. Denney, E., Pai, G.: A lightweight methodology for safety case assembly. In: Ortmeier, F., Daniel, P. (eds.) SAFECOMP 2012. LNCS, vol. 7612, pp. 1–12. Springer, Heidelberg (2012). https://doi.org/10.1007/978-3-642-33678-2_1

26. Denney, E., Pai, G., Pohl, J.: Advocate: an assurance case automation toolset. In: Proceedings of Workshop SASSUR (Next Generation of System Assurance Approaches for Safety-Critical Systems) of the 31st International Conference on Computer Safety, Reliability and Security SAFECOMP, pp 8–21 (2012)

27. Armengaud, E.: Automated safety case compilation for product-based argumentation. In: Embedded Real Time Software and Systems Conference (ERTS 2014), Toulouse, France (2014)

28. Hawkins, R., Habli, I., Kolovos, D., Paige, R., Kelly, T.: Weaving an assurance case from design: a model-based approach. In: 16th IEEE International Symposium on High Assurance Systems Engineering – HASE2015. Florida (2015)

29. Armoush, A.: Design Patterns for Safety-Critical Embedded Systems. Ph.D. Thesis, RWTH-Aachen (2010)

30. ISO/IEC/IEEE 15288: Systems and software engineering – System life cycle processes Standard. https://www.iso.org (2015)

31. Gamma, E., Helm, R., Johnson, R., Vlissides, J.: Design Patterns: Elements of Reusable Object-Oriented Software. Addison-Wesley, Boston, MA, USA (1994)

32. Prieto Rodriguez, A.A.: Exploration of a pattern-based approach for the reuse of safety mechanisms in embedded systems. Master's Thesis. Technische Universität München. Faculty of Informatics. Chair of Software and Systems Engineering (2014)
33. Khalil, M.: Design patterns to the rescue: guided model-based reuse for automotive solutions. In: 2018. 25th Pattern Languages of Programming Conference. PLoP2018. Portland. Oregon, USA. In review
34. Zverlov, S., Khalil, M., Chaudhary, M.: Pareto-efficient deployment synthesis for safety-critical applications. In: Embedded Real Time Software and Systems Conference (ERTS 2016), Toulouse, France (2016)
35. AADL. Architecture Analysis and Design Language. SAE International Standard AS-5506 Ver. 2.1. 2102 (2018). www.aadl.info
36. Hamid, B.: A model-driven approach for developing a model repository: methodology and tool support. Future Gen. Comput. Syst. **68**, 473–490 (2017). ISSN 0167-739X
37. Hauge, A., Stølen, K.: An analytic evaluation of the SaCS pattern language—Including explanations of major design choices. In: Patterns, pp. 79–88 (2014)
38. Hauge, A.A.: SaCS: a method and a pattern language for the development of conceptual safety designs. Doctoral Dissertation. Series of dissertations submitted to the Faculty of Mathematics and Natural Sciences, University of Oslo. No. 1568. ISSN 1501-7710 (2014)
39. Habli, I., Kelly, T.: Process and product certification arguments – getting the balance right. SIGBED Rev. **3**(4), 1–8 (2006)
40. Hamid, B.: SEMCO Project, System and software Engineering for embedded systems applications with Multi- COncerns support, http://www.semcomdt.org
41. Schmidt, D.: Model-driven engineering. IEEE Comput. **39**(2), 41–47 (2006)
42. Crnkovic, I., Chaudron, M.R.V., Larsson, S.: Component-based development process and component lifecycle. In: Proceedings of the International Conference on Software Engineering Advances, ICSEA 2006, p. 44. IEEE Computer Society (2006)
43. Frakes, W., Kang, K.: Software reuse research: status and future. IEEE Trans. Softw. Eng. **31**(7), 529–536 (2005)

Enabling Performance Modeling for the Masses: Initial Experiences

Abel Gómez[1]([⊠])(iD), Connie U. Smith[2], Amy Spellmann[2], and Jordi Cabot[1,3](iD)

[1] Internet Interdisciplinary Institute (IN3),
Universitat Oberta de Catalunya (UOC), Barcelona, Spain
agomezlla@uoc.edu, jordi.cabot@icrea.cat
[2] L&S Computer Technology, Inc, Austin, USA
{cusmith,amy}@spe-ed.com
[3] ICREA, Barcelona, Spain

Abstract. Performance problems such as sluggish response time or low throughput are especially annoying, frustrating and noticeable to users. Fixing performance problems after they occur results in unplanned expenses and time. Our vision is an MDE-intensive software development paradigm for complex systems in which *software designers* can evaluate performance early in development, when the analysis can have the greatest impact. We seek to empower designers to do the analysis themselves by automating the creation of performance models out of standard design models. Such performance models can be automatically solved, providing results meaningful to them. In our vision, this automation can be enabled by using model-to-model transformations: First, designers create UML design models embellished with the *Modeling and Analysis of Real Time and Embedded systems* (MARTE) design specifications; and secondly, such models are transformed to automatically solvable performance models by using QVT. This paper reports on our first experiences when implementing these two initial activities.

Keywords: Experience · Performance engineering · UML · MARTE · QVT

1 Introduction

Poor performance of cyber-physical systems (CPS) is exemplified by: (*i*) noticeably sluggish response time that becomes frustrating and unacceptable to users; (*ii*) low throughput that, in the worst case, cannot keep pace with the arrival and processing of new information; (*iii*) jitter such as flickering of displays, pixelation, irregular unpredictable responses, pauses while the system catches up, etc.; (*iv*) lack of response to user inputs because the system is busy with the previous request; or (*v*) timeouts and error messages.

Performance problems are obvious to users, and especially annoying and frustrating. Performance has become a competitive edge. The consequences of

© Springer Nature Switzerland AG 2018
F. Khendek and R. Gotzhein (Eds.): SAM 2018, LNCS 11150, pp. 105–126, 2018.
https://doi.org/10.1007/978-3-030-01042-3_7

poor performance range from complaints or rejection of new products to a system failure that, in the worse case, may involve loss of life [18]. Social media and online product reviews expose these performance problems in a way not previously possible, so product failures are much more visible. Extreme cases raise the potential of a business failure.

However, more often than not, performance problems are tackled after they occur, resulting in unplanned expense and time for refactoring. Instead, we advocate for a Model-driven Engineering (MDE) [15] approach to CPS systems development in which stakeholders evaluate the performance of systems early in development when the analysis can have the greatest impact [34]. We seek to move system performance analysis from an isolated set of tools, that require experts to do laborious manual transfers of data among design and analysis tools, to an integrated framework in which independent tools share information automatically and seamlessly [32].

Our vision is a framework which takes advantage of ① *Model Interchange Formats (MIF)*, which are a common representation for data required by performance modeling tools. The MIFs we use were originally proposed in 1995 [35, 37] and have been broadened in scope over the years to incorporate performance-determining factors found in most performance modeling tools and techniques [19, 33]. Using a MIF, tools in the framework may exchange models by implementing an import/export mechanism and need not be adapted to interact with every other tool in the framework. In fact, tools need not know of the existence of other tools thus facilitating the addition of new tools in the framework. This framework exploits model-to-model (M2M) transformations from design models to a MIF and thus provides an automated capability for analyzing the performance of CPS architectures and designs, enabling stakeholders to obtain decision support information – quickly and economically – during the early stages of development.

Our envisioned framework is ② *design-driven* rather than *measurement-driven*. *Measurement-driven* approaches use metrics of performance behavior and find ways to reduce resource usage to improve performance. On the contrary, our *design-driven* approach ties the performance metrics to the aspects of the design that cause excessive demands, so it is also possible to change the way the software implements functions. This often leads to more dramatic improvements than those achievable solely with measurement-driven approaches. The design-driven approach also leads to the resource-usage-reduction improvements so a combination of both types of improvements are attainable.

Finally, we envision an approach exploiting ③ *design specifications* as the source for the performance models, as opposed to *performance specifications* (see Sect. 4 for a description, and Sect. 8 for a comparison with similar previous approaches). Developing *performance modeling annotations* to designs – such as those in the *Modeling and Analysis of Real Time and Embedded Systems / Performance Analysis Model* (MARTE/PAM) [25] – requires expertise in performance engineering, and we seek to enable system designers to evaluate the performance of their designs without requiring performance-modeling experts.

System designers – software architects, designers, modelers, developers, etc. – are *the masses* to whom our approach is targeted[1]. We do not envision eliminating performance specialists altogether: experts should be used when system designers find high performance risk or serious problems requiring performance expertise, when successful project completion is vital, and other high-profile concerns exist. This makes effective use of scarce performance-expertise resources.

This paper reports on our experience on implementing the first version of the design to MIF transformation for our MDE-based performance modeling framework supporting our vision to bring performance assessment closer to system designers. The starting point of this experience is the *Implementation of a Prototype UML to S-PMIF+ model-to-model transformation (UML to S-PMIF+)* project. This UML to S-PMIF+ transformation is a core element of our approach and key to study the feasibility of the approach. This *L&S Computer Technology* project, supported by the MDE experts at the *Universitat Oberta de Catalunya*, aims at implementing the transformation to generate performance models – that can be automatically verified – from design models. As the title of the project specifies, design models are specified using UML [27], which are enriched with design modeling stereotypes from the *Modeling and Analysis of Real-time Embedded Systems* (MARTE) [25] standard. These design models are transformed to the *Software Performance Model Interchange Format+* (S-PMIF+) [33]. S-PMIF+ is an XML-based, MOF-compliant interchange format that can be fed into performance engineering analysis tools such as RTES/Analyzer [20].

The rest of the paper is structured as follows. Section 2 introduces a classical – i.e., not automated – performance analysis process, which serves as the basis to our automated proposal presented in Sect. 3. Section 4 presents our approach to model performance by using UML and MARTE, and Sect. 5 presents how such UML/MARTE models can be transformed to an automatically solvable performance model by using the QVT transformation language. Section 6 exemplifies how the concepts introduced in the two previous Sections are put in practice. Section 7 discusses our findings and lessons learned during this experience. Section 8 discusses related work and Sect. 9 presents our conclusions.

2   *Software Performance Engineering* in a Nutshell

Software Performance Engineering (SPE) [34] is a systematic, quantitative approach to the cost-effective development of software systems to meet performance requirements. Presented more than 25 years ago, it is a clear example of a classical and well established performance analysis process. The SPE process focuses on the system's use cases and the scenarios that describe them. From a development perspective, use cases and their scenarios provide a means of understanding and documenting the system's requirements, architecture, and design. From a performance perspective, use cases allow the identification of workloads that are significant from a performance point of view, that is, the collections of requests

---

[1] From this point on, we will use the generic term *system designers* to refer to any stakeholder taking advantage of our approach.

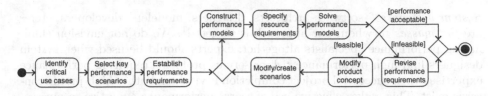

Fig. 1. SPE process (adapted from [34])

made by the users of the system. Traditionally, SPE processes have been conducted by performance analysts – assisted by software architects or developers – who use existing functional models of the system as their starting point. Figure 1 describes typical steps in a simplified SPE process from the modeling point of view:

1. A performance analyst *identifies the critical use cases*, which are those that are important to the operation of the system, or to responsiveness as seen by the user.
2. The analyst *selects the key performance scenarios* – i.e., **UML Sequence Diagrams** in design models. The key performance scenarios are those that are executed frequently, or those that are critical to the perceived performance of the system.
3. The analyst *establishes the performance requirements*, i.e., identifies and defines the performance requirements – expressed in terms of response time, throughput, or resource usage – and workload intensities for each scenario selected in step 2.
4. The performance analyst *constructs the performance models* by translating the sequence diagrams of the key performance scenarios into execution graphs [34].
5. The analyst *specifies the resource requirements*, i.e., the amount of service that is required from key devices in the execution environment. This is typically done in two separate steps: first, by specifying the *software resource requirements*, i.e., the computational needs that are meaningful from a software perspective; and secondly, by mapping those software resource requirements onto the *computer resource requirements*. Software resource requirements can be extracted from the functional description of the system (e.g., from **UML Class Ciagrams**), while computer resource requirements depend on the environment in which the software executes (e.g., typically specified in **UML Deployment Diagrams** and other documentation).
6. Finally, the analyst *solves the performance models*. Solving the execution graph characterizes the resource requirements of the proposed software in isolation. If this solution indicates that there are no problems, the analyst proceeds to solve the system execution model. If the model solution indicates that there are problems, there are two alternatives:(*i*) *revise performance*

requirements, modifying them to reflect this new reality – in this case, all stakeholders should decide if the new requirements are acceptable – or, (*ii*) *modify the product concept*, looking for feasible, cost-effective alternatives for satisfying this use case instance. This latter option may require modifying existing scenarios or creating new ones – again, involving other stakeholders such as software architects or developers.

These steps describe the SPE process for one phase of the development cycle, and the steps repeat throughout the development process. At each phase, the analyst refines the performance models based on increased knowledge of details in the design.

Despite many successes applying the SPE methods, there are key barriers to its widespread adoption and use: (*i*) it requires considerable experience and knowledge of performance modeling and there is a small pool of these experts; (*ii*) it is time consuming to manually develop performance models of a large, complex system; and (*iii*) a substantial amount of time is required to keep performance models in sync with evolving design models.

3   Towards Automated *Software Performance Engineering*

As mentioned above, a traditional SPE process is a labor-intensive approach requiring considerable expertise and effort: performance engineers work side by side with system designers to understand their design, and then create performance models of the design using a performance modeling tool, such as SPE-ED [20]; when problems are detected, performance engineers recommend solutions to system designers who do a refactoring in order to improve performance. Clearly, automating the production of performance models would make early design assessment viable and enable system designers to conduct many of their own analyses without requiring extensive performance expertise.

Fortunately, as electronic systems have become more and more complex and software intensive [36], new engineering practices have been introduced to advance productivity and quality of these cyber-physical systems [16]. Model-Driven Engineering (MDE) [15] is a powerful development paradigm based on software models which enables automation, and promises many potential benefits such as increased productivity, portability, maintainability, and interoperability [10].

Although SPE relies on some design models, it does not exploit all their potential. Thus, our vision for SPE is a MDE-intensive software development paradigm based on MDA standards such as UML [27], MARTE [25], QVT [23] and MOF [24]. In this paradigm, automatic model transformation plays a key role in the development process, allowing system designers to evaluate the performance of systems early in development, when the analysis can have the greatest impact. Thus, we seek to empower system designers to do the analysis themselves by automating the creation of performance models, invoking the model

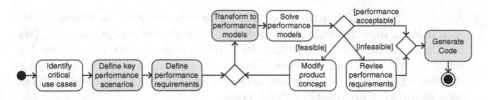

Fig. 2. An automated SPE process

solver, and getting the analysis results in a format meaningful to them. This quantifies the performance of system design options and identifies performance risks.

Achieving such empowerment, however, presents two important challenges:

C1 — We need to provide system designers with **model specifications** which allow them to express performance-determining design elements such as communication, constrained resources, etc. in their design models

C2 — We need to provide system designers with automatic tools able to **transform system design models** into analyzable performance models.

Thus, resolving these challenges accomplishes the objective of providing performance predictions without the performance expertise previously required.

Informally, our proposed renovated process can be seen as an evolution of SPE in which we introduce automation as shown in Fig. 2[2]. An important aspect to be noted (Fig. 2) with respect to a classical SPE process (Fig. 1) is that the main actors involved are now *system designers* as opposed to *performance engineers*. Our process consists of the following Activities:

1. As in traditional SPE, a performance assessment process starts by *identifying the critical use cases*.
2. System designers *define the key performance scenarios*. As opposed to Fig. 1, in which the key performance scenarios were selected by performance engineers from design models, here system designers use UML modeling tools to directly create them as we will describe later in Sect. 4.
3. System designers *define performance requirements* directly in the design models. This can be done by enriching the UML functional models with non-functional properties, using MARTE stereotypes, as we also describe in Sect. 4. Here, *performance requirements* are thus part of system models, and not a separate artifact as in traditional SPE.
4. Design models are *transformed to performance models*. As opposed to traditional SPE, where performance models were manually created by performance engineers, here performance models are automatically generated by executing a model-to-model transformation specified in QVT, as we outline in Sect. 5.

---

[2] We have indicated with a gray background the activities that are different from those in Fig. 1.

5. From here on, the process is similar to traditional SPE: performance models are solved, and after obtaining the analysis results three possibilities arise: (*i*) the results are acceptable; (*ii*) the results are unacceptable but the performance requirements are infeasible; and (*iii*) the results are unacceptable but the performance requirements are feasible. In the first and the second case the process continues as in traditional SPE. In the third case, system designers may modify the product concept (i.e., the models) and regenerate/reevaluate the performance models without intermediate steps.

6. Finally, as in any MDE process, system designers may automatically generate the application code for the system models. This latter step is out of the scope of this paper.

4   Defining Performance Scenarios and Requirements with UML/MARTE

In Sect. 2 we informally introduced some of the different UML diagrams that are useful from the SPE point of view. However, since traditional SPE design models do not need to be machine readable, no specific design rules are enforced in that approach. Our approach aims to achieve automation, and thus, it advocates for – and enforces – the use of four different UML diagrams to specify design models including performance characteristics.

An important aspect of UML is that customization is possible by using profiles. *Modeling and Analysis of Real-time Embedded Systems* (MARTE) [25] is an OMG standard defining foundations for model-based descriptions and analysis of real time and embedded systems. To facilitate its adoption, MARTE has been defined as a UML profile.

We advocate for the use of MARTE to include performance information and requirements in design models. Thus, system designers can make use of tools they are familiar with, without requiring performance engineers to manually create performance models. Although the use of MARTE stereotypes to enable the generation of performance models is not novel (see Sect. 8), the use of *design specifications* in favor of *performance modeling annotations* is. Thus, we propose the use of design modeling annotations – such as those from the *Generic Resource Modeling (GRM)*, *Software Resource Modeling (SRM)*, *Hardware Resource Modeling (HRM)* or *Allocation modeling (Alloc)* MARTE [25] subprofiles – as opposed to *performance modeling annotations* – such as those from the *Generic Quantitative Analysis Modeling (GQAM)*, *Performance Analysis Modeling (PAM)* or *Schedulability Analysis Modeling (SAM)* MARTE subprofiles.

Below we specify the UML diagrams to be used in our automated approach and their purpose, which are later exemplified in the case study in Sect. 6.

Structural View – Deployment Diagrams (DD) specify elements defining the execution architecture of systems. In our modeling approach, DDs specify hardware elements of the system, i.e., those capable of providing any kind of processing service.

Structural View – Class Diagrams (CD) specify the main logical entities participating in a system. In our modeling approach, CDs are used to define software elements of the system, as well as other communication and synchronization entities.

Examples of MARTE stereotypes that can be applied on class diagrams are those applicable to *Operations*, such as `MARTE::MARTE_Foundations::GRM::Acquire` and `MARTE::MARTE_Foundations::GRM::Release`. Such stereotypes can be used to specify that the stereotyped operations acquire or release a *mutex*, respectively.

Structural View – Composite Structure Diagrams (CSD) allow modeling the internal structure of a given *Classifier*. In our modeling approach CSDs are used to represent how the specific instances participating in a system – modeled as *Properties* – relate to each other from a static point of view. Such participants instantiate the classifiers representing either hardware or software elements (specified in a DD or a CD respectively). CSDs specify resources and their allocations for performance analysis. Typical stereotypes used in CSDs are (non exhaustive): `MARTE::MARTE_DesignModel::SRM::SW_Concurrency::SwSchedulableResource`, to annotate software elements generating a workload, and which execute concurrently with other software elements; `MARTE::MARTE_DesignModel::HRM::HwLogical::HwComputing::HwComputingResource`, to annotate active hardware execution resources such as CPUs or FPGAs; `MARTE::MARTE_Foundations::Alloc::Allocate`, typically applied on *Abstractions*[3] between software resources and hardware resources; or `MARTE::MARTE_Foundations::Alloc::Allocated`, typically applied to software and hardware elements related by an `Allocated` *Abstraction*.

Behavioral View – Sequence Diagrams (SD) allow describing precise inter-process communication by specifying execution traces. In our proposal, *Lifelines* in a SD represent elements declared in a CSD. SDs are the main means to specify *key performance scenarios* in our modeling approach. SDs typically also include fine grained resource usage information by using the `MARTE::MARTE_Foundations::GRM::ResourceUsage` stereotype. This stereotype may be applied to a *Message* or to an *ExecutionSpecification* to indicate that a given operation effectively requires the usage of the resource represented by the *Lifeline* – either receiving the *Message* or covered by the *ExecutionSpecification*, respectively – for a specific amount of time.

5   Automatic Transformation to Performance Models

With the aim of automating the transformation of software design models into performance models, we have implemented a transformation in a M2M transformation language. As Sect. 4 describes, the source models to be transformed are UML design models enriched with MARTE annotations.

---

[3] `Allocate` can only be applied to *Abstractions*, which are a specific kind of UML *Dependency*.

We have chosen the *Software Performance Model Interchange Format+* (S-PMIF+) as the target representation for our performance models. S-PMIF+ is a Model Interchange Format (MIF) to exchange Real-Time and Embedded Systems (RTES) and Internet of Things (IoT) performance models among modeling tools proposed by Smith et al. [33]. S-PMIF+ is an extension of the S-PMIF, which is MOF-compliant since 2010 [22].

We have chosen MOF 2.0 Query/View/Transformation (QVT) [23], and specifically its *Operational* language (QVTo)[4], to encode the transformation rules between UML/MARTE and S-PMIF+. While a plethora of other existing transformation languages could have been chosen to implement this project, we chose QVTo for the following reasons:

Consistency — Almost all the languages in this work are OMG standards (UML [27], MARTE [25], MOF [24]). Using QVT allows us to stay inside the OMG stack.

Standardization — QVT has a normative document describing the semantics of the language, alleviating any future *vendor lock-in* problem.

Availability — Eclipse provides an interpreter of this language. Eclipse is the ideal platform to implement this transformation, since it provides (open source) tools to cover all the modeling steps of our proposed process.

Adequacy to the problem — The transformation from UML to S-PMIF+ involves sequence diagrams, where ordering is an important property. Managing ordering with declarative languages is hard, thus an imperative language such as QVTo provides a better control of the transformation logic (however, at the expense of abstraction).

Table 1 shows the subset of the transformation rules of the UML to S-PMIF+ transformation that are relevant for the case study presented in Sect. 6. The first column indicates the UML elements (see [27]) involved in the rule; the second column the MARTE stereotypes (see [25]) that have to be applied so that the rule matches; and the third column indicates the S-PMIF+ element (see [22,33] for a full reference) that should be generated.

The UML to S-PMIF+ transformation follows a top-down approach. Starting from the UML top-level element – i.e., the *Interaction* corresponding to the SD – traverses the containment tree processing the contained elements. In this navigation, one of the most relevant properties of *Interaction* is *fragment*, which contains – in the order they occur – all the events happening in the *Interaction*. Simplifying, once an interesting event – i.e., an event that should be transformed – is found, the corresponding transformation rule is applied.

Listing 1 shows the *QVT mappings* implementing the rule specified in the fourth row of Table 1. Rule `executionSpecification2Node` (lines 1–4) is a *mapping* that is called when an *ExecutionSpecification* contained within an *Interaction* is found. This mapping is indeed a *disjunction* of

---

[4] In fact, the QVT specification defines three transformation languages: *Core*, *Operational* and *Relations*, being the main difference among them their declarative or imperative nature.

Table 1. High-level transformation mappings

SOURCE ELEMENT	MARTE STEREOTYPE	TARGET ELEMENT
Property represented by a Lifeline	SwSchedulableResource (isActive=true)	PerformanceScenario
Property represented by a Lifeline	SwSchedulableResource	ExecutionGraph (contained within the corresponding Scenario)
Property represented by a Lifeline	TimingResource	PassiveEntity (type=timer)
ExecutionSpecification whose covered Lifeline does not receive neither sync nor async Messages	—	BasicNode
MessageOccurrenceSpecification	SwSchedulableResource (applied on the Property represented by the Lifeline receiving the message); and ResourceUsage (applied on the ExecutionSpecification whose start event is the receive event of the current message)	ActiveService
MessageOccurrenceSpecification of a self-message	SwSchedulableResource (applied on the Property represented by the Lifeline receiving the message); and ResourceUsage (applied on the Message whose start event is the current MessageOccurrenceSpecification)	ActiveService
MessageOccurrenceSpecification whose corresponding Message is invoking a method called 'start'	TimingResource (applied on the Property represented by the Lifeline receiving the message)	PassiveService (command=start)
MessageOccurrenceSpecification whose corresponding Message is invoking a method called 'stop'	TimingResource (applied on the Property represented by the Lifeline receiving the message)	PassiveService (command=stop)
Property (receiving an Abstraction)	Allocated and HwComputingResource or DeviceResource. Additionally, the Abstraction pointing to the Property must have Allocate.	Server

three other mappings: `executionSpecification2BasicNode` (lines 18–29), `executionSpecification2ReplyNode` (not shown) and `executionSpecification2NoReplyNode` (not shown). A disjunction indicates that only the first *mapping* whose *when* clause holds will be executed. As it can be observed, `executionSpecification2BasicNode` inherits from the *abstract mapping* `executionSpecification2abstractNode` (lines 6–16). This abstract mapping cannot be executed by itself (in fact, `SPMIF::Node` is an abstract class, which prevents its execution), but can specify transformation actions that can be reused and extended by other mappings (such as the `executionSpecification2Node` disjoint mappings). In this case, the *abstract mapping* is executed before the instruction in line 28, and triggers the execution of the mappings between lines 9–14 for the events returned by the helper `events()`. This helper is declared in the context of `ExecutionSpecification` so that it can be used as shown in line 8. It returns the list of events that occurr in the *Lifeline* covered by the *ExecutionSpecification* while it is active. As it can be observed, we rely on the order of the events to determine whether an event occurrs during the execution. Lines 34–36 show an interesting feature of QVTo: the possibility to specify assertions. This is a specially useful feature as we will discuss in Sect. 7. Finally, the *when* clause between lines 20–27 specifies that the mapping will only be executed when the Lifeline covered by the *ExecutionSpecification* does not receive neither synchronous nor asynchronous messages while the *ExecutionSpecification* is active.

This Listing is only a small demonstration of what our M2M transformation – of nearly 2000 lines of code (LOC) – looks like. In Sect. 7 we provide more information about its characteristics and numbers.

6 An Illustrative Case Study: Cyber Physical Systems Analysis

We illustrate our approach by analyzing an existing *data acquisition system* (*SensorNet*) and predicting its performance when encryption is added. Encryption is critical to ensure that data is securely transferred from *servers* to a *data store* in the cloud. We chose this case study to show how both security and performance can be analyzed before implementation.

Our *SensoreNet* case study involves both hardware and software elements as shown in Fig. 3. Figure 3a shows the DD with the processors used in execution:

Listing 1. Excerpt of the UML/MARTE to S-PMIF+ QVTo transformation

```
1  mapping UML::ExecutionSpecification::executionSpecification2Node() : SPMIF::ProcessingNode
2  disjuncts UML::ExecutionSpecification::executionSpecification2BasicNode,
3    UML::ExecutionSpecification::executionSpecification2ReplyNode,
4    UML::ExecutionSpecification::executionSpecification2NoReplyNode;
5
6  abstract mapping UML::ExecutionSpecification::executionSpecification2abstractNode() : SPMIF::
       Node {
7    var index : Index = new Index();
8    self.events()->forEach(s) {
9    serviceReq += s[UML::ExecutionSpecification]
10             .map executionSpecification2ServiceSpec(index);
11   serviceReq += s[UML::MessageOccurrenceSpecification]
12             .map messageOccurrenceSpecification2PassiveService(index);
13   serviceReq += s[UML::MessageOccurrenceSpecification]
14             .map messageOccurrenceSpecification2ActiveService(index);
15   }
16 }
17
18 mapping UML::ExecutionSpecification::executionSpecification2BasicNode() : SPMIF::BasicNode
19 inherits UML::ExecutionSpecification::executionSpecification2abstractNode
20 when { -- Generate Basic Node when the Lifeline does not receive neither sync nor async
       messages
21   self.events()[UML::MessageOccurrenceSpecification].message[ --> Select messages that:
22   receiveEvent.covered() = self.covered() --> Are received by this Lifeline
23     and receiveEvent.covered() <> sendEvent.covered() --> Are not self-messages
24     and (messageSort = UML::MessageSort::synchCall
25       or messageSort = UML::MessageSort::asynchCall) --> Are sync or async messages
26     ]->isEmpty()
27 }{
28   name := self.name;
29 }
30
31 helper UML::ExecutionSpecification::events() : OrderedSet(UML::InteractionFragment) {
32   var start : Integer = self.covered().events()->indexOf(self.start);
33   var finish : Integer = self.covered().events()->indexOf(self.finish);
34   assert fatal (start < finish)
35       with log ('Malformed input model in ExecutionSpecification "{1}": its "start" event
           ({2}) appears after its finish ent ({3}).'._format(self, self.start, self.finish
           ));
36   return self.covered().events()->subOrderedSet(start, finish);
37 }
```

Servers are hardware elements, with computing and communication capabilities, that read information from simple hardware *Sensors* – 2700 in our case study – and send this information via a communication media to the cloud (represented by *CloudData*). Figure 3b depicts the software elements in a CD: *Analytics* reads information from a *Sensor*[5], later processes it by using the *Advanced Encryption Standard (AES)* and *Filter* software artifacts; and finally sends it to a *CloudTable*. Additionally, *Analytics* makes use of a *LatencyTimer*, which tracks the beginning and the end of this process.

Figure 4 shows the actual instances of these hardware and software elements of our *SensorNet* case study in a CSD: *cloudData*, *server* and *sensors* are instances of the *Nodes* specified in Fig. 3a; while *filter*, *aes*, *analytics*, *sensor* and *latencyTimer* are instances of the *Classes* specified in Fig. 3b. As it can be observed, we used MARTE stereotypes to specify additional data that is needed to build the performance model[6]: `SwSchedulableResource` specifies workload in *analytics* by using the VSL [25] expression `closed(population=10, extDelay=(500,ms))`, i.e., 10 requests in an interval of 500ms; `HwComputingResource` designates the processors for the *Servers*, i.e., 80 instances; `DeviceResource` represents a server that does not model contention delays (a so-called *delay server* in the performance model); and the `TimingResource` designates the *latency timer*. The *Allocate* shows how processes are allocated to the processors: *cloudTable* is hosted on *cloudData*; *filter*, *aes* and *analytics* tasks are executed on a *server*; and the software representation of *sensors* lie on hardware *sensors*.

Finally, we modeled two scenarios: the first adds security/encryption using basic *sensors*, where the *encryption* and *filtering* happen on the servers; and the second evaluates replacing the *basic sensors* with *smart sensors*, capable of doing the encryption on the sensor itself. In both cases, we use the *CloudTable* database for storing data.

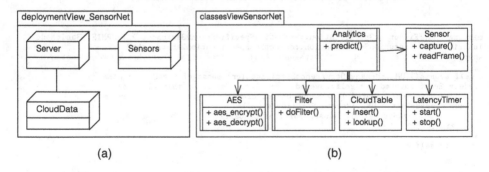

(a)   (b)

Fig. 3. Deployment diagram (a) and class diagram (b)

---

[5] *Sensor* here represents the software element used to access hardware *Sensors*.
[6] We obtained processing times and data/network transfer bytes specified in Figs. 4 and 5 from the analysis of benchmark data.

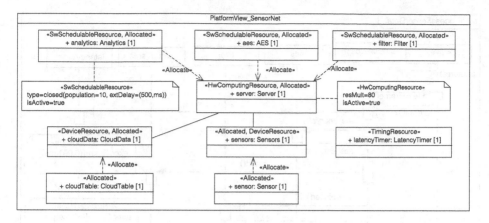

Fig. 4. Composite structure diagram

The sequence diagram for the first scenario is shown in Fig. 5: *analytics* reads a frame of captured data from a specific basic *sensor*, starts the *latencyTimer*, *encrypts*[7] the frame, and *inserts* it into the *cloudTable*. Then, it *filters* the data, does a *lookup* from the *cloudTable* to get recent activity discovered by the sensor, *decrypts* it, and makes *predictions* of future behavior. Results are finally *encrypted* and *inserted* into the *cloudTable*, and the *latencyTimer* is stopped. The figure shows the MARTE annotations for the execution time required for some – not all for readability purposes – steps.

We do not show the sequence diagrams for the second scenario (i.e., using the smart sensors) for the sake of conciseness. In summary, this second sequence diagram lacks the encryption and filter steps, and has a lower value in the specification for the data rate. All the other structure diagrams remain unchanged.

Once the scenarios are modeled, our prototype is able to transform them to the corresponding S-PMIF+ specifications by applying the rules introduced in Sect. 5. Figure 6 shows the resulting S-PMIF+ model for the first scenario. A *Performance Scenario* – with its corresponding *Execution Graph* – is generated for the *analytics* property, which was stereotyped as SwSchedulableResource. Additionally, a *Basic Node* is generated from the *ExecutionSpecification* sending the *insert* message to *cloudTable*. This message, in turn, generates an *Active Service* which executes on the *CloudData Server* with a *service time* of $1.0 \cdot 10^{-6}$ (seconds). All the other elements are generated according to the transformation rules listed in Table 1.

The S-PMIF+ models are sent to the RTES/Analyzer solver. RTES/Analyzer is the tool allowing the developer to study the performance of the modeled system with different parameter settings for the *data rate*, *number of processors*, *time for encryption*, and *time for CloudTable processing*.

---

[7] We based the encryption and decryption on an open source version of the Advanced Encryption Standard (AES) [8].

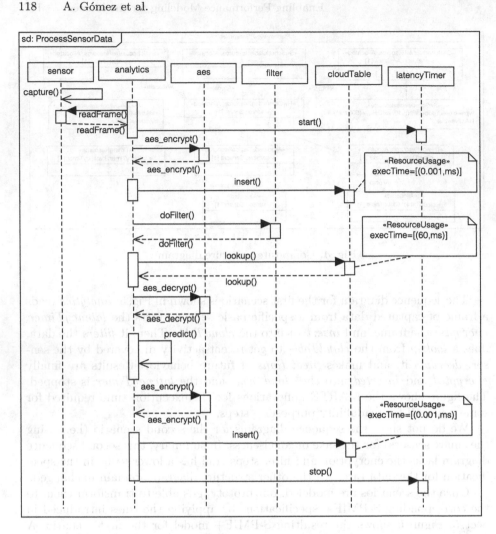

Fig. 5. Sequence diagram

From our experiments using RTES/Analyzer, we obtained that the first scenario using the *basic sensors* requires 80 CPUs to meet the performance requirement (for the 2700 sensors of the case study); while the second scenario using *smart sensors* requires only 50 CPUs. Additional valuable information from the RTES/Analyzer model shows that we need more processors in the cloud to speed up the *insert* and *lookup* tasks. For the case study, we used a single instance in the cloud. There are many other options for both platforms and designs that can be explored with the model, such as: (*i*) reducing the time required for encryption by tuning the algorithm to the application; (*ii*) using asynchronous *cloudTable* inserts; (*iii*) using a pipeline architecture; or (*iv*) using cloud vs.

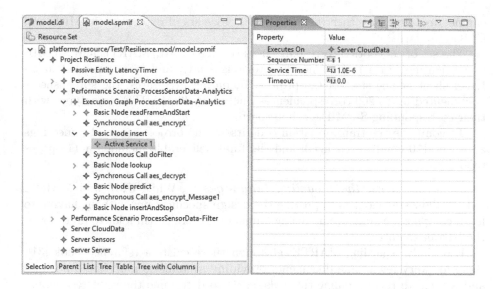

Fig. 6. Generated S-PMIF+ model

on-premises storage. In any case, the evaluation process is the same: the design model is revised, transformed and solved.

7   Discussion

This section reports on the some of the lessons learned during the realization of this work, mainly linked to the realization of the technology transfer project between *L&S Computer Technology* and the *Universitat Oberta de Catalunya*.

While the specific goal of the project was to "simply" write a transformation between UML/MARTE and S-PMIF+ (i.e., implementing Activity 4 of Sect. 3), we quickly realized that clearly defining the inputs and outputs of such a transformation indeed impacted the whole process. This led us to redraw the initial scope of the transformation, having a wider vision of the project, and coming out with a set of modeling guidelines (which in turn support Activities 2–3 in Sect. 3) that, together with the transformation itself, make up the core of the framework. A transformation project is, in the end, a software development project (where *the software* is the transformation) and, as such, it is not without similar challenges.

In the following, we provide some facts about this project, and reflect about the decisions taken and the experience we gained. We believe this could be useful to other teams developing projects involving industry-level transformations. This is the first take-away for anybody starting a transformation project.

Project size and effort — The project lasted for 2 months and was lead by two main technical contacts, one with nearly 30 years of experience in performance engineering, and the other with more than 13 years of experience in MDE and OMG standards.

The set of conceptual correspondences between UML/MARTE and S-PMIF were identified in a several-months previous study, and were provided in an Excel sheet at the start of the project. Including attributes, the spreadsheets documented up to 200 correspondences, including 40 MARTE stereotypes with their corresponding S-PMIF+ counterparts.

To complete the transformation code itself, the project required 8 meetings and over 150 emails exchanged; and the final deliverable included a 118-pages report.

Barrier to entry: the modeling languages — While UML and MARTE indeed allow stakeholders to provide the design specifications without having to learn complex performance modeling languages, there is still a lot to do to lower the barrier to entry.

Especially regarding MARTE, although there exists a reference book [31], there are very few online documents providing systematic modeling guidelines and we had to rely on online tutorials [9,21] to determine the right recommendations for users of our approach. We based our specifications on the design methods of Selic et al. [31] because they are a big step forward on *how* to specify typical design characteristics, particularly those that impact performance such as communication, synchronization, etc. This work provides performance feedback on the desirability of design options. This and other work that provides design-assessment feedback makes UML/MARTE more attractive going forward. If another, more promising MDE design language emerges it should be straightforward to adapt our approach to transform it to our MIFs to provide performance predictions.

As a consequence of the scarce documentation available, 34 pages out of the 118 of the report mentioned above were dedicated to explain our recommended use of UML and MARTE to support Activities 2–3 of our approach. This is necessary to resolve some of the language ambiguities (e.g., regarding the specification of VSL expressions[8]).

Our thoughts on using QVTo — Although imperative transformation languages do not have an especially good reputation, in this special case QVTo was a very good choice for our project thanks to the following features of the language:

- Its imperative character facilitated the processing of ordered elements (required for the transformation of sequence diagrams) in a very natural way.
- Its logging facilities and support for assertions are specially useful to control ill-formed models produced by the tools (more on this below).
- It has explicit support to organize transformations in libraries which helps when developing complex transformations and facilitates reusability.

---

[8] See http://issues.omg.org/issues/MARTE12-4.

- Helpers can be used to add new operations to meta-elements dynamically, without changing the metamodels (similar to the concept of extension functions in Kotlin [14] and other languages). Again, this simplifies the writing of complex transformations.
- QVTo allows the definition of intermediate classes, which only live within the transformation execution scope. This is very useful to reify VSL expressions – Strings – in their corresponding in-memory complex datatypes (the so-called *NFP types* [25]).

We have been pleasantly surprised with QVTo, especially after previous bad experiences with its declarative counterpart. QVTo is definitely an option to be considered when choosing the transformation language for your project, particularly if you require some of the complex requirements above.

Repetitive Transformation code — The transformation was spread out in 4 files for a total of 2027 lines of code (LOC) excluding empty lines. These LOC were distributed as follows:

- 243 LOC dedicated to check the presence/absence of MARTE stereotypes (58 helpers were written to deal with MARTE stereotypes);
- 272 LOC (in 30 helpers) devoted to string manipulations;
- 448 LOC to deal with VSL expressions and NFP types (21 helpers to deal with them);
- 305 LOC in UML helpers (47 helpers to deal with UML elements);
- 759 LOC for the actual implementation of the transformation mappings;

As you see, more than 60% of the transformation code dealt with auxiliary tasks. This must be taken into account when estimating the effort required to implement transformations. Too often we based that estimation on the analysis of the mappings forgetting that this will be only a small part of the total LOC.

Nevertheless, this repetitive code could be simplified by importing external libraries (a clear example would be a QVTo library for String manipulation). These ready-made libraries do not exist at this time, but we believe it is in the best interest of the community to develop and share them.

Limitations of the modeling tools — Within the Eclipse ecosystem, Papyrus is the most popular tool for UML modeling. Still, it also has known limitations when it comes to SDs and this had a negative impact on our project. Ordering of events is crucial in SDs (see Sect. 5), however Papyrus is not always able to maintain it correctly in the underlying model as soon as the user moves messages around. Papyrus models get corrupt very easily, and *ExecutionSpecifications* – among other primitives – lose their start and finish events easily. Garbage elements are also commonly left around.

Limitations of this approach — The design specifications follow the methods in [31] for specifying communication, synchronization and other coordination, resource constraints, etc. using the rules in Sect. 5. These guidelines must be followed for the resulting performance model to represent the intended behavior of the system. Likewise, the performance models only contain features that are expressed in the design models; developers should be aware that early predictions tend to be optimistic, and only represent details that have been specified in the design models. This follows the SPE method of adding features as the software evolves: early models may not represent all aspects of performance (best-case models); details are added as the software specifications evolve to get a more precise prediction of performance.

All the previous facts and issues, beyond delaying the project, also forced us to write additional *sanity check code* to ensure the correctness of the input models before actually transforming them.

On the positive side, the interpreter of QVTo provided all the expected facilities of a modern IDE: content-assist, line-by-line debugging, and watch expressions, which helped us in detecting the above issues.

8   Related Work

The assessment of non-functional requirements, such as performance, of software systems is a well-established discipline in the software engineering field [1,4,7,34]; however, different formalisms, techniques, and levels of automation have been achieved.

Other design-based approaches can also be found in the literature. *Performance by Unified Model Analysis* (PUMA) is a framework for transforming data from a UML-based software design to performance tools [28,39]. It uses the *Core Scenario Model* (CSM) as the intermediate representation. CSM was originally based on the UML profile for *Schedulability, Performance, and Time* (SPTP) [26] and later adapted to MARTE/PAM both of which closely correspond to the information requirements of the *Layered Queueing Model* (LQN) tool. This simplifies the M2M transformations, but because the MARTE/PAM input specifications so closely resemble the performance model itself, it requires performance expertise to create those specifications. Our work uses MIFs that were originally proposed for a model interchange paradigm in 1995 [35,37]. They have been updated and generalized [19,33] to include performance modeling features found in a variety of performance modeling tools and techniques that have proven to be useful over the years, including those in LQN. Another key difference is that we do not require the performance-specific annotations in MARTE/-PAM; we use the MARTE design specifications provided by developers instead. Nevertheless, these approaches are similar in concept, and useful insights on the challenges of developing transformations are also described in [38].

Palladio [2] is an example that also uses MDE techniques. Its simulation tool is implemented using the same technologies as the prototype presented in this work (e.g., Eclipse, Eclipse Modeling Framework, etc.). Unlike our proposal, Palladio provides a domain specific modeling language, the so-called *Palladio Component Model* (PCM), to specify component-based software architectures. Nevertheless, it is worth mentioning that PCM resembles UML in some parts (e.g., component, activity and deployment diagrams).

Kounev et al. [17] propose a model-based approach to designing self-aware IT systems using the *Descartes Modeling Language* (DML). DML is a domain-specific architecture-level language that allows specifying adaptation points to reconfigure the application architecture at runtime. The Descartes approach is fully automated, it is also based on Eclipse, and enables on-line performance predictions and model-based adaptation. DML has been applied to several industrial case studies [13].

These and other approaches differ in that they transform to one specific tool rather than to a MIF. E.g., both PCM and DML transform to Queueing Petri Nets (QPN) to solve their models using the QPME tool; while our prototype transforms our UML/MARTE models to S-PMIF+, which serves as a pivot language for different formalisms and tools.

On the other hand, these tools still require an expert in the use of that performance analysis tool: e.g., Palladio and DML require learning a new performance model specification language. While this is not a problem for performance modeling experts, it is a barrier to system developers who wish to evaluate their own design with minimal extra work. It is also noteworthy that the contents of these meta-models (PCM and DML) were considered and incorporated when possible in the development of the MIFs used in our approach.

The DICE framework [6] is an MDE-based solution using UML specifically designed to focus on the specific challenges of quality-assurance for data-intensive applications using big data technologies. Its DICE Simulation component [3] is also built using Eclipse Papyrus, and is able to transform annotated UML models to both performance and reliability models to stochastic Petri nets using QVTo. The main difference with respect to the work presented here is that, in order to fully support the specificities of data-intensive applications, DICE provides its own profile – the so-called *DICE Profile*. This profile provides performance modeling annotations – as opposed to the design specifications of our approach – which extend and reuse constructs from the GQAM, PAM and SAM MARTE subprofiles, as well as from the DAM [4] profile.

Process mining techniques are a clear example of measurement-based approaches (as described earlier) and several tools are available (e.g., [5,11,12,29, 30]). These approaches try to bridge the gap between the resulting performance metrics and the design itself, however, this is still a challenging task requiring significant expertise. Our approach is design-based, and uses M2M transformations to bridge such a gap by automatically generating performance models from UML diagrams, which are compliant with the standard OMG MARTE [25] profile.

9   Conclusions

This experience has proved the viability of automating SPE processes based on MDE techniques and MIFs. The heart of this automated approach, the transformation from UML/MARTE, shows that a renovated SPE process can be based on the models produced by system designers without requiring extensive knowledge and experience in performance engineering. By automating the transformation of software designs to performance models, we eliminate the need for laborious and error-prone manual translation of software design information into performance models, and the effort in keeping the design and performance models in sync throughout development and operation. The results are also presented in a format that can be easily evaluated by system designers. Automation and usability are key if system designers are to use the technology.

The prototypes we created demonstrated that the end-to-end process is clearly viable even if we learned a few hard lessons along the way. We developed screens that make the transformation of designs to performance models, automated solution of experiments, and the conversion of tool output into a results format that is easy to comprehend, highlights potential problems, allows evaluation of tradeoff in design parameters, and allows user customization of results and formats.

The focus of this effort was on performance analysis of CPS systems; however, as further work, we plan to *plug in* other tools to support additional types of design analysis, such as safety, reliability/availability, fault tolerance and others.

References

1. Balsamo, S., Di Marco, A., Inverardi, P., Simeoni, M.: Model-based performance prediction in software development: a survey. IEEE Trans. Softw. Eng. **30**(5), 295–310 (2004)
2. Becker, S., Koziolek, H., Reussner, R.: The palladio component model for model-driven performance prediction. J. Syst. Softw. **82**(1), 3–22 (2009)
3. Bernardi, S., et al.: A systematic approach for performance assessment using process mining. Empir. Softw. Eng. (2018). https://doi.org/10.1007/s10664-018-9606-9
4. Bernardi, S., Merseguer, J., Petriu, D.C.: Dependability modeling and analysis of software systems specified with UML. ACM Comput. Surv. **45**(1), 1–48 (2012)
5. Celonis PI (2011). https://www.celonis.com. Accessed June 2018
6. Consortium, D.: Getting started with DICE: developing data-intensive cloud applications with iterative quality enhancements (2018). http://www.dice-h2020.eu/getting-started/. Accessed June 2018
7. Cortellessa, V., Marco, A.D., Inverardi, P.: Model-Based Software Performance Analysis, 1st edn. Springer Publishing Company, Incorporated (2011)
8. Daemen, J., Rijmen, V.: The Design of Rijndael. Springer-Verlag New York Inc., Secaucus (2002)
9. Demathieu, S.: MARTE tutorial: An OMG UML profile to develop Real-Time and Embedded systems. http://www.uml-sysml.org/documentation/marte-tutorial-713-ko/at_download/file. Accessed June 2018
10. Di Ruscio, D., Paige, R.F., Pierantonio, A.: Guest editorial to the special issue on success stories in model driven engineering. Sci. Comput. Program. **89**(PB), 69–70 (2014). https://doi.org/10.1016/j.scico.2013.12.006
11. Diwan, A., Hauswirth, M., Mytkowicz, T., Sweeney, P.F.: TraceAnalyzer: a system for processing performance traces. Softw. Pract. Exp. **41**(3), 267–282 (2011)
12. Günther, C.W., Rozinat, A.: Disco: discover your processes. BPM (Demos) **940**, 40–44 (2012)
13. Huber, N., Brosig, F., Spinner, S., Kounev, S., Bähr, M.: Model-based self-aware performance and resource management using the descartes modeling language. IEEE Trans. Softw. Eng. **43**(5), 432–452 (2017)

14. JetBrains: Extensions-Kotlin Programming Language. https://kotlinlang.org/docs/reference/extensions.html. Accessed June 2018
15. Kent, S.: Model driven engineering. In: Proceedings of the Third International Conference on Integrated Formal Methods, IFM 2002. pp. 286–298. Springer-Verlag, London, UK (2002)
16. Khaitan, S.K., McCalley, J.D.: Design techniques and applications of cyberphysical systems: a survey. IEEE Syst. J. **9**(2), 350–365 (2015)
17. Kounev, S., Huber, N., Brosig, F., Zhu, X.: A model-based approach to designing self-aware IT systems and infrastructures. IEEE Comput. **49**(7), 53–61 (2016). https://doi.org/10.1109/MC.2016.198
18. Leveson, N.G.: Safeware-System Safety and Computers: A Guide to Preventing Accidents and Losses Caused by Technology. Addison-Wesley (1995)
19. Lladó, C.M., Smith, C.U.: PMIF+: extensions to broaden the scope of supported models. In: Balsamo, M.S., Knottenbelt, W.J., Marin, A. (eds.) EPEW 2013. LNCS, vol. 8168, pp. 134–148. Springer, Heidelberg (2013). https://doi.org/10.1007/978-3-642-40725-3_11
20. L&S Computer Technology Inc: SPE-ED+. http://spe-ed.com/. Accessed June 2018
21. Medina, J.: The UML profile for MARTE: modelling predictable real-time systems with UML. http://www.artist-embedded.org/docs/Events/2011/Models_for_SA/01-MARTE-SAM-Julio_Medina.pdf. Aaccessed June 2018
22. Moreno, G.A., Smith, C.U.: Performance analysis of real-time component architectures: an enhanced model interchange approach. Perform. Eval. **67**(8), 612–633 (2010). Special Issue on Software and Performance
23. OMG: Meta Object Facility (MOF) 2.0 Query/View/Transformation Specification, Version 1.3. http://www.omg.org/spec/QVT/1.3/
24. OMG: Meta Object Facility (MOF), Version 2.5.1. http://www.omg.org/spec/MOF/2.5.1/
25. OMG: Modeling and Analysis of Real-time Embedded Systems (MARTE), Version 1.1. http://www.omg.org/spec/MARTE/1.1/
26. OMG: UML Profile for Schedulability, Performance, & Time (SPTP), Version 1.1. http://www.omg.org/spec/SPTP/1.1/
27. OMG: Unified Modeling Language (UML), Version 2.5. http://www.omg.org/spec/UML/2.5/
28. Petriu, D.B., Woodside, M.: An intermediate metamodel with scenarios and resources for generating performance models from uml designs. Softw. Syst. Model. **6**(2), 163–184 (2007). https://doi.org/10.1007/s10270-006-0026-8
29. ProM Tools (2017). http://www.promtools.org/doku.php. Accessed June 2018
30. QPR Process Analyzer (2011). https://www.qpr.com. Accessed June 2018
31. Selic, B., Gérard, S.: Modeling and Analysis of Real-Time and Embedded Systems with UML and MARTE: Developing Cyber-Physical Systems, 1st edn. Morgan Kaufmann Publishers Inc., San Francisco (2013)
32. Smith, C.U., Lladó, C.M., Puigjaner, R.: Model interchange format specifications for experiments, output and results. Comput. J. **54**(5), 674–690 (2011). https://doi.org/10.1093/comjnl/bxq065
33. Smith, C.U., Lladó, C.M.: SPE for the internet of things and other real-time embedded systems. In: Proceedings of the 8th ACM/SPEC on International Conference on Performance Engineering Companion, pp. 227–232. ACM, New York 2017). https://doi.org/10.1145/3053600.3053652

34. Smith, C.U., Williams, L.G.: Performance Solutions: A Practical Guide to Creating Responsive, Scalable Software. Addison Wesley Longman Publishing Co., Inc. (2002)
35. Smith, C., Williams, L.: A performance model interchange format. J. Syst. Softw. **49**(1), 63–80 (1999). https://doi.org/10.1016/S0164-1212(99)00067-9
36. Wallin, P., Johnsson, S., Axelsson, J.: Issues related to development of E/E product line architectures in heavy vehicles. In: 42nd Hawaii International Conference on System Sciences (2009)
37. Williams, L.G., Smith, C.U.: Information requirements for software performance engineering. In: Beilner, H., Bause, F. (eds.) TOOLS 1995. LNCS, vol. 977, pp. 86–101. Springer, Heidelberg (1995). https://doi.org/10.1007/BFb0024309
38. Woodside, M., Petriu, D.C., Merseguer, J., Petriu, D.B., Alhaj, M.: Transformation challenges: from software models to performance models. Softw. Syst. Model. **13**(4), 1529–1552 (2014). https://doi.org/10.1007/s10270-013-0385-x
39. Woodside, M., Petriu, D.C., Petriu, D.B., Shen, H., Israr, T., Merseguer, J.: Performance by unified model analysis (PUMA). In: Proceedings of the 5th International Workshop on Software and Performance, WOSP 2005. pp. 1–12. ACM, New York (2005). https://doi.org/10.1145/1071021.1071022

Realizability of Service Specifications

Mohammad F. Al-hammouri$^{(\boxtimes)}$ and Gregor von Bochmann

School of Electrical Engineering and Computer Science (EECS),
University of Ottawa, Ottawa, ON, Canada
{m.alhammouri,bochmann}@uottawa.ca

Abstract. This paper considers a global requirements model in the form of partially ordered actions of UML collaborations, or a high-level MSC (UML interaction sequences), and then studies the derivation of a distributed design model which may include coordination messages exchanged between the different system components. Different problems for the direct realization (without coordination messages) of a design model for special cases of alternatives followed by strict or weak sequence are discussed and solutions provided. Then the case of a weak while loop is considered. While previous work proposes the addition of sequence numbers in the involved messages, we show that in most cases such sequence numbers are not required. We consider message FIFO transmission or without order, and identify two potential problems: loop termination race, and message overtaking. A proposition is given which states under which conditions the directly realized distributed design model does not have these problems and therefore does not need additional sequence numbers. Another proposition provides certain modifications (including the addition of sequence numbers) that can be applied to the design model when these problems are present, and such that the resulting design model conforms to the requirements. These results can be viewed as an improvement of the previous work in [1] by minimizing the number of additional sequence numbers that must be included in the messages of a weak while loop collaboration.

Keywords: Direct realizability
Deriving a distributed implementation · Distributed applications
Partial order specifications · Distributed design models
Weak sequencing

1 Introduction

In this paper, we are concerned of the transformation from a global requirements model, which describe the behavior of a distributed system in an abstract manner by defining the local actions to be performed by the different system components, to a distributed design model, which defines the behavior of each system component separately, including its local actions plus the exchange of coordination messages which are necessary to assure that the actions of the different components are performed in the required order. This problem is often

© Springer Nature Switzerland AG 2018
F. Khendek and R. Gotzhein (Eds.): SAM 2018, LNCS 11150, pp. 127–143, 2018.
https://doi.org/10.1007/978-3-030-01042-3_8

called realizability of service specifications where the service specification is the global requirements model and the specification is said to be directly realizable if a design model can be constructed without any coordination messages. Many difficulties are associated with the realizability of service specifications like non-local choice [2], non-deterministic choice [3], and race conditions [4]. Most of the work in this area uses Message Sequence Charts (MSC) [5] or UML interaction sequences [6] as a modeling paradigm for the global requirements model. We have proposed to use the concept of collaborations for defining the requirements model [6–9]. A collaboration identifies a certain number of system components that play certain roles in the collaboration and defines a global behavior to be performed by these roles. The behavior is defined in terms of actions to be performed by the roles, and a partial order that defines constraints on the order in which these actions may be performed. Normally, the behavior of a collaboration is defined in terms of sub-collaborations that are performed in a specified order. The ordering relationships are strict or weak sequential order, alternatives, concurrency and looping behavior. This formalism is similar to HMSC [10] and UML [11].

In [1], an algorithm is proposed to derive a distributed design model from a global requirements model with a behavior defined by sub-collaborations in sequential, alternative, concurrent or looping composition. As in [12,13], the algorithm may introduce coordination messages for strict sequencing. It also deals with weak sequencing and introduces a choice indication (*cim*) message if one of the roles does not participate in all alternatives of a choice, and introduces sequence numbers in all the messages in the body of a loop with weak sequencing between the repetitions. The algorithm assumes that each component has a message pool where received messages are stored until they are consumed in the order required by the component.

In this paper we investigate this problem in more detail. The main contributions are as follows:

- We show that in many cases the *cim* message is not required.
- We discuss the reception of coordinating messages if an alternative with different sets of terminating roles is followed in strict sequence by another sub-collaboration; a case which was not covered in [1].
- We discuss in detail under which conditions sequence numbers in the messages of a weak while loop are required for coordination. In particular, we have a proposition which states under which condition a weak while loop is *directly realizable* (without sequence numbers nor additional coordination messages); we distinguish between networks message delivery with and without FIFO order; and we point out that, in general, not all messages need sequence numbers when the loop is not *directly realizable*.
- We show that the distributed design model for a weak while loop may be constructed such that for certain components the direct realization approach can be taken, while the approaches of [1] or of [14] may be used independently for the other components. The approach of [1] assumes that the message pool has an interface that allows to wait for a message with a specific sequence

number. If such a function is not available, as for instance in typical programming languages interfaces, the approach of [14] (which is more complex) can be used.
- We discuss in detail the functions that the interface of the message pool of a component should provide for the different behavior composition rules.

The paper is organized as follows: In Sect. 2, we present the concept of collaboration which is used for the modeling the behavior of systems. The order of execution of actions is defined in terms of partial orders. We first give an intuitive explanation and some simple examples, then we discuss the formalization of these concepts following Pratt [15] and complement this formal model with the concept of roles which represent the different system components. We also define what it means that a more detailed behavior model (e.g. a distributed design model) conforms to a more abstract requirement model. In Sect. 3, we discuss the some issues related to the realizability of a global requirements model, give a short literature review, discuss two issues related to alternatives, and propose an interface for the message reception pool. Then in Sect. 4, we discuss in detail the derivation of a distributed design model for a weak while loop behavior. Section 5 is the conclusion.

2 Definitions and Notations

2.1 The Concept of Collaboration

As mentioned above, a collaboration is a collection of actions that are performed by a distributed system. In the requirements model, a certain number of roles are identified, and each action is performed by one of these roles such that their execution satisfies a given partial order. Figure 1(a) shows the example of a collaboration X using a graphical notation borrowed from [9]. Collaboration X has three roles, x, y, and z, and includes 6 actions, a_i $(i = 1, 2, \ldots 6)$. The partial order for the execution of these actions is shown in Fig. 1(b), where $a_i \rightarrow a_j$ means that the execution of action a_i is performed before the execution of action a_j.

For the composition of two collaborations A and B in strict sequence, written "A $;_s$ B", any action of B may only executed when all actions of A have completed. Therefore it is important to identify the initial actions (those for which there are no earlier actions in the partial order) and the final actions (those for which there are no later actions in the partial order). As discussed in [13], for ensuring strict sequencing between A and B, it is sufficient to ensure that all initial actions of B start after all final actions of A have completed. Figure 1(c) shows a more abstract view of collaboration X showing only the initial and final actions of the collaboration. The order of execution of the actions of collaboration X is also be presented in Fig. 1(d) using the notation proposed in [8] (adapted from Activity Diagrams). Here the A_i $(i = 1, 2, \ldots 6)$ are sub-collaborations, and each A_i contains a single action, namely a_i.

Figure 2 shows two other compositions of collaborations. Figure 2(a) shows a collaboration including two decision points: the possible execution orders are $C_0 \; ;_s C_1 \; ;_s C_3$, $C_0 \; ;_s C_2 \; ;_s C_3$, and $C_0 \; ;_s C_2 \; ;_s C_4 \; ;_s C_3$, where the C_i are arbitrary sub-collaborations. Figure 2(b) shows a weak while loop where sub-collaboration C_2 is performed after zero, one or more executions of sub-collaboration C_1. The sequencing between successive executions of C_1 and the final execution of C_2 are weak sequences, which means that sequencing is only enforced locally by each role, but not globally.

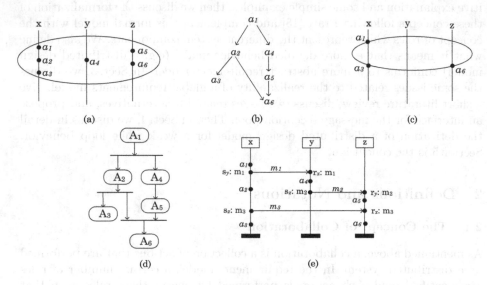

(a)   (b)   (c)

(d)   (e)

Fig. 1. (a) Example of a collaboration X. (b) The partial order for the execution of the actions of X. (c) An abstract view of the collaboration X, showing only initial and final actions. (d) Another representation for the order of actions executions (adapted from Activity Diagrams). (e) Distributed implementation for collaboration X using MSC notation

2.2 Behavior of Collaborations: A Formalization

As pointed out by Lamport [16], partial order is a natural concept for describing the execution of distributed systems. Pratt [15] proposed to use labelled partially ordered set (lposet) [17] for this purpose. A (strict) lposet, also called pomset (partially ordered multi-set) is a tuple $(E, \sum, <, l)$, where E is a set of events, $\sum$ is a set of action labels, $< \subseteq E \times E$ is a irreflexive, asymmetric, and transitive order on E (where "$e_1 < e_2$" means that event e_2 is after event e_1, or $e_1 \rightarrow e_2$ and l is a labeling function $l: E \rightarrow \sum$.

The behavior of the collaboration X shown in Fig. 1(a) can be modelled by a lposet $(E, \sum, <, l)$, where $E = \{e_i | i = 1, 2, \dots 6\}$, $\sum = \{a_i | i = 1, 2, \dots 6\}$, $<$ is as shown in Fig. 1(b), and $l(e_i) = a_i$ for $| i = 1, 2, \dots 6$. Note that the events in the figure are labelled with the action labels, not with the event names.

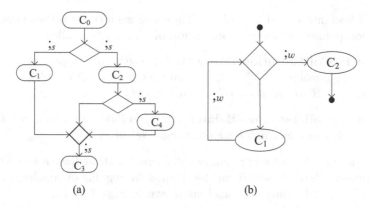

Fig. 2. (a) An example of a composition of collaborations including two decision points. (b) Weak while loop

The collaboration $\mathbb{X}$ shown above is a special case of a requirements model which has a behavior defined by a single pomset. However, in general, the behavior of a collaboration consists of several pomsets. Gischler [18] uses the term "process" to designate a behavioral model, such as a collaboration, and the term "behavior" for the set of pomsets that are allowed for the execution by that model. The following rules are defined for the behavior of process (or collaboration) compositions (see for instance [18]):

The **strict sequence** of two processes C_1 and C_2, written $C_1; s\ C_2$, has the following behavior: the set of all strict concatenations of one pomset in the behavior of C_1 with one pomset in the behavior of C_2 (where the strict combination of two pomsets P_1 and P_2 means that all events of P_2 are after all events of P_1.

The **concurrent** execution of two processes C_1 and C_2, written $C_1 \| C_2$, has the following behavior: the set of all concurrent combinations of one pomset in the behavior of C_1 with one pomset in the behavior of C_2 (where the concurrent combinations of two pomsets P_1 and P_2 is the pomset that contains the union of events and actions, and no order dependencies between the events of P_1 and P_2.

A **choice** between two alternative processes C_1 and C_2, written $C_1 + C_2$, has the following behavior: it is the union of the pomsets in the behavior C_1 and the behavior of C_2.

For an arbitrary number of repetitions of a process C, the Kleene star operator is defined as usual. The behavior of C^{*s} is defined to be strict sequence of zero, one or more repetitions of C in strict sequence.

As an example, the behavior of the collaboration shown in Fig. 2(a) can be defined by the expression $C_0\ ;_s (C_1 + C_2\ ;_s (C_4 + 1));_s\ C_3$, where 1 represents the pomset with an empty set of events. We note that the literature on pomsets usually only considers strict sequencing, which makes abstraction of system components and roles. These concepts are necessary for the derivation of a distributed system design model, and for the definition of weak sequencing (which was first introduced for MSCs). Therefore we introduce the concept of a collaboration-pomset, which is an extension of a pomset as follows:

Definition 1 (Collaboration-Pomset). *A collaboration-pomset is a tuple* $(E, \sum, <, l, \mathbb{R}, \rho)$, *where* $(E, \sum, <, l)$ *is a pomset,* $\mathbb{R}$ *is a set of roles, and* ρ *is a mapping* $\rho : E \to \mathbb{R}$. ρ *assigns a role to each event.*

Definition 2 (Collaboration-Behavior). *A collaboration-behavior is a set of collaboration-pomsets which have a common set of roles* $\mathbb{R}$.

We consider in the following mainly collaborations that have a behavior (i,e, a collaboration-behavior) which can be defined by regular expressions, such as discussed above, or by diagrams, such as shown in Figs. 1 and 2.

Definition 3 (Weak Sequence). *The weak sequence of two collaborations* C_1 *and* C_2, *written* $C_1 ;_w C_2$, *has the following behavior: the set of all weak concatenations of one collaboration-pomset in the behavior of* C_1 *with one collaboration-pomset in the behavior of* C_2 *(where the weak concatenation of two collaboration-pomsets* P_1 *and* P_2 *means that, for any role* r, *all events of* P_2 *that are assigned to the role* r *are after all events of* P_1 *that are assigned to* r.

Note: It was shown in [19] that associativity does not always hold for multiple strict and weak sequencing.

Like the Kleene operator for strict sequencing C^{*s} (mentioned above), we also define arbitrary, multiple weak sequencing using the notation C^{*w} . We consider in Sect. 4 the distributed design model for a weak while loop, as shown in Fig. 2(b), which is defined by the expression "$C_1^{*w} ;_w C_2$".

2.3 Comparing Two Behavior Models

We use the same modeling concepts for requirement models and distributed system design models, namely collaborations (as defined in Sect. 2.2). In this subsection we ask the question: Does a given design model C_2 conform to a given requirement model C_1? The conformance relation should be defined such that if C_2 conforms to C_1, then any implementation that conforms to C_2 will also conform to C_1.

We assume that a design model C_2 conforming to a more abstract model C_1 should include all events of C_1 associated with the same actions and roles as in C_1, but it may contain additional events that are introduced during the refinement process. We also assume that the partial order defined by C_1 should be realized by C_2, but the order of C_2 may be stronger. Therefore we provide the following definitions.

Definition 4 (Conformance of Pomsets). *Given two collaboration-pomsets* P_1 *and* P_2, *we say that* P_2 *conforms to* P_1 *if the events of* P_2 *include the events of* P_1, *the order of* P_2 *is a refinement of the order of* P_1 *and the restriction of the labelling and role mapping functions of* P_2, *restricted to the events of* P_1, *are equal to the functions of* P_1.

Definition 5 (Conformance of Collaborations). *Given two collaborations C_1 and C_2, we say that C_2 conforms to C_1 if for each collaboration-pomset P in the behavior of C_2, there is a collaboration-pomset in the behavior of C_1 to which P conforms.*

3 Deriving Conforming Distributed Design Models

3.1 Basic Ideas

Since the early work in this area [13,20], the following basic ideas were proposed for the derivation of a distributed design model from a global requirements model:

1. The distributed design consists of processes for each role. The processes performed by different roles communicate through the exchange of messages.
2. The process of a given role r is obtained from the global requirements collaboration by projecting its behavior onto role r, that is, by deleting all events that are associated with other roles $r' \neq r$.
3. If an order should be introduced between two actions $a_1 \rightarrow a_2$ associated with different roles r_1 and r_2, respectively, one should introduce a coordination message (called "flow message" in [1]) to be sent by r_1 after the execution of a_1, and to be received by r_2 before the execution of a_2.
4. Each role has a reception pool where received messages are stored until their consumption is requested by the local behavior. We distinguish the following cases:
   (a) A single input queue which receives the messages from all other roles.
   (b) For each other role, messages are transmitted in FIFO order and stored in the pool in separate FIFO queues.
   (c) A simple pool of messages which can be requested for consumption in any order (for instance [20]).

If we apply these principles to the global requirements model of Fig. 1(a) and (b), we obtain the distributed design model of Fig. 1(e), which is shown in the form of a MSC. The messages in this design are introduced according to point (3) above. For the message sending and receiving actions, we use the notation "$s_x : m_1$" and "$r_y : m_2$", respectively, where x and y are the roles to which the message is sent, and the role from where the message was received, and m_1 and m_2 represent the types of the message involved.

It is important to note, that the messages m_2 and m_3 may lead to a race condition at reception by role z, that is, m_3 may arrive before m_2, although it is expected to arrive afterwards. A reception pool of type (b) or (c) (see above) is introduced in order to deal with such race conditions. If such a pool is used by role z, then it may consume these two messages in the order it expects, that is, first m_2 then m_3. (If m_3 arrives before m_2, it will be stored in the pool; z will wait for m_2; and then it will request the consumption of m_3). We note that a reception pool type (a) will lead to a deadlock if m_3 arrives before m_2. Therefore, this type of pool should be avoided.

One says that a global requirements model is **realizable** if a conforming distributed design model can be found. We call **basic implementation** the design model obtained by the basic approach above without any additional coordination message (using point (3)). We say that the requirements model is **directly realizable** if the basic implementation with reception pool conforms to the global requirements. We note that in the case that the global requirements are given in the form of the simple MSC without alternatives, the specification is directly realizable since it contains already all messages required for enforcing the order of the distributed actions (for instance, if we take Fig. 1(e) as the global requirements model).

3.2   Review of Work on Realizability

Realizability of global specifications has been extensively studied by many authors. Different formalisms have been used for defining the global specification, while for the definition of the local behavior of each role normally state machine models were used. The conditions for the realizability of High-level MSC (HMSC for short) have been proposed in [21], for Message Sequence Graph (MSG for short) in [22], and for Compositional MSCs in [20]. Some authors have discussed the pathologies in HMSCs that prevent their realization like non-local choice [2,10].

Global specifications in the form of a set of MSC are considered in [23]. This is related to the problem of implied scenarios. This work is extended in [22] by studying the realizability of MSC-graphs under FIFO communication. In both papers, the specification is realizable if there exist concurrent automata which implement the set of MSCs. Two types of realizability are considered: weak realizability (where the distributed design may deadlock) and safe realizability where no additional deadlock is introduced. In both cases, the behavior for each role is modelled by a finite state machine and communication is through FIFO queues.

In [20], they formally study under which conditions the global specification (compositional MSC) is directly realizable, they prove that the absence of non-deterministic, race and non-local choice lead to sound choice which is directly realizable. Different composition operators (i.e., weak and strong sequence, alternative and parallel) between sub-collaborations are studied in [7,8], and how they affect realizability.

In many cases the specifications are not directly realizable, however, they are realizable by including additional coordination messages or parameter in the implementation. Additional data is added to the messages to achieve safe realizability for MSC specifications [24]. In [25], they consider the realizability of local-choice HMSCs and proof that the implementation strongly conforms to the specification using messages parameters. The authors of [7,8] report when strong and weak sequence need coordination messages to achieve realizability, and [1] introduces the *cim* message for the realization of alternatives. In [1,14], race conditions in weak while loops are studied and an additional message parameter is introduced for obtaining realizability.

3.3   Alternatives with Different Terminating Roles

For enforcing a weak sequence between two collaborations C_1 ;$_w$ C_2, no coordination messages are required in the distributed design model since the ordering defined by weak sequence is a local order only. This is different for the strict sequence C_1 ;$_s$ C_2 which defines globally that all actions of C_2 must be after all actions of C_1. This can be ensured by introducing coordination messages from all roles performing a final action of C_1 (called terminating roles of C_1) to all roles performing an initial action of C_2 (called initiating roles of C_2) [1,12].

In the case of a collaboration with alternatives C_1 and C_2, followed in strict sequence by another collaboration C_3, the situation is in general more complex, as shown by the example of Fig. 3. This case is not mentioned in [13], and it is excluded from the discussion in [1,12], If the alternatives have different sets of terminating roles, the initiating roles of C_3 have to wait for two alternative sets of coordinating messages. In the example of Fig. 3, the choice between the two alternatives is made by role y (local choice), and role w has to consume, before the action e_6 in collaboration C_3, either two coordination messages from roles x and z, or another message from role z (we assume that all coordination messages can be distinguished by their type).

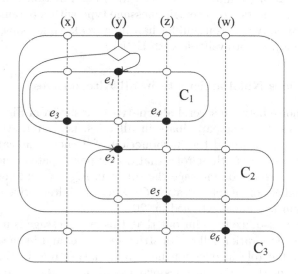

Fig. 3. Alternatives with different terminating roles

3.4   Interface Provided by the Reception Pool

The reception pool should provide an interface to the local behavior at the given role which allows to specify which messages are candidate for consumption. For avoiding the race condition in the behavior of Fig. 1(e), the local behavior at role z would request the consumption of message m_2, and then of message m_3. In the case of the local behavior of role z in the alternative of Fig. 3, the first action in both alternatives would be the reception of a message. The local behavior would request the consumption of one of these messages and would be informed which message was received. We note that we assume that the messages can all be distinguished by their type (and/or by the sending role). We call such an interface a **basic pool interface**. It can be constructed using the basic Internet socket interface for communication with a single partner. Such an interface is for instance provided by the BPEL programming environment, which is often used for the distributed implementation of Web Service Applications.

We note, however, that this basic interface is not natural for handling strict order between two collaborations. In this case, an initiating role of the second collaboration would start with requesting the consumption of a set of messages, namely all messages to be received from the terminating roles of the first collaboration. The situation becomes even more complex for strict sequence after alternatives with different sets of terminating roles, as discussed above. In this case, the initiating role after the alternative would naturally request two or more alternative sets of messages to be consumed. In the example of Fig. 3, the behavior of role w for sub-collaboration C_3 would start with requesting either the set of messages $\{r_x : m_1, \ r_z : m_2\}$ or $\{r_z : m_3\}$. Such an interface is unfortunately not provided for BPEL programming. Also the interface function which allows for requesting the consumption of a certain message type with a parameter that has a given integer value (which is useful for handling weak while loops, as discussed in the next section), is not available with BPEL.

3.5   A Role Does Not Participate in all Alternatives

In the case of choice between several alternatives, as shown in Fig. 4, where one of the alternatives does not participate in all roles, i.e., alternative A doesn't participate in z, [1] suggested the introduction of a choice indication message cim to indicate the choice to those roles that do not participate in the alternative. Without such a coordination message the role z in Fig. 4 would not know when to start the initial action of collaboration C_3 when this alternative is chosen. We note that problem was not mentioned in [20].

Here we would also like to point out that this cim message is not required if the subsequent collaboration follows in strict sequence, and in the case of weak sequence only if the role in question has an initiating role in the subsequent collaboration. If in Fig. 4 the m_6 message would go in the opposite direction (and role z would not be initiating), role z could simply request the pool for the consumption of m_5 or m_6.

4   Weak While Loop

We consider in this section a requirements model including a weak while loop as shown in Fig. 2(b). We assume that the decision of repeating collaboration C_1 or finishing with C_2 is a local choice. In the example of Fig. 5, this is done

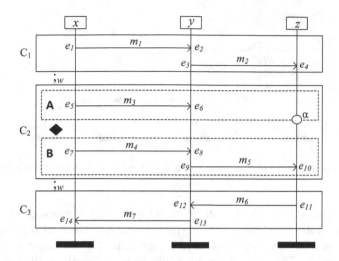

Fig. 4. An example where role z does not participate in all alternatives (α is part of the design model where *cim* must be received)

by role x. We call this role the **initiator** of the loop. The other roles are called **dependent roles**. It is important to note that the first event of a dependent role in C_1 or in C_2 is always the reception of a message (since otherwise the role would be initiating, and the choice would not be local). We also assume that all collaboration-pomsets of C_1 and C_2 involve the same set of roles.

It has been pointed out in the literature that a race may occur for a dependent role between the reception of the first messages of C_1 and C_2. For instance in Fig. 5, if the transmission of m_2 during the last repetition of C_1 is delayed for some reason, the role z may receive m_5 before the last message m_2. We call such a race a **termination race** of the loop.

Another problem that may occur is the following: If a given type of message of C_1 is not transmitted over a FIFO channel from the sending role to the receiving role, then it may happen that the message instance of the nth repetition of C_1 is overtaken by the instance of the next repetition. If the message has no parameters, then there is no problem, but otherwise the parameter values would arrive out of order. We call this problem **message overtaking**. For instance, we note that message type m_8 in Fig. 5 may have message overtaking in the case that C_1 is repeated twice and the transmission of the first message m_8 is very slow.

Proposition 1. *A weak while loop with local choice is directly realizable if it does not contain any termination race nor message overtaking.*

Proof. The absence of termination race means: For any dependent role r that receives the first messages m_1 and m_2 in C_1 and C_2, respectively, it can never happen that the message m_2 is received by r while m_1 still in transit. Also, the absence of message overtaking means: For any dependent role r and any message

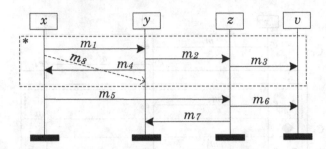

Fig. 5. An example of a weak while loop where role x is the loop initiator

type m received within C_1, it can never happen that a message of type m is overtaken by another instance of that type belonging to the next repetition of C_1. There is no need for any coordination messages since the messages are consumed in the right order. Therefore the weak while loop is directly realizable.   □

In the following we discuss under what conditions there are no such problems and how a given role can be implemented in the distributed design model in the case that there are problems.

4.1   Checking the Requirements Model for Problems

We analyse in this subsection the requirements model and give some propositions that ensure the absence of termination race and message overtaking.

Proposition 2 (Absence of termination race). *A dependent role r of a weak while loop has no termination race if one of the following conditions is satisfied:*

(a) *The reception of the first message m by r in C_1 is before that last event in C_1 of the initiator.*

(b) *The first messages received by r in C_1 and C_2 are sent by the same role r', and the communication is over a FIFO channel. Note that it is assumed here that role r' has no termination race.*

Proof. **For (a):** If the first message m in C_1 to be received by r is in transit, then it must have been sent and not yet received. Since the reception is before the last event in C_1 of the initiator, the initiator must be involved in the execution of C_1 when a message m is in transit. Therefore there can never be the first message received by r in C_2 in transit at the same time. Therefore there cannot be a race.

For (b): Since we assume that the sending role r' has no termination race, the first messages in C_1 will be sent before the first message in C_2. Because they are sent over a FIFO channel, they will also be received in this order.   □

Proposition 3 (Absence of message overtaking). *For the reception of a message type m by a role r during the repetitions of C_1, there is no danger of message overtaking, if one of the following conditions is satisfied:*

(a) The reception of the message is before the last event in C_1 of the initiator.
(b) The message is received over a FIFO channel from the sending role.
(c) The receiving role is the initiator of the loop.

Proof. The proof for **(a)** is similar to the previous proposition. Point **(b)** is evident. Point **(c)** follows from the fact that the initiator waits for receiving all messages related to one repetition of C_1 before it starts another repetition.   □

4.2   Deriving a Distributed Design Model for a Weak While Loop

To get a conforming distributed design model in the case of a termination race, it was suggested in the literature to include in the first messages received by a role in C_1 and in C_2 a sequence parameter which indicates the number of repetitions of C_1, and accept the first message of C_2 only if it contains the right sequence number. This approach was also used in [1], however, for all roles and with sequence parameters in all messages. This, by the way, also solves the message overtaking problem.

In this section we discuss how a conforming design model can be constructed by introducing a minimum number of sequence parameters in messages.

As pointed out by Proposition 1, the basic implementation provides a conforming design model if there are no problems of termination race nor message overtaking. We propose to construct a conforming design model by starting out with the basic implementation, and then performing modifications to the behavior of those roles that have any of these problems.

For a role r that has termination race (TR), one of the following modifications can be used:

– **Modification-TR-1:**
  (a) A sequence parameter is introduced into the first message receive in C_2.
  (b) The behavior has a local variable N which is initialized to 0 before the while loop starts. Each time the first message of C_1 is received, N is incremented.
  (c) In the request to the message pool for consuming the first message of C_1 or C_2, a condition is added to the consumption of the first message of C_2, namely that the parameter value is equal to N.
  (d) This assumes that the behavior of the sending role also has a modification introducing a local variable N (which is incremented) and sending the value of N as message parameter.

This modification-TR-1 corresponds to what is proposed in [1]. It presents the difficulty that a message pool providing a suitable interface must be used. To avoid this difficulty, the following modification was proposed in [14].

- **Modification-TR-2:** Points (a), (b) and (d) as above. Instead of (c), we have the following:
  - A request is given to the message pool to consume the first message of C_1 or of C_2. If the first message in C_2 is received, the message is stored in a buffer and its parameter is stored in a second local variable M. If (M = N), the behavior of C_2 starts using the first message in the buffer. Otherwise the local behavior of C_1 is performed. Then the process goes back to the beginning of the loop and waits again for an instance of first message for C_1 or C_2,

For a role r that has message overtaking(MO) for a message type m, the following modifications can be used:

- **Modification-MO-1:** Points (b) and (d) as in Modification-TR 1. Instead of (a) and (c), we have the following:
  - A sequence parameter is introduced into the message type that has the problem of overtaking.
  - In the request for consumption to the message pool of message m, a condition is added to the consumption, namely that the parameter value is equal to N.

- **Modification-MO-2:** Ensure that the message m is received through a FIFO channel.

Modification-MO-1 has the disadvantage that an additional message parameter must be introduced and the message pool needs to support consumption requests with parameter conditions. It is often much easier to ensure FIFO delivery between the sending and receiving roles.

Proposition 4 (Conforming design model). *Given a requirements model R and a distributed design model D. D conforms to R if the following condition is satisfied: D is obtained from the basic implementation of R by applying the following modifications:*

(a) *For each responding role that has a termination race according to R, apply Modification-TR-1 or Modification-TR-2.*

(b) *For each reception by some depending role of some message with the problem of message overtaking according to R, apply Modification-MO-1 or Modification-MO-2.*

Proof. We have to show that the following conditions are satisfied:

(a) Collaboration C_1 is executed by all roles the same number of times.

(b) During the Nth execution of C_1 by a given role r, each message m consumed by r was sent by the sending role r' during its Nth execution of C_1.

Condition (b) follows from point (b) of the Proposition. It is straightforward to prove that the Modification-MO-1 or Modification-MO-2 assures that there is no message overtaking in the design model. For proving Condition (a), we have to prove that if Modification-TR-1 or Modification-TR-2 are introduced for a role r, this ensures that C_2 is executed by r only after C_1 has been executed N times, where N is the number of time that the loop initiator executed C_1.

For this purpose, we group the roles into role-sets RS(i) ($i = 0, 1, 2, ...$). The initiator is in RS(0) and any dependent role that receives the first message of C_2 from a role in RS(i) is in RS(i+1). Now we do the proof by induction over i. Suppose that the roles in RS(i) execute C_1 the same number of times N as the initiator, then any role in RS(i+1) receives the first message of C_2 with the parameter N. It is easy to see that Modification-TR-1 or Modification-TR-2 ensure that the role will also executed C_1 N times before it executes C_2. When it executes C_2 and sends an initial message to another role, then this message will also include the parameter N. We conclude that all first messages of C_2 will include the same parameter value and therefore all roles will execute C_1 the same number of times. □

5 Conclusion

We consider the derivation of a distributed design model from a global requirements model which identifies the different actions to be performed by the different system components and a partial order that determines the order in which these actions may be performed. The distributed design model defines for each component the local actions to be performed and their order. We call basic implementation a design model obtained by projection of the requirements model onto each component. If this design model conforms to the requirements, we say that the requirements are directly realizable. However, in most cases additional coordination messages or parameters must be introduced to coordinate the order of actions at different components. We study special cases of alternatives followed by strict or weak sequence. We show that the choice indication message *cim*, introduced in [1] is not required in many cases.

We also study the implementation of the weak while loop, which may have the problems of termination race and message overtaking. We show under which conditions these problems are absent, and the loop is directly realizable. For the other cases, we show how a conforming design model can be obtained by introducing minimal changes to the basic implementation. Overall, this is an important improvement over what is proposed in [1].

This work is important in the context of distributed system design where the designers and developers should consider these problems and know how to solve them. This work is also important for the construction of tools that generate code for distributed applications in order to generate code without design flaws.

In the near future, we plan to use the formal partial order description to prove the conformance of the derived design model and to implement the derivation algorithm in a tool environment.

References

1. von Bochmann, G.: Deriving component designs from global requirements. In: CEUR Workshop Proceedings, vol. 503, pp. 55–69 (2008)
2. Ben-Abdallah, H., Leue, S.: Syntactic detection of process divergence and non-local choice in message sequence charts. In: Brinksma, E. (ed.) TACAS 1997. LNCS, vol. 1217, pp. 259–274. Springer, Heidelberg (1997). https://doi.org/10.1007/BFb0035393
3. Mooij, A.J., Goga, N., Romijn, J.M.T.: Non-local choice and beyond: intricacies of MSC choice nodes. In: Cerioli, M. (ed.) FASE 2005. LNCS, vol. 3442, pp. 273–288. Springer, Heidelberg (2005). https://doi.org/10.1007/978-3-540-31984-9_21
4. Alur, R., Holzmann, G.J., Peled, D.: An analyzer for message sequence charts. In: Margaria, T., Steffen, B. (eds.) TACAS 1996. LNCS, vol. 1055, pp. 35–48. Springer, Heidelberg (1996). https://doi.org/10.1007/3-540-61042-1_37
5. ITU-TS, Recommendation Z.120 (02/11), Message Sequence Chart (MSC). ITU, Geneva. Technical report (2011)
6. Castejón, H.N., Bræk, R.: Formalizing collaboration goal sequences for service choreography. In: Najm, E., Pradat-Peyre, J.-F., Donzeau-Gouge, V.V. (eds.) FORTE 2006. LNCS, vol. 4229, pp. 275–291. Springer, Heidelberg (2006). https://doi.org/10.1007/11888116_21
7. Castejon, H.N., Braek, R., von Bochmann, G.: Realizability of collaboration-based service specifications. In: Proceedings - Asia-Pacific Software Engineering Conference, APSEC, pp. 73–80 (2007)
8. Castejón, H.N., von Bochmann, G., Bræk, R.: On the realizability of collaborative services. Softw. Syst. Model. 12(3), 597–617 (2013)
9. Israr, T., von Bochmann, G.: Performance modeling of distributed collaboration services. In: ICPE 2011-Proceedings of the 2nd Joint WOSP/SIPEW International Conference on Performance Engineering, January 2011, pp. 475–480 (2011)
10. Hélouët, L.: Some pathological message sequence charts, and how to detect them. In: Reed, R., Reed, J. (eds.) SDL 2001. LNCS, vol. 2078, pp. 348–364. Springer, Heidelberg (2001). https://doi.org/10.1007/3-540-48213-X_22
11. Object Managment Group: UML 2.5.1 specification. Technical report (2017)
12. Khendek, F., von Bochmann, G., Kant, C.: New results on deriving protocol specifications from service specifications. In: Proceedings of the ACM SIGCOMM 1989, pp. 136–145 (1989)
13. Gotzhein, R., von Bochmann, G.: Deriving protocol specifications from service specifications including parameters. ACM Trans. Comput. Syst. 8(4), 255–283 (1990)
14. Mustafa, N.M.F., von Bochmann, G.: Transforming dynamic behavior specifications from activity diagrams to BPEL. In: Proceedings of the 6th IEEE International Symposium on Service-Oriented System Engineering, SOSE 2011, pp. 305–311 (2011)
15. Pratt, V.: Modeling concurrency with partial orders. Int. J. Parallel Program. 15(1), 33–71 (1986)
16. Lamport, L.: Time, clocks, and the ordering of events in a distributed system. Commun. ACM 21(7), 558–565 (1978)
17. Katoen, J.P., Lambert, L.: Pomsets for message sequence charts. In: Proceeding of First Workshop SDL and MSC (SAM 1998), pp. 197–208 (1998)
18. Gischer, J.L.: The equational theory of pomsets. Theor. Comput. Sci. 61(2–3), 199–224 (1988)

19. von Bochmann, G.: Associativity between weak and strict sequencing. In: Amyot, D., Fonseca i Casas, P., Mussbacher, G. (eds.) SAM 2014. LNCS, vol. 8769, pp. 96–109. Springer, Cham (2014). https://doi.org/10.1007/978-3-319-11743-0_7

20. Mooij, A., Romijn, J., Wesselink, W.: Realizability criteria for compositional MSC. In: Johnson, M., Vene, V. (eds.) AMAST 2006. LNCS, vol. 4019, pp. 248–262. Springer, Heidelberg (2006). https://doi.org/10.1007/11784180_20

21. Hélouët, L., Jard, C.: Conditions for synthesis of communicating automata from HMSCs. In: Proceedings of 5th International Workshop on Formal Methods for Industrial Critical Systems, March 2000

22. Alur, R., Etessami, K., Yannakakis, M.: Realizability and verification of MSC graphs. Theor. Comput. Sci. **331**(1), 97–114 (2005)

23. Alur, R., Etessami, K., Yannakakis, M.: Inference of message sequence charts. IEEE Trans. Softw. Eng. **29**(7), 623–633 (2003)

24. Baudru, N., Morin, R.: Safe implementability of regular message sequence chart specifications. In: ACIS 4th International Conference on Software Engineering, Artificial Intelligence, Networking and Parallel/Distributed Computing (SNPD 2003) (2003)

25. Genest, B., Muscholl, A., Seidl, H., Zeitoun, M.: Infinite-state high-level MSCs: model-checking and realizability. J. Comput. Syst. Sci. **72**(4), 617–647 (2006)

An Arithmetic Semantics for GRL Goal Models with Function Generation

Yuxuan Fan, Amal Ahmed Anda, and Daniel Amyot(✉) (iD)

EECS University of Ottawa, Ottawa, ON K1N 6N5, Canada
{yfan035,aanda027,damyot}@uottawa.ca

Abstract. Goal models are used to support early requirements engineering activities by capturing system and stakeholder objectives and their links, and by enabling what-if and trade-off analysis in a decision-making context. They are also increasingly used in system monitoring and self-adaptation contexts. Yet, automatically converting goal models to code for supporting analysis and adaptation activities remains an issue. This paper presents a new arithmetic semantics for the standard Goal-oriented Requirement Language (GRL), supported by a transformation to functions in multiple programming languages. Such code allows for quantitative GRL model evaluations to be performed outside of modeling tools, including in running systems. The transformation makes use of a Python-based intermediate representation (SymPy), with function generation in Java, JavaScript, C, C++, Python, R, and Matlab. The semantics and transformation, implemented in the jUCMNav plug-in for Eclipse, entirely cover GRL, including goals, indicators, actors, and any combination of links.

Keywords: GRL model · Self-adaptation · Mathematical analysis

1 Introduction

Goal modeling is a requirements engineering activity that targets the understanding and specification of the goals of systems and their stakeholders, the various means of achieving these goals, and other types of relationships between these elements. Goal models support functional and non-functional aspects of systems and enable what-if analysis as well as an evaluation of trade-offs between the often conflicting goals of different stakeholders. There exist many goal modeling languages [13], including i*, Tropos, KAOS, as well as ITU-T's Goal-oriented Requirement Language (GRL), part of the User Requirements Notation (URN) standard [2,14]. Goal model analysis can be used not only at design time [1,12], but also at runtime in systems that exhibit some context monitoring or self-adaptation functionalities [27].

In emerging adaptive systems, systems of systems, as well as socio-cyber-physical systems (SCPSs), including autonomous vehicles, smart homes, and smart cities, goal-based reasoning often needs to be performed by the systems

© Springer Nature Switzerland AG 2018
F. Khendek and R. Gotzhein (Eds.): SAM 2018, LNCS 11150, pp. 144–162, 2018.
https://doi.org/10.1007/978-3-030-01042-3_9

themselves, outside goal modeling environments. Such runtime reasoning can help manage the complexity and uncertainty of the development and execution processes of these kinds of systems [4,6]. Some SCPSs may also need to adapt dynamically to reach an optimal symbiosis with their users and contexts. Managing goal models at runtime is an increasingly popular solution for conducting trade-off analysis and selecting the best adaptation strategy using data monitored in real time [6]. In this context, how to transform a goal model into a representation that can be evaluated at runtime by systems becomes an important issue.

Transforming goal models into executable functions could also be useful in modeling environments that support simulations. For example, the Systems Modeling Language (SysML) [20] could embed such functions in its models in order to simulate adaptive systems. This is also in line with the recent request for proposal for SysML v2 [19], which is looking to integrate goal concepts.

As runtime adaptation is based on a quantitative evaluation of monitored data contributing to goals of different stakeholders, the source modeling language must support a representation of stakeholders and their goals, some means of representing quantitative data and their corresponding satisfaction level, as well as automated mechanisms for quantitative evaluation. GRL is the only standardized language that meets these requirements. GRL helps capturing stakeholders (roles, organizations, systems, etc., collectively named actors), their intentions (goals, softgoals, tasks, and resources), their relationships (AND/OR decomposition, positive/negative contributions, and dependencies), and indicators to measure intention satisfaction based on external evidence. In GRL, goals and other intentional elements can also be partially satisfied. A GRL indicator assesses a current observable data value in a given unit against target, threshold, and worst value parameters, and outputs a satisfaction level that can be propagated to goals, softgoals, tasks and resources in the rest of the model. Indicators can be used (1) at design time via GRL evaluation strategies or external data sources (database, web server, Excel sheet, etc.) and (2) at runtime using monitoring sensors and real-time data [21]. GRL hence supports quantitative and qualitative trade-off and what-if analyses usable at design time but also at runtime in an adaptation context [13,21]. Although GRL has been previously used to model context-aware systems [25], no transformation from GRL to code executable by systems currently exists to support run-time adaptation.

This paper proposes a new arithmetic semantics for GRL and a method for transforming entire GRL models into mathematical functions. Seven target programming languages (Java, JavaScript, C, C++, Python, R, and Matlab) are currently supported for efficient and effective model evaluations in different contexts, including running systems but also other modeling environments that support simulations (e.g., with SysML [20]). The transformation is implemented in the jUCMNav modeling environment [3] and exploits an intermediate arithmetic representation in the SymPy language [23]. The rest of this paper is organized as follows. Section 2 highlights related work, including modeling approaches but also tools used in our own approach. Section 3 explains the methodology and the proposed tool-supported transformation. Section 4 provides an illustrative example. Finally, Sect. 5 discusses conclusions, including limitations and future work.

2   Related Work

2.1   Existing Approaches

To support design selection processes through simulation and runtime adaptation, some approaches attempted to transform goal models and/or feature models into mathematical functions. Ramirez and Cheng [22] proposed the *Athena* approach, which uses the KAOS [24] and RELAX [26] goal languages to monitor environmental conditions and determine whether requirements are violated or not. In order to monitor the surrounding environment, Athena generates fuzzy functions automatically for softgoals while using templates that return Boolean values for functional goals. The values of the generated functions are propagated to calculate the overall satisfaction level and determine whether goals are violated. However, the approach does not cover contribution relationships or the relative importance of goals to actors in the analysis process. In addition, limiting the satisfaction of goals to Boolean values is at times perceived as too restrictive for run-time adaptation [8].

Nguyen et al. [17] proposed the *Constrained Goal Model (CGM)* approach, which formalizes and expands conventional goal model concepts with conditions and numerical variables in order to automate reasoning. Preconditions are assigned to goals and other elements. Numerical variables are used as constraints and parameters (e.g., cost and performance) of the multi-objective function used to reason upon goals. Although the conditions were shown to speed up the reasoning process, they also limit the flexibility of the process in dealing with unknown situations. Moreover, the reasoning process: (1) does not represent goal-based reasoning that propagates satisfaction levels using indicators, goals, and their relationships, and (2) is based on the values and constraints that are assigned by users for each model element, including penalties, rewards, attributes, and preconditions. Such assignment is not simple for large and complex systems.

Similarly, in order to support adaptive and complex systems in their evolution, Chatzikonstantinou and Kontogiannis [8] presented a framework that is based on a conditional goal model to express extra information about system goals and their dependencies, as well as to automate the reasoning process. They presented the *ReqRV* approach, which is an adaptive requirement-based view that aims to verify systems while running. In order to decide whether requirements are fulfilled or not, conditions that include domain assumptions as well as current satisfaction values are assigned to each requirement. A fuzzy approach is used to monitor the environment and determine, based on quantitative weights, whether the related goals are violated. Although the proposed method can monitor its environment and verify its requirements, it is unable to deal with unknown situations at runtime because of the predetermined conditions.

The approach also does not support trade-off analysis or the selection of best-suited adaptations among alternatives. Moreover, assigning valid conditions to each goal is, again, not simple for large and complex models.

Because of the difficulty of conducting goal-based reasoning of a large goal model to select a suitable solution at design time, Chitra et al. [9,10] use a multi-objective optimization based on the satisfaction levels of goals in a model. They identify the quantitative weights of the leaf goals automatically without the analyst's intervention. Next, these weights are propagated to calculate the satisfaction level of the top goal. The satisfaction level of each goal is used as an argument of the main multi-objective function to select the solution that maximizes the satisfaction level of the model's goals. The score and the weight of the leaf goals are the constraints of this function. However, this function could generate unfeasible solutions caused by invalid combinations of alternatives. Moreover, functional goals, relationships between goals, indicators and importance values of model elements are not involved in the analysis.

Mathematical functions are also generated from goal models in contexts other than adaptive systems. For example, in order to support software product lines (SPL) and product reuse, Noorian et al. [18] consider goals, softgoals, and features in building feature models and selecting a product using an optimization model. Conventional feature models can indicate whether a product configuration is valid or not, but the introduction of goals in such models can help determine which valid configurations are satisfying softgoals better than others. The required goals and softgoals of the new product are selected by a user and an objective function is then built by summing up the impact of each feature on the selected softgoals and goals. Three types of constraints (features, goals, and their integration) are used as rules with the proposed utility function to eliminate invalid configurations. Yet, only part of the goal model is involved in the optimization model and the utility function does not represent goal-based reasoning in which the softgoals, the goals and their relationships are involved.

As shown above, although goal and feature models have been transformed into mathematical functions to deal with the complexity and scalability of large models, their reasoning processes have often been: (1) *incomplete* (i.e., using only part of the goal model), (2) *imprecise* (i.e., using qualitative values, or using a mix of numerical and Boolean values for softgoals and goals, respectively), and (3) *not truly goal-based* (e.g., using only conditions and utility functions).

2.2   Existing Tools

In order to translate GRL models into arithmetic functions in different programming languages, we exploited two existing tools: jUCMNav and SymPy.

jUCMNav is a free, Eclipse-based graphical editor and analysis tool for URN and GRL models [3]. jUCMNav supports the bottom-up evaluation of GRL strategies (i.e., initial values associated with some of the goals/indicators) using different quantitative, qualitative, and hybrid algorithms [1]. jUCMNav also offers an extensible architecture where model transformations are implemented as plug-ins. Such a transformation was previously defined for exporting a constraint-based representation of GRL models [16], enabling tools to solve models instead of just propagating satisfaction values to higher-level goals and to actors. However, a constraint-based approach is often much too computationally expensive for usage by running systems in an adaptation context.

SymPy is a free, lightweight Python library for symbolic mathematics [23]. This library is used to symbolically simplify mathematical expressions, and it includes *code printers* that convert SymPy expressions into target languages such as Java, JavaScript, and C. SymPy is used here as the the target language for our transformation from GRL, and then code printers (existing ones, as well as new ones) enable efficient and maintainable code generation to multiple target programming languages.

3   Methodology

This section describes the arithmetic semantics of GRL and a transformation to SymPy expressions. The latter are themselves transformed into executable functions in different programming languages.

3.1   Overview

Goal models can be developed to describe how systems should adapt to their environment. Once a model is developed and validated (e.g., through the techniques described by Horkoff et al. [13]), it needs to be transformed into a format executable by running systems and/or by simulation engines. Figure 1 illustrates the main steps involved in transforming a model in standard GRL into arithmetic functions in multiple programming languages. A new jUCMNav plug-in first traverses the GRL model and generates a SymPy file conforming to the proposed arithmetic semantics for GRL. This intermediate representation exploits the SymPy Python library to symbolically simplify the generated functions (e.g., by computing the results of sub-expressions involving constants). Then, a new Python script we produced invokes existing or new SymPy code printers to generate mathematical expressions in target programming languages, as separate files.

Fig. 1. The flow of entire transformation process

Three contributions can be observed here: a new arithmetic semantics for standard GRL, a transformation from GRL to SymPy mathematical functions, and the provision or extension of code generators from SymPy to seven target programming languages. These contributions are described in the subsections.

3.2   Arithmetic Semantics for Standard GRL

There are three main categories of concepts in GRL:

1. **Intentional elements**, including goals, softgoals, tasks, resources, and indicators. Intentional elements have a satisfaction value v computed at runtime based on a selected GRL strategy or on external inputs. They also have an importance value representing their weight in the computation of the satisfaction of their containing actor, if any. An indicator additionally includes four parameters (current value, target value, threshold value, and worst value) used to transform an external input (current value) into a satisfaction value.
2. **Intentional links**, including AND/OR decomposition links, (weighted) contribution links, and dependency links.
3. **Actors**, which also have a satisfaction value, as well as an importance value used in the computation of the satisfaction of the entire model.

Figures 2, 3, 4 and 5 show the different types of links between source intentional elements (S) and destination intentional elements (D_x).

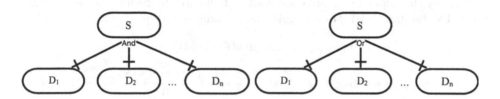

Fig. 2. AND-decomposition link   Fig. 3. OR-decomposition link

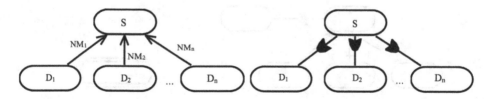

Fig. 4. Contribution link   Fig. 5. Dependency link

The quantitative satisfaction value of a leaf **intentional element** is provided as explicit input in a strategy. For the other intentional elements, the satisfaction value of the source ($v(S)$) is a function of the destination ($v(D_x)$) of its **intentional links**. Satisfaction is evaluated over [0...100].

1. For the AND-decomposition (Fig. 2), the minimum is propagated.

$$v(S) = Min(v(D_1), v(D_2), ..., v(D_n)) \tag{1}$$

2. For OR-decomposition (Fig. 3), the maximum is propagated.

$$v(S) = Max(v(D_1), v(D_2), ..., v(D_n)) \tag{2}$$

3. For contribution links (Fig. 4), NM_x represents the quantitative contribution/weight (over $[-100..100]$) of destination intentional element D_x to the source intentional element S. A truncated weighted sum is propagated. Note that in GRL, contributions are additive and convey contributions to the satisfaction of the target intentional element, not probabilities or confidence levels.

$$v(S) = Max(0, Min(100, \frac{\sum_{x=1}^{n}(v(D_x) \times NM_x)}{100})) \tag{3}$$

4. For dependency links (Fig. 5), the current element's satisfaction (defaulted to 0) is truncated to the minimum satisfaction of its dependees.

$$v(S) = Min(v(S), v(D_1), v(D_2), ..., v(D_n)) \tag{4}$$

In GRL, an intentional element can have decomposition (one type), contribution, and dependency links simultaneously. In such cases, first the satisfaction from decomposition links is computed, then the contribution satisfactions are added, and finally the dependency links are used to truncate the result (as specified in the URN standard [14]). For example, the arithmetic interpretation of Fig. 6 is:

$$v(S_{decomp}) = Min(v(D_1), v(D_2)) \tag{5}$$

$$v(S_{contrib}) = Max(0, Min(100, \frac{25 \times v(D_3) + 100 \times v(S_{decomp})}{100})) \tag{6}$$

$$v(S) = Min(v(S_{contrib}), v(D_4)) \tag{7}$$

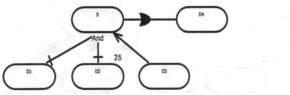

Fig. 6. Multiple types of link   **Fig. 7.** Indicator

Figure 7 shows an **indicator** element I that can also be linked to other intentional elements (except that an indicator cannot be decomposed or receive contributions). The satisfaction value of an indicator is computed by comparing its current value against it target, threshold, and worst values. The threshold value is always between the target and worst values, and the target, threshold, and worst values cannot be equal. The satisfaction is: 100 if the current value reaches the target value (or does better), 50 if it equals the threshold value, and 0 if it reaches the worst value (or is even worse). Linear interpolations are used in the other cases.

In this context, when the target value of an indicator is higher than its worst value, the satisfaction value of this indicator (where C represents the current value, T is the target value, TH is the threshold, and W is the worst value) becomes:

$$v(I) = \begin{cases} 100 & \text{if } C \geq T \\ 0 & \text{if } C \leq W \\ Abs(\frac{C-TH}{T-TH}) \times 50 + 50 & \text{if } TH \leq C < T \\ -Abs(\frac{C-TH}{W-TH}) \times 50 + 50 & \text{if } W < C < TH \end{cases} \tag{8}$$

When its target value is inferior to the worst value (which happens, for example, when an indicator represents a wait time where the smaller the current value, the better), the satisfaction value of the indicator becomes:

$$v(I) = \begin{cases} 100 & \text{if } C \leq T \\ 0 & \text{if } C \geq W \\ Abs(\frac{C-TH}{TH-T}) \times 50 + 50 & \text{if } T < C \leq TII \\ -Abs(\frac{C-TH}{TH-W}) \times 50 + 50 & \text{if } TH < C < W \end{cases} \tag{9}$$

Finally, the satisfaction of a GRL **actor** depends of the satisfaction of its contained intentional elements with non-null importance values (the latter being specified over $[0..100]$). A weighted average is used if the sum of the weights is greater than 100, otherwise a weighted sum is used. Figure 8 illustrates an actor A containing n intentional elements E_x with importance weights W_x. The arithmetic semantics of an actor is:

$$v(A) = Max(0, Min(100, \frac{\sum_{x=1}^{n}(v(E_x) \times W_x)}{Max(100, \sum_{x=1}^{n}(W_x))})) \tag{10}$$

If none of the top-level (root) intentional elements of an actor has a strictly positive weight, then these top-level elements are considered to be weighted equally, with the weights summing up to 100.

Actors themselves can also be weighted in order for the satisfaction of the entire GRL **model** to be computed. The satisfaction of the model has a semantics similar to that of an actor (a weighted sum or average). In Fig. 9, A_x is one of n actors in a GRL model and AW_x is the weight of actor A_x. The quantitative evaluation value of a GRL *Model* is:

$$v(Model) = Max(0, Min(100, \frac{\sum_{x=1}^{n}(v(A_x) \times AW_x)}{Max(100, \sum_{x=1}^{n}(AW_x))})) \tag{11}$$

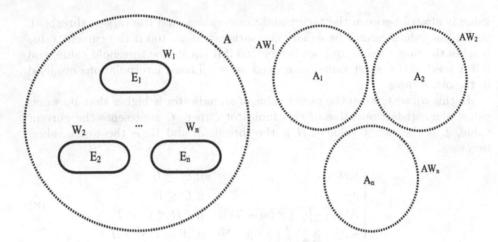

Fig. 8. Actor containing intentional elements with importance weights

Fig. 9. Actors with importance weights in a model

Additional semantic rules for GRL models include:

1. If there is no actor present in the model, then a default actor containing all intentional elements and that has an importance weight of 100 is assumed to exist.
2. If there are actors but they have no weight, then these actors are considered to be weighted equally, with the weights summing up to 100.

This arithmetic semantics for GRL enables the generation of executable mathematical functions for any valid GRL model.

3.3   SymPy Code Generation

In order to transform a GRL model to a mathematical function according to our new arithmetic semantics, we developed a new export plug-in for jUCMNav. As systems and simulations are implemented using many different languages, it quickly becomes impractical to define one transformation for each target language. One way to reduce this complexity is to use an intermediate representation supporting mathematical functions for which there are transformations to common programming languages already existing. Then, only one transformation from GRL to that intermediate language would be needed.

We selected SymPy [23] as the intermediate representation (see Sect. 2.2). SymPy is an open-source Python-compatible language and library that already comes with a variety of code printers (generators). In addition, it symbolically simplifies functions, which leads to improved performance during evaluations. The SymPy export plug-in is freely available online [11]. It supports the entire semantics discussed in the previous section. It currently generates one global function for the entire GRL model (which composes all functions from its actors and other elements). However, the export also generates individual mathematical functions for the model's non-leaf intentional elements and actors, for future use (e.g., to support the implementation of only one part of a large model, or to enable testing parts separately).

3.4 Transformation to Programming Languages

SymPy mathematical expressions can be transformed to many target languages. We selected common implementation languages (Java, JavaScript, Python, C, and C++) as well as simulation languages (R and Matlab), some of which can be used embedded in other modeling languages (e.g., SysML).

We had to extend existing code printers to support generic $Max()$ and $Min()$ functions, heavily used in our semantics. We also (surprisingly) had to add a simple Java code printer as none was available. The Java code printer generates a model class with one static method corresponding to the global model function. We also had to fix a few small bugs discovered in the Matlab code printer.

For convenience, mathematical functions in different target languages are exported in different files with the appropriate extensions (e.g., Java mathematical functions in .java files). We created a Python module library named MathTo, which can be imported into SymPy files. This MathTo module enables the selection of target languages to export and the generation of corresponding files.

The module and a test suite that covers all GRL model elements and their transformation to the seven target languages are available online [11].

4   Illustrative Example

To illustrate our function generation, we use a simplified GRL model of a hybrid car's engine system described in [20] and its related user goals. This example was selected because the conflicts between its goals (e.g., comfortable driving for the user, and acceleration for the system) require the software to control and manage the engine's overall performance [15].

Figure 10 shows the concerns of the System and its User (with short names, for simplicity). The overall goal of the system is Drive, decomposed into two sub-goals: Acceleration and Control. These two goals can be realized by two pairs of tasks. The acceleration goal can be satisfied by the engine(s), which may be electric, fuel-based, or a combination of the two. The control goal aims to regulate the car's speed, managing the distance between the car and surrounding objects. User concerns are represented by softgoals (i.e., Comfortable driving and Reduce the cost). The system monitors its environment using sensors, modeled as indicators, to measure Distance and car Vibration. These sensors identify problem symptoms using target, threshold, and worst value parameters (see Table 1). Calculating the overall model satisfaction is performed to decide whether to change the task selection in the system. If yes, the system selects the combination

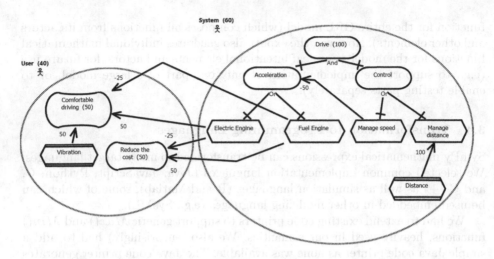

Fig. 10. GRL model of a simple hybrid car system example.

of tasks that satisfies the driving goal while maximizing driving comfort and minimizing costs, depending on observed environmental conditions.

Table 1. Indicator parameter values

Indicator	Target	Threshold	Worst	Unit
Distance	25	10	5	Meter
Vibration	0	10	20	Hertz

To transform the GRL model of the simplified hybrid car's engine into mathematical functions, we invoked the new SymPy export mechanism in jUCMNav. A file named AdaptiveCar.py was generated automatically. Based on Rule 11, the global mathematical function of the model is:

$$v(AdaptiveCar) = \frac{(v(User) \times 40 + v(System) \times 60)}{100} \tag{12}$$

where (from Rules 3 and 10 applied to the User actor):

$$v(User) = (Max(0.0, Min(100.0, (50 \times Fuel\_engine + -25 \times \\ Electric\_engine)/100.0)) * 100.0 + Max(0.0, Min(100.0, (50 \times \\ v(Vibration) + 50 \times Electric\_engine + -25 \times Fuel\_engine)/100.0)) \\ \times 100.0)/100 \tag{13}$$

and (from Rule 9 because the target value of the Vibration indicator is less than its worst value):

$$v(Vibration) = \begin{cases} 100 & \text{if } C \leq 0 \\ 0 & \text{if } C \geq 20 \\ Abs(\frac{C-10}{10-0}) \times 50 + 50 & \text{if } 0 < C \leq 10 \\ -Abs(\frac{C-10}{10-20}) \times 50 + 50 & \text{if } 10 < C < 20 \end{cases} \tag{14}$$

and where (from Rules 2, 3, and 4 applied to the System actor):

$$\begin{aligned} v(System) &= v(Drive) \\ &= Min(Max(Max(0.0, Min(100.0, (100 * v(Distance))/100)), \\ &\quad Manage\_speed), Max(0.0, Min(100.0, (-50 \times Manage\_speed + \\ &\quad Max(Fuel\_engine, Electric\_engine) \times 100.0)/100.0)))) \end{aligned} \tag{15}$$

and finally (from rule 8 because the target value of the Distance indicator is higher than its worst value):

$$v(Distance) = \begin{cases} 100 & \text{if } C \geq 25 \\ 0 & \text{if } C \leq 5 \\ Abs(\frac{C-10}{25-10}) \times 50 + 50 & \text{if } 10 \leq C < 25 \\ -Abs(\frac{C-10}{5-10}) \times 50 + 50 & \text{if } 5 < C < 10 \end{cases} \tag{16}$$

The Python/SymPy code in Listing 1 was generated by jUCMNav for the model. Note that the tool renames the variables to avoid clashes. It also embeds translation code that can be used to invoke language-specific SymPy code printers. When operations on known constants are involved (e.g., $T - TH$ in Rule 8), then the precomputed result is directly exported by jUCMNav, for efficiency.

Listing 1. Python/SymPy code generated in AdaptiveCar.py

```
from MathTo import *
from sympy import *
import sys

# Initialize the variables
Reduce_the_cosT=Symbol('Reduce_the_cosT')
Comfortable_drivinG=Symbol('Comfortable_drivinG')
DrivE=Symbol('DrivE')
ControL=Symbol('ControL')
AcceleratioN=Symbol('AcceleratioN')
Fuel_enginE=Symbol('Fuel_enginE')
Electric_enginE=Symbol('Electric_enginE')
```

```
Manage_distancE=Symbol('Manage_distancE')
Manage_speeD=Symbol('Manage_speeD')
VibratioN=Symbol('VibratioN')
DistancE=Symbol('DistancE')

# Functions for intentional elements
Reduce_the_cosT=Max(0.0,Min(100.0,(50*Fuel_enginE+-25*
    Electric_enginE)/100.0))

Comfortable_drivinG=Max(0.0,Min(100.0,
  (50*Piecewise(
   (100,VibratioN<=0.0),
   (abs((VibratioN-10.0)/10.0)*50+50,(0.0<VibratioN)&(
       VibratioN<=10.0)),
   (-abs((VibratioN-10.0)/-10.0)*50+50,(10.0<VibratioN)&(
       VibratioN<20.0)),
   (0,True))
 + 50*Electric_enginE+-25*Fuel_enginE)/100.0))

DrivE=Min(Max(0.0,Min(100.0,(-50*Manage_speeD+Max(
  Fuel_enginE,Electric_enginE)*100.0)/100.0)),Max(Max(0.0,
    Min(100.0,(100*Piecewise(
    (100,DistancE>=25.0),
    (abs((DistancE-10.0)/15.0)*50+50,(10.0<=DistancE)&(
       DistancE<25.0)),
    (-abs((DistancE-10.0)/-5.0)*50+50,(5.0<DistancE)&(
       DistancE<10.0)),
    (0,True)))/100.0)),
  Manage_speeD))

ControL=Max(Max(0.0,Min(100.0,(100*Piecewise(
    (100,DistancE>=25.0),
    (abs((DistancE-10.0)/15.0)*50+50,(10.0<=DistancE)&(
       DistancE<25.0)),
    (-abs((DistancE-10.0)/-5.0)*50+50,(5.0<DistancE)&(
       DistancE<10.0)),
    (0,True)))/100.0)),
  Manage_speeD)

AcceleratioN=Max(0.0,Min(100.0,(-50*Manage_speeD+ Max(
    Fuel_enginE,Electric_enginE)*100.0)/100.0))

Manage_distancE=Max(0.0,Min(100.0,(100*Piecewise(
    (100,DistancE>=25.0),
    (abs((DistancE-10.0)/15.0)*50+50,(10.0<=DistancE)&(
       DistancE<25.0)),
    (-abs((DistancE-10.0)/-5.0)*50+50,(5.0<DistancE)&(
       DistancE<10.0)),
    (0,True)))/100.0))
```

```
# Functions for actors
SysteM=(Min(Max(0.0,Min(100.0,(-50*Manage_speeD+Max(
      Fuel_enginE , Electric_enginE ) *100.0) /100.0) ) ,Max(Max
      (0.0,Min(100.0,(100*Piecewise(
      (100,DistancE>=25.0),
      (abs(  (DistancE-10.0)/15.0)*50+50,(10.0<=DistancE)&(
          DistancE<25.0)),
      (-abs(  (DistancE-10.0)/-5.0)*50+50,(5.0<DistancE)&(
          DistancE<10.0)),
      (0,True)))/100.0)),
   Manage_speeD)) *100.0) /100
```

```
UseR=(Max(0.0,Min(100.0,(50*Fuel_enginE+-25*Electric_enginE
      )/100.0))*100.0+Max(0.0,Min(100.0,(50*Piecewise(
      (100,VibratioN<=0.0),
      (abs(  (VibratioN-10.0)/10.0)*50+50,(0.0<VibratioN)&(
          VibratioN<=10.0)),
      (-abs(  (VibratioN-10.0)/-10.0)*50+50,(10.0<VibratioN)&(
          VibratioN<20.0)),
      (0,True))
   +50*Electric_enginE+-25*Fuel_enginE)/100.0))*100.0)/100
```

```
# Function for the Model
AdaptivecaR=((Min(Max(0.0,Min(100.0,(-50*Manage_speeD+
   Max(Fuel_enginE , Electric_enginE ) *100.0) /100.0)),
   Max(Max(0.0,Min(100.0,(100*Piecewise(
      (100,DistancE>=25.0),
      (abs(  (DistancE-10.0)/15.0)*50+50,(10.0<=DistancE)&(
          DistancE<25.0)),
      (-abs(  (DistancE-10.0)/-5.0)*50+50,(5.0<DistancE)&(
          DistancE<10.0)),
      (0,True)))/100.0)),Manage_speeD))*100.0)/100*60+(Max
          (0.0,Min(100.0,(50*Fuel_enginE+-25*
   Electric_enginE)/100.0))*100.0+Max(0.0,Min(100.0,  (50*
   Piecewise(
      (100,VibratioN<=0.0),
      (abs(  (VibratioN-10.0)/10.0)*50+50,(0.0<VibratioN)&(
          VibratioN<=10.0)),
      (-abs(  (VibratioN-10.0)/-10.0)*50+50,(10.0<VibratioN)&(
          VibratioN<20.0)),
      (0,True))+50*Electric_enginE+-25*
   Fuel_enginE)/100.0))*100.0)/100*40)/100
```

```
# Code to translate the function of the model from SymPy
      into several programming languages . The model name is
      used as the name of the generated files , with different
      extensions .
modelName = 'AdaptivecaR '
List=['Manage_speeD ','VibratioN ','Electric_enginE ','
      DistancE ','Fuel_enginE '] # Variable list
```

```
LANG = ''
langList = ['python','c','c++','java',"javascript",'matlab'
    ,'r']
def allPrint():
    for j in langList:
        LANG = str(j)
        Translate('((Min(Max(0.0,Min(100.0,(-50*
        Manage_speeD+Max(Fuel_enginE , Electric_enginE)
        *100.0)/100.0)),Max(Max(0.0,Min(100.0,(100*
        Piecewise((100,DistancE>=25.0),(abs( (DistancE
        -10.0)/15.0)*50+50,(10.0<=DistancE)&(DistancE
        <25.0)),(-abs( (DistancE-10.0)/-5.0)
        *50+50,(5.0<DistancE)&(DistancE<10.0)),(0,True)
        ))/100.0)),Manage_speeD))*100.0)/100*60+(Max
        (0.0,Min(100.0,(50*Fuel_enginE+-25*
        Electric_enginE)/100.0))*100.0+Max(0.0,Min
        (100.0,(50*Piecewise((100,VibratioN<=0.0),(abs(
        (VibratioN-10.0)/10.0)*50+50,(0.0<VibratioN)&(
        VibratioN<=10.0)),(-abs( (VibratioN-10.0)
        /-10.0)*50+50,(10.0<VibratioN)&(VibratioN<20.0)
        ),(0,True))+50*Electric_enginE+-25*Fuel_enginE)
        /100.0))*100.0)/100*40)/100 ',modelName,List ,
        LANG)
if(len(sys.argv)==1):
    allPrint()
else:
# Print the code for the specified target language. Not
    shown here.
```

By executing the AdaptiveCar.py file using Python (and specifying the target language), the function can be translated to Java, JavaScript, Python, C, C++, R, or Matlab. As an example, Listing 2 shows the code generated for Java (AdaptiveCar.java). Note that only the leaf intentional elements from the GRL model are left as method parameters (Manage Speed, Vibration, Electric Engine, Fuel Engine, and Distance); this is the information that must be provided upon invocation. Note also that SymPy symbolically simplified constant expressions. For example, the 40/100 and 60/100 of equation 12 and kept as is in the SymPy code were converted in Java to 0.4 and 0.6, respectively. Listing 3 shows a second example of generated code, this time for C++ (AdaptiveCar.cpp), where there are some small rounding differences in the real numbers due to the symbolic processing done by SymPy.

Listing 2. Java mathematical function in AdaptiveCar.java

```
public class Model{
  public double AdaptivecaR (double Manage_speeD ,double
    VibratioN ,double Electric_enginE ,double DistancE ,
    double Fuel_enginE ){
    double expr = 0.4*Math.max(0, Math.min(100.0,
        -0.25*Electric_enginE + 0.5*Fuel_enginE )) +
    0.4*Math.max(0, Math.min(100.0, 0.5*Electric_enginE
        - 0.25*Fuel_enginE + 0.5*
    ((VibratioN <= 0.0) ? ( 100.0 )
    : ((VibratioN <= 10.0 && VibratioN > 0) ?
    (50.0*Math.abs(0.1*VibratioN - 1.0) + 50.0 )
      : ((VibratioN > 10.0 && VibratioN < 20.0) ?
      (-50.0*Math.abs(0.1*VibratioN - 1.0) + 50.0 )
        : ( 0)))))) +
    0.6*Math.max(0, Math.min(100.0, Math.min(-0.5*
        Manage_speeD + 1.0*Max(Electric_enginE ,
        Fuel_enginE ), Math.max(Manage_speeD , 1.0*
    ((DistancE >= 25.0)    ? ( 100.0 )
    : ((DistancE >= 10.0) ?
    (50.0*Math.abs(0.0666666666666667*DistancE -
        0.666666666666667) + 50.0 )
      : ((DistancE > 5.0) ?
      (-50.0*Math.abs(0.2*DistancE - 2.0) + 50.0 )
        : (0))))
    ))));
  return expr;
  }
}
```

Listing 3. C++ mathematical function in AdaptiveCar.cpp

```
#include <iostream>
using namespace std ;

double AdaptivecaR ( double Manage_speeD ,double VibratioN ,
    double Electric_enginE ,double DistancE ,double
    Fuel_enginE ){
    double expr = 0.4*std ::max(0, std ::min(100.0, -0.25*
        Electric_enginE + 0.5*Fuel_enginE )) + 0.4*std ::max
        (0, std ::min(100.0, 0.5*Electric_enginE - 0.25*
        Fuel_enginE + 0.5*((VibratioN <= 0.0) ? (
100.0 )
      : ((VibratioN <= 10.0 && VibratioN > 0) ? (
        50.0*std ::fabs (0.1*VibratioN - 1.0) + 50.0 )
      : ((VibratioN > 10.0 && VibratioN < 20.0) ? (
```

```
                −50.0∗std :: fabs (0.1∗VibratioN − 1.0) + 50.0 )
          : (
             0 )
          ))))) + 0.6∗std :: max(0 , std :: min(100.0 , std :: min(−0.5∗
               Manage_speeD + 1.0∗Max( Electric_enginE , Fuel_enginE
               ) , std :: max(Manage_speeD , 1.0∗((DistancE >= 25.0) ?
               (
   100.0 )
      : ((DistancE >= 10.0) ? (
          50.0∗std :: fabs (0.066666666666666666∗DistancE −
               0.66666666666666663) + 50.0 )
      : ((DistancE > 5.0) ? (
          −50.0∗std :: fabs (0.2∗DistancE − 2.0) + 50.0 )
      : (
          0 )
      )))))));
      return expr;
}
```

5   Conclusions and Future Work

This paper provides a new arithmetic semantics for GRL together with a tool-supported transformation from GRL models to compact mathematical functions in multiple programming languages. This enables GRL models to be analyzed quantitatively outside goal modeling tools. These generated functions can be embedded in (1) system implementations, to support adaptive systems in monitoring context changes and selecting the most suitable adaptation; and (2) other models (e.g., in SysML) supporting simulations. SymPy was used as an intermediate representation to simplify the support of multiple target programming languages (seven of which are currently generated), and to provide symbolic simplifications improving the performance of the generated functions.

The approach currently does not generate code for GRL strategies, which would initialize some value parameters when invoking the functions. Transforming them could be useful when the possible system adaptations are predefined.

Other potentially useful extensions of this work include the generation of functions for feature models, which are combined to GRL models in jUCMNav. Transformations to optimization languages (e.g., CPLEX) could also enable GRL models to be solved for optimal solutions rather than simply propagate initial values to compute model satisfaction. A transformation to spreadsheets such as Microsoft Excel could even be considered, to support model analytics and visualization.

Changes to the arithmetic semantics could be investigated as well. For example, the simple weighted sum/average for model satisfaction used in rule 11 could be changed in favor of more sophisticated multi-criteria decision analysis functions, for example the distance-based TOPSIS [7], recently used for GRL [5].

Acknowledgment. A. Anda thanks the Libyan Ministry of Education for its financial support. This work was also supported by D. Amyot's Discovery Grant from NSERC.

References

1. Amyot, D., Ghanavati, S., Horkoff, J., Mussbacher, G., Peyton, L., Yu, E.: Evaluating goal models within the goal-oriented requirement language. Int. J. Intel. Syst. **25**(8), 841–877 (2010)
2. Amyot, D., Mussbacher, G.: User requirements notation: the first ten years, the next ten years. JSW **6**(5), 747–768 (2011)
3. Amyot, D., et al.: Towards advanced goal model analysis with jUCMNav. In: Castano, S., Vassiliadis, P., Lakshmanan, L.V., Lee, M.L. (eds.) ER 2012. LNCS, vol. 7518, pp. 201–210. Springer, Heidelberg (2012). https://doi.org/10.1007/978-3-642-33999-8_25
4. Anda, A.A., Amyot, D.: Self-adaptation driven by SysML and goal models: a literature review. Syst. Eng. (2018), (submitted)
5. Baslyman, M., Amyot, D.: A distance-based GRL approach to goal model refinement and alternative selection. In: 2017 IEEE 25th International Requirements Engineering Conference Workshops (REW), pp. 16–20. IEEE (2017)
6. Bocanegra, J., Pavlich-Mariscal, J., Carrillo-Ramos, A.: On the role of model-driven engineering in adaptive systems. In: Computing Conference (CCC), 2016 IEEE 11th Colombian, pp. 1–8. IEEE (2016)
7. Ceballos, B., Lamata, M.T., Pelta, D.A.: A comparative analysis of multi-criteria decision-making methods. Prog. AI **5**(4), 315–322 (2016). https://doi.org/10.1007/s13748-016-0093-1
8. Chatzikonstantinou, G., Kontogiannis, K.: Run-time requirements verification for reconfigurable systems. Inf. Softw. Technol. **75**, 105–121 (2016)
9. Chitra, Subramanian, M., Krishna, A., Kaur, A.: Optimal goal programming of softgoals in goal-oriented requirements engineering. In: PACIS 2016 Proceedings, p. 202. AISEL (2016)
10. Chitra, S., Krishna, A., Kaur, A.: Optimal reasoning of goals in the i* framework. In: Asia-Pacific Software Engineering Conference, APSEC, pp. 346–353 (2015)
11. Fan, Y.: GRLToMath plugin for jUCMNav (2018). https://github.com/AAmberFan/GRLToMath
12. Horkoff, J., Aydemir, F.B., Cardoso, E., Li, T., Maté, A., Paja, E., Salnitri, M., Piras, L., Mylopoulos, J., Giorgini, P.: Goal-oriented requirements engineering: an extended systematic mapping study. Requir. Eng., Sep 2017. https://doi.org/10.1007/s00766-017-0280-z
13. Horkoff, J., Yu, E.: Comparison and evaluation of goal-oriented satisfaction analysis techniques. Requir. Eng. **18**(3), 199–222 (2013). https://doi.org/10.1007/s00766-011-0143-y
14. International Telecommunication Union: Recommendation Z.151 (10/12) User Requirements Notation (URN)—Language definition (2012). https://www.itu.int/rec/T-REC-Z.151/en
15. Ito, Y., Tomura, S., Moriya, K.: Vibration-reducing motor control for hybrid vehicles. R&D Rev. Toyota CRDL **40**(2), 37–43 (2005)
16. Luo, H., Amyot, D.: Towards a declarative, constraint-oriented semantics with a generic evaluation algorithm for GRL. In: 5th International i* Workshop (iStar 2011). CEUR-WS, vol. 766, pp. 26–31 (2011)

17. Nguyen, C.M., Sebastiani, R., Giorgini, P., Mylopoulos, J.: Multi-objective reasoning with constrained goal models. Requir. Eng. **23**(2), 189–225 (2018)
18. Noorian, M., Bagheri, E., Du, W.: Toward automated qualitycentric product line configuration using intentional variability. J. Softw. Evoluti. Process **29**(9), e1870 (2017)
19. Object Management Group: Systems Modeling Language (SysML) v2 Request For Proposal (RFP). OMG Document Number: ad/17-12-02 (2017). http://www.omg. org/cgi-bin/doc.cgi?ad/2017-12-2
20. Object Management Group: Systems Modeling Language (SysML). Version 1.5. OMG Document Number: formal-17-05-01. (2017). https://www.omg.org/spec/ SysML/1.5/
21. Pourshahid, A., Johari, I., Richards, G., Amyot, D., Akhigbe, O.S.: A goal-oriented, business intelligence-supported decision-making methodology. Decis. Anal. **1**, 9 (2014)
22. Ramirez, A.J., Cheng, B.H.C.: Automatic derivation of utility functions for monitoring software requirements. In: Whittle, J., Clark, T., Kühne, T. (eds.) MODELS 2011. LNCS, vol. 6981, pp. 501–516. Springer, Heidelberg (2011). https://doi.org/ 10.1007/978-3-642-24485-8_37
23. SymPy Development Team: SymPy (2018). http://www.sympy.org/
24. Van Lamsweerde, A.: Requirements Engineering: From System Goals to UML Models to Software, vol. 10. Wiley, Chichester, UK (2009)
25. Vrbaski, M., Mussbacher, G., Petriu, D., Amyot, D.: Goal models as run-time entities in context-aware systems. In: Proceedings of the 7th Workshop on Models@Run.Time, pp. 3–8. MRT 2012. ACM (2012). https://doi.org/10.1145/ 2422518.2422520
26. Whittle, J., Sawyer, P., Bencomo, N., Cheng, B.H.C., Bruel, J.M.: RELAX: a language to address uncertainty in self-adaptive systems requirement. Requir. Eng. **15**(2), 177–196 (2010)
27. Yang, Z., Li, Z., Jin, Z., Chen, Y.: A systematic literature review of requirements modeling and analysis for self-adaptive systems. In: Salinesi, C., van de Weerd, I. (eds.) REFSQ 2014. LNCS, vol. 8396, pp. 55–71. Springer, Cham (2014). https:// doi.org/10.1007/978-3-319-05843-6_5

Textual User Requirements Notation

Ruchika Kumar and Gunter Mussbacher[✉]

Department of Electrical and Computer Engineering, McGill University,
Montréal, Canada
ruchika.kumar@mail.mcgill.ca,
gunter.mussbacher@mcgill.ca

Abstract. The User Requirements Notation (URN) is a requirements engineering standard published by the International Telecommunication Union that combines goal and scenario modeling in support of the elicitation, specification, analysis, and validation of requirements. The URN standard focuses on a graphical notation. This paper introduces a textual notation for URN called TURN (Textual User Requirements Notation). The main objective of TURN is to support the modeling of very large URN specifications where thousands of separate goal graphs or scenarios become unwieldy to navigate. In addition, the entering of large specifications in graphical tools has proven tedious, as the modeler must be concerned with layout issues that are unrelated to the information that is attempted to be modeled. In general, TURN offers an alternative input medium for URN specifications which aims to be easier, faster, and more scalable. Xtext is the defacto standard for the specification of textual metamodel-based software languages. To validate the feasibility of TURN, it is specified as an Xtext grammar, resulting in a metamodel tailored to TURN and covering a large subset of URN. The differences between the URN standard and TURN are elaborated, a multi-phased model-to-model transformation from TURN to URN is described, and conformance to URN is demonstrated with a rather exhaustive set of test cases for TURN specifications and their transformations.

Keywords: Textual User Requirements Notation · Goal modeling
Goal-oriented Requirement Language · Scenario modeling · Use Case Maps
Textual syntax · Language specification · Xtext
Model-to-model transformation

1 Introduction

The User Requirements Notation (URN) [2] is a lightweight graphical language for modeling and analyzing requirements in the form of goals and scenarios. Currently, URN supports only a concrete graphical syntax supported by the jUCMNav tool [13], which has some advantages as it is easier to grasp and requires less mental effort [16]. We propose the Textual URN (TURN) to take advantage of the many benefits of a textual language. For example, it may promote usability, productivity, and scalability of URN models. The entering of large specifications in graphical tools has proven tedious, as the modeler must be concerned with layout issues that are unrelated to the information that is attempted to be modeled. Other advantages of textual notation

© Springer Nature Switzerland AG 2018
F. Khendek and R. Gotzhein (Eds.): SAM 2018, LNCS 11150, pp. 163–182, 2018.
https://doi.org/10.1007/978-3-030-01042-3_10

include fast editing style, usage of error markers, providing auto-completion, and quick fixes. Furthermore, they can easily be integrated into existing tools such as diff/merge or information interchange through e-mail, or blogs. Textual languages may also improve the analyzability and modifiability of a model [6], may have a shorter learning curve [15], and may have efficient consistency checking [11].

Xtext (eclipse.org/Xtext) is the defacto standard for the specification of textual metamodel-based software languages. Xtext automatically generates a text editor, parser, and metamodel from an Xtext grammar specification. Typically, the same abstract syntax (defined by a metamodel) is used for different concrete representations. However, experience has shown that it is not so straightforward to add a textual syntax to an existing graphical language [1]. Therefore, we define a separate metamodel for TURN, one that is automatically generated from the Xtext grammar, and a multi-phase model-to-model transformation from TURN to URN to demonstrate conformance with the URN standard.

The contributions of the paper are as follows: (i) the definition of an Xtext-based textual syntax for URN that covers most of its concepts and informs an effort at ITU to standardize a textual syntax for URN, (ii) a tailored metamodel for TURN, generated from the Xtext grammar for TURN and using the notion of *Path* which does not explicitly exist in the URN metamodel, (iii) a transformation from TURN to URN to demonstrate conformance to URN, and (iv) a rather exhaustive set of test cases that validates TURN specifications and their transformation to URN.

The remainder of this paper presents background on the User Requirements Notation in Sect. 2, focusing on its graphical syntax. Section 3 discusses the differences between the Textual URN and URN with the help of concrete examples and highlights those parts of the TURN metamodel that differ the most from the URN metamodel. Section 4 explains a multi-phased transformation from TURN to URN including a rather exhaustive set of test cases to validate the feasibility of TURN and demonstrate conformance to URN. Section 5 briefly summarizes related work, while Sect. 6 concludes the paper and states future work.

2 Background on User Requirements Notation

The User Requirements Notation (URN) [2] is a graphical language intended for the elicitation, analysis, specification, and validation of requirements. It combines two complementary notations: the Goal-oriented Requirement Language (GRL) [7] for modeling goal-oriented and intentional concepts including non-functional requirements; and Use Case Maps (UCMs) [7] for functional and operational requirements. It is the first and currently only standard which explicitly addresses goals (with GRL) in addition to scenarios (with UCMs) in a graphical way in one unified language. The International Telecommunication Union standardizes URN in the Z.15x series [7].

URN models are used to specify and analyze various types of reactive systems, business processes, and goals of organizations, and telecommunications standards. It provides insight at the requirements level that enables designers to reason about feature interactions and trade-offs early in the design process.

2.1   GRL Notation

A GRL goal model shows the high-level business goals and non-functional requirements of interest to a stakeholder and the alternative solutions that can accomplish
these goals and high-level requirements. A stakeholder of a system is represented as an
Actor (◯, e.g., "Telecom Provider" in Fig. 1). An actor holds the intentions, i.e., the
actor wants goals to be achieved, tasks to be performed, resources to be available, and
softgoals to be satisfied. Various intentional elements (softgoal, goal, task, and
resource) capture the mentioned concerns. Objectives and qualities are modeled with
softgoals and goals. A *Softgoal* (◯, e.g. "High Reliability") is used to represent
objectives that have no definite measure of satisfaction, whereas a *Goal* (◯, e.g.,
"Voice Connection Be Setup") is used when the objective is clear and quantifiable.
Softgoals are typically related to non-functional requirements, whereas goals are related
to functional requirements and measurable non-functional requirements. A *Task* (◯,
e.g., "Make Voice Connection Over Wireless") is a proposed solution that achieves a
goal or satisfies a softgoal. A goal model may also document facts or *Beliefs* (◯, e.g.,
"Wireless is less reliable than Internet") to capture the rationale. Softgoals, goals, and
tasks may require *Resources* (▢, e.g., "Logging Equipment") to be achieved or completed. *Key Performance Indicators* (KPIs) (e.g., "Failure Rate for Voice Connection
Over Internet") allow real-life measured values to be integrated into the analysis of a
goal model, hence improving the accuracy of the analysis.

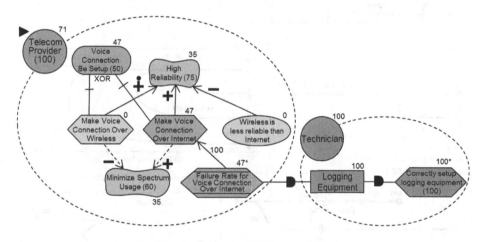

Fig. 1. Excerpt of GRL model [7]

Element links connect various elements in a goal model using structural and
intentional relationships. *Decomposition* links (+——, e.g., between "Voice Connection
Be Setup" and "Make Voice Connection Over Wireless") allow an element to be
decomposed into sub-elements. GRL supports AND, XOR, and IOR decompositions.
A *Dependency* link (—▶—, e.g., between "Failure Rate for Voice Connection Over
Internet" and "Logging Equipment") is used to model dependency of one element on

another element, typically across actor boundaries. Impacts of one element on another are represented using a *Contribution* link (→, e.g., between "Make Voice Connection Over Internet" and "High Reliability"). Contributions can be qualitative (e.g., + or −) or quantitative (integer value between 100 and −100).

2.2   UCM Notation

A Use Case Map (UCM) models causal relationships involving concurrency and partial ordering of steps in a scenario. A UCM links causes to effects and abstracts from the details of component interactions that are generally expressed as message sequences. Moreover, UCMs provide their users with the ability to dynamically refine capabilities for variations of scenarios and structures, and they allow incremental development and integration of complex scenarios. A UCM can also be transformed into sequence diagrams/MSCs, performance models, and test cases.

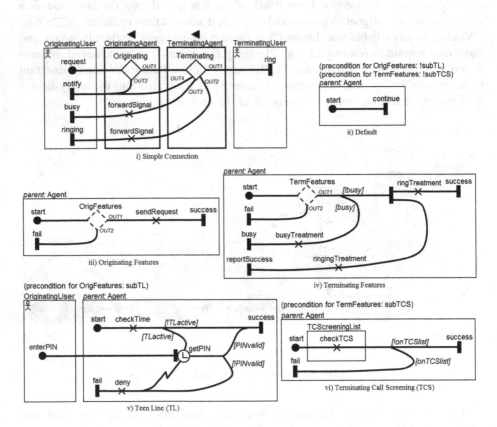

Fig. 2. Examples of UCMs [7]

In UCMs, a *Scenario* is used to partially describe a system usage that is defined as a set of partially-ordered responsibilities performed by the system to transform inputs to outputs while satisfying preconditions and postconditions. UCM *Responsibilities* (**x**, e.g., "forwardSignal" in Simple Connection UCM in Fig. 2) are activities that represent something to be performed (operation, action, task, function, etc.), i.e., the steps in a scenario. A responsibility can also be associated or allocated to a component. A *Component* (□, e.g., "Originating User") can represent software entities like objects, processes, databases etc. as well as non-software entities like actors and hardware. A *Start Point* (●, e.g., "request") captures pre-conditions and triggering events while an *End Point* (▮, e.g., "busy") captures resulting events and post-conditions. Scenarios progress along paths from start points to end points that can also support responsibilities, alternatives (OR-fork), and concurrent behavior (AND-fork) and may also join (OR-join and AND-join). An *OR-join* indicates overlapping of scenarios that share common paths while an *AND-join* synchronizes two or more paths that must have been traversed for the scenario to progress. An alternative branch is guided by a *Condition* (e.g., "[!busy]" in Terminating Features UCM) that needs to be true for the guarded path to be followed.

A *Stub* is a container for sub-maps or plugin maps. Any map can be a plugin with its start points and end points connected to identifiable input and output segments of a stub. This binding relationship ensures that the paths flow from parent maps to plugin maps, and back to parent maps. Two variants of stubs exist – a *Static Stub* (◇, e.g., "Originating" in Simple Connection UCM) that can contain only one plugin map and a *Dynamic Stub* (◇, e.g., "OrigFeatures" in Originating Features UCM) that can contain more than one plugin map with pre-conditions used to choose the correct map(s) for run-time traversal. In UCM, waiting can be done using *Waiting Places* and *Timers* (⊙, e.g., "getPIN" in Teen Line UCM). The waiting period ends when there is an event received by the waiting place or the timer from the environment or another scenario. A timer also has a timeout path (↗, e.g., the path from the timer to the "deny" responsibility) that can be followed when it does not receive a trigger in time.

For traceability reasons, URN allows typed links to be defined between model elements. Typically, GRL model elements such as actors and tasks are connected to UCM model elements such as components and responsibility or stubs with URN links (▶, e.g., actor "Telecom Provider" in Fig. 1 is linked to components "OriginatingAgent" and "TerminatingAgent" in Fig. 2). Outgoing URN links are indicated by a triangle pointing to the right, while incoming URN links are indicated by a triangle pointing to the left.

3 Differences Between TURN and URN

Study Group 17 of the International Telecommunication Union is currently tasked to define a textual syntax for the URN standard. The TURN specification introduced in this paper resembles the current status of the textual syntax for GRL and the long form syntax of UCM. Study Group 17 is also exploring a short form syntax for UCM, which omits most keywords for UCM model elements (e.g., `start` and `stub`) in favor of more terse symbols. In general, the TURN specification strikes a balance between supporting as many language features of URN as possible and the usability, convenience, and expediency of the textual syntax. Therefore, not all URN concepts are supported and hence, a model based on a TURN specification cannot specify everything that can be specified with URN. A URN model, on the other hand, can specify everything that can be specified with TURN. The main differences between TURN and URN are highlighted in this section, first for GRL and then for UCM, with the help of concrete examples.

TURN uses a different approach to uniquely identify its model elements compared to URN. In URN, unique numerical identifiers are assigned automatically, which is impractical for TURN. Therefore, TURN allows the specification of short and long unique names. For example, the goal's short name in line 02 of Listing 1 is `Voi-ceConn`, while its long name is `Voice Connection Be Setup`. The short name makes it easier to reference a model element from different parts of the TURN spec-ification, e.g., the task `MakeVoiceOverInternet` references `VoiceConn` in line 08. Ideally, short names are optional and long names may also be used to reference model elements (and this is the currently proposed approach in Study Group 17). However, the current Xtext implementation of the TURN grammar always requires the short name and allows optional long names, because the Xtext's built-in ID feature used for short names does not allow spaces.

3.1   Overview of Differences Between TGRL and GRL

In general, the Textual GRL (TGRL) matches GRL to a large degree as illustrated in Fig. 3. All GRL concepts are supported by TGRL, but there are minor differences related to (i) containment structure, (ii) indicators, and (iii) the dual modeling of qualitative and quantitative values.

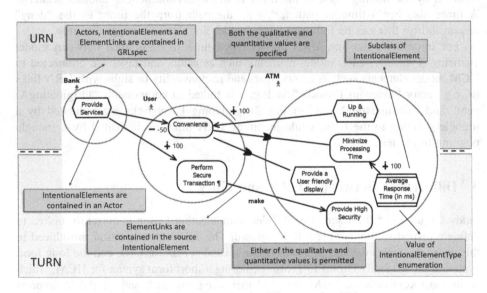

Fig. 3. Overview of main differences for GRL

3.2   Containment Structure

The containment structure in TGRL is more restrictive, but results in a well-nested textual specification that is easier to comprehend and maintain. In GRL, intentional elements and element links may be specified outside an actor, while in TGRL each intentional element is contained in an actor and each element link is contained in the source intentional element of the link as shown below. For example in Listing 1, the actor `TelP` in lines 01–14 contains all intentional elements and the task `MakeVoiceOverInternet` in lines 05–09 contains all three elements links originating from it in a TGRL model that correspond to excerpts of the GRL model introduced in Fig. 1.

Listing 1. General Form of TGRL Model

```
01 actor TelP#"Telecom Provider" {
02     goal VoiceConn#"Voice Connection Be Setup" {}
03     softgoal HighRel#"High Reliability" {}
04     softgoal SpecUsage#"Minimize Spectrum Usage" {}
05     task MakeVoiceOverInternet#"Make Voice Connection Over Internet" {
06         contributesTo HighRel with somePositive
07         contributesTo SpecUsage correlated with somePositive
08         xor decomposes VoiceConn
09     }
10     indicator VCFRate#"Failure Rate for Voice Connection Over Internet" {
11         unit "failures/week/10000 connections"
12         contributesTo MakeVoiceOverInternet with 100
13     }
14 }
```

3.3   Indicators

An indicator in TGRL is identified by the type attribute of intentional element, just like all other intentional elements in GRL, instead of being a subclass of intentional element as is the case for the jUCMNav [13] implementation of GRL. jUCMNav differs from the URN standard in the handling of indicators, because an indicator is not a subclass of intentional element in the URN standard. Instead, they are both subclasses of GRLContainableElement. Since the inheritance structure is flattened in TURN, we opted to treat an indicator just like all other intentional elements. This allows for a more uniform handling of all intentional elements compared to the URN standard. For example in Listing 1, the indicator `VCFRate` in lines 10–13 is treated exactly the same way as the other intentional elements, except that the optional unit attribute is only allowed for indicators. This is a small trade-off which could have been addressed by making indicator a subclass of intentional element, but we opted for a more concise TURN grammar plus a simple validation check instead.

3.4   Dual Modeling of Qualitative and Quantitative Values

It does not make sense to specify qualitative and quantitative values in TGRL at the same time (e.g., `contributesTo MakeVoiceOverInternet with 100/make`), as this only conveys redundant information. TGRL hence allows either qualitative or quantitative importance/contribution values to be specified but not both at the same time for the same model element. In GRL, it is possible to specify both and the enforcement of consistency rules for qualitative and quantitative values is the responsibility of URN tools, which is avoided with TGRL.

3.5   Overview of Differences Between TUCM and UCM

The Textual UCM (TUCM), on the other hand, exhibits significant differences to UCM as depicted in Fig. 4. Some differences are due to the fact that specific concepts are not supported by TUCM. Empty points are used to control the shape of a path in UCM, and are hence not required in a textual notation. Component types and performance specifications are not supported because they are rarely used (as observed from personal experience with UCM over the last two decades), while scenario definitions are left for future work[1]. All other concepts are covered by TUCM with minor differences related to (i) parent components and (ii) the specification of element containment in components, while major differences relate to (iii) component and responsibility definitions and (iv) the notion of path, which does not exist explicitly in the UCM metamodel but plays a crucial role in the TUCM metamodel.

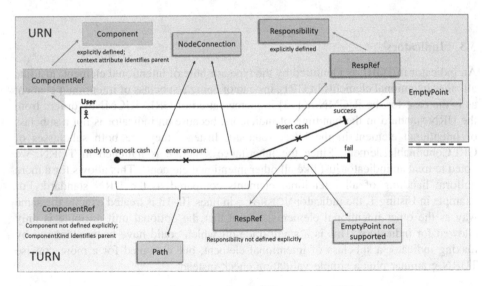

Fig. 4. Overview of main differences for UCM

---

[1] A textual syntax for scenario definitions has already been defined that closely matches the URN standard. However, the textual syntax for scenario definitions has not yet been tested thoroughly enough to be included in this paper.

The general form of a TUCM model is shown in Listing 2, using the -> notation to separate path nodes. For example in line 02, a start point (start) s is followed by a responsibility (X) r and then an end point (end) e. In line 03, all of these path nodes are contained in the component (team) C.

Listing 2. General Form of a TUCM Model

```
01 map Example1 {
02     start s -> X r -> end e.
03     team C: s, r, e
04 }
```

3.6 Parent Components

A parent component is a placeholder on a plugin map that is replaced by a component of the parent map according to component bindings specified by the stub using the plugin map. UCM uses the context attribute of a component to indicate a parent component, while TUCM uses the additional value "parent" in the component kind enumeration of a component. This allows a more consistent treatment of all components, i.e., the team keyword in line 03 of the example in Listing 2 is simply replaced by the parent keyword, if a parent component is to be modeled (see line 03 in Listing 3). This is possible, because the component kind is not used for a parent component, i.e., in UCM either the context attribute or the component kind enumeration is used but not both at the same time.

3.7 Specification of Element Containment in Components

Furthermore, TUCM allows the ·· notation (see line 03 in Listing 3) as a shortcut. Instead of enumerating all contained path nodes, only the first and last path node have to be specified. This alternative specification of element containment in components is not supported by UCM.

Listing 3. Shortcut Notation for Components

```
01 map Example2 {
02     start s -> X r -> end e.
03     parent C: s..e
04 }
```

3.8 Component and Responsibility Definitions

In TUCM, component and responsibility definitions are not specified directly as is the case in UCM but indirectly based on the short name and long name of a component and responsibility, respectively. Two components or responsibilities with the same short name (e.g., rA in lines 02 and 03 of the example in Listing 4) always refer to the same definition. In addition, two components or responsibilities with a different short name (e.g., rB_1 and rB_2 in lines 02 and 03) refer to the same definition, if their long names are the same (e.g., `Beta` in lines 02 and 03). This approach keeps the speci-fication short and concise, if component references and responsibility references do not need to be differentiated. This is the case for `rA`, because all references are contained in component `C1` (see line 04). However, if there is a need to differentiate references, then this is also possible, as is shown with `rB_1` and `rB_2`, which are contained in components `C1` and `C2`, respectively (see lines 04 and 05).

Listing 4. Naming and Referencing of Responsibilities

```
01 map Example3 {
02     start s -> X rA -> X rB_1#"Beta" -> end e.
03     start s2 -> X rA -> X rB_2#"Beta" -> end e2.
04     team C1: rA, rB_1
05     team C2: rB_2
06 }
```

3.9   Notion of Path

The most important difference is that the TUCM metamodel is structured around the notion of path, which does not exist in the UCM metamodel. To motivate this approach, the Terminating Call Screening (TCS) map from Fig. 2 is modeled with TUCM (see Listing 5) with one start point, one responsibility, one OR-fork and its two branches with one condition and one end point each. A node where a path splits into several branches is described by nesting its branches inside the node as shown below for the OR-fork (`or`). This results in three paths (the one from start point to the OR-fork and the two nested branches inside the OR-fork).

Listing 5. Terminating Call Screening

```
01 map TCS #"Terminating Call Screening (TCS)" {
02     start startPoint -> X checkTCS -> or {
03         [!onTCSlist] -> end success.
04         [onTCSlist] -> end failPoint.
05     }
06 }
```

Consider an extension of the TCS map in Listing 5, by introducing a logging service that, if enabled, logs calls before also ending in success. This requires the addition of the `logCall` responsibility and an OR-join (see line 03 in Listing 6). A node where several paths join is described by one path defining the join node and the other path(s) referencing this join node as shown in Listing 6.

Listing 6. Extended Terminating Call Screening

```
01 map TCS #"Terminating Call Screening (TCS)" {
02     start startPoint -> X checkTCS -> or {
03         [!onTCSlist && log] -> X logCall -> join j -> end success.
04         [!onTCSlist && !log] -> j;
05         [onTCSlist] -> end failPoint.
06     }
07 }
```

In this example, the first branch defines the OR-join (join) j (see line 03 in Listing 6) while the second branch references j (see line 04 in Listing 6) as indicated by the semi-colon (;), resulting in one additional path. This approach is used for all branching nodes (i.e., OR-forks, AND-forks, and stubs) and all nodes that join branches (i.e., OR-joins, AND-joins, and stubs).

In summary, instead of a UCM map containing path nodes and their node connections, a TUCM map consists of paths which in turn consist of path body nodes, regular ends, and referenced ends. Whereas node connections connect source and target path nodes with each other in UCM, a path contains an ordered list of path body nodes in TUCM. A path represents a segment of a UCM map. Segments correspond to the path body nodes of a UCM map that lie between branching and join nodes. A branch is typically treated as a separate path body in TUCM. This is done because a textual representation requires a tree-based format, and hence the graph-based representation of a UCM map is broken down into individually specifiable segments in TUCM. This difference is further illustrated in Fig. 5.

The UCM map in Fig. 5 contains the following seven segments when modeled with TUCM: (i) from start point to OR-fork, (ii) from OR-fork to AND-fork via "swipe card", (iii) from OR-fork to OR-join via "insert card", (iv) from AND-fork to stub via "enter PIN", (v) from AND-fork to stub via "enter captcha", (vi) from stub to end point via out-path 1, and (vii) from stub to AND-join via out-path 2. The last node in a segment may either be a regular end, i.e., the actual definition of a node, or a referenced end, i.e., a reference to an already specified path body node.

The concept of a Path as shown in Fig. 6 and all other concepts mentioned in this paragraph except for UCM path nodes do not exist in the UCM metamodel. A Path contains a StartPoint and a PathBody where a *PathBody* contains a set of PathBody-Nodes, which cover all supported URN path nodes. In addition, a PathBody can have a RegularEnd, a ReferencedEnd, or a ReferencedStub. A *RegularEnd* denotes the end of

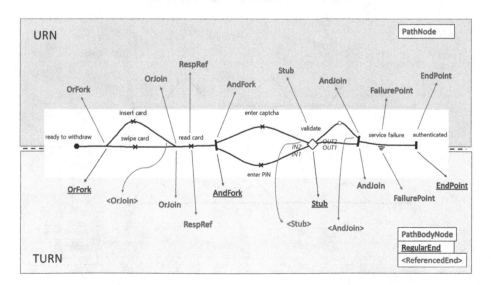

Fig. 5. Key difference between UCM and TUCM – paths

a path segment, which can either be an EndPoint or a node where new branches start (i.e., an OrFork, AndFork, or Stub). A *ReferencedEnd* and *ReferencedStub* denote the end of a path that ends at a path node defined in a different path (OrJoin, AndJoin, RespRef, FailurePoint, and Stub, respectively).

RespRef, FailurePoint, or EndPoint may be referenced as a shortcut notation, because TUCM does not require OR-joins to be specified that are implied by the structure of the UCM model as explained in Fig. 7. Instead, the transformation from TURN to URN ensures that the representation of a TUCM model with implicit OR-joins shown at the bottom of Fig. 7 is properly translated into a valid UCM model with explicit preceding OR-joins shown at the top.

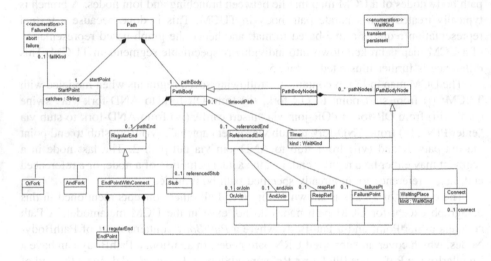

Fig. 6. Xtext metamodel for TUCM path

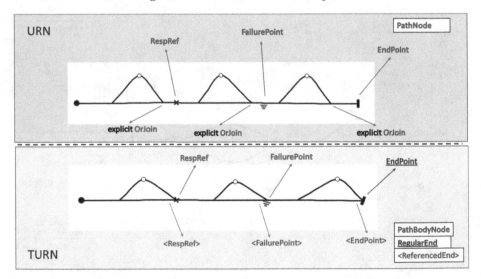

Fig. 7. Key difference between UCM and TUCM – implicit OR-joins

As a consequence of the path-based TUCM metamodel, the metamodel elements for OR-forks, AND-forks, and stubs also reflect the notion of path, i.e., these elements contain explicit path bodies to capture their outgoing branches and out-paths.

In addition as another shortcut notation, OR-forks, AND-forks, and stubs may define the continuation of one or more branches, i.e., a *connecting path body*. This situation is depicted by a branch or several branches continuing after the closing curly brackets of OR-forks, AND-forks, or stubs as shown in the example in Listing 7, hence simplifying the earlier specification.

Listing 7. Connecting Path Body for OR-fork

```
01 map TCS #"Terminating Call Screening (TCS)" {
02    start startPoint -> X checkTCS -> or {
03       [!onTCSlist && log] -> X logCall -> ;
04       [!onTCSlist && !log] -> ;
05       [onTCSlist] -> end failPoint.
06    } -> end success.
07 }
```

The branches that end with a semi-colon are joined by an implicit OR-join (AND-join in case of an AND-fork) before the connecting path body (i.e., `-> end success.` in line 06 in Listing 7) resulting in the same URN model as shown in Fig. 2. Implicit OR-joins and AND-joins simplify the specification of well-nested OR-forks and AND-forks, respectively. Just like URN, TURN allows arbitrary combinations of OR-forks, OR-joins, AND-forks, and AND-joins that do not need to be well-nested, but these forks and joins then usually need to be specified explicitly. For a Stub, out-paths that end with a semi-colon are joined implicitly with an OR-join before the Stub's connecting path body.

4 Multi-phased Transformation from TURN to URN

To validate the feasibility of the proposed TURN specification, TURN is implemented with Xtext, the defacto standard for metamodel-based definitions of textual languages. Furthermore, a TURN specification is transformed into a URN model to demonstrate conformance to URN. The TURN-URN transformation unfolds in three phases (see Fig. 8).

Phase 0. The input of this phase is a TURN model specified with the Xtext editor automatically generated from the Xtext grammar for TURN. It makes use of the Eclipse Modeling Framework (EMF) to save the TURN model in an XMI file conforming to the TURN metamodel, also automatically generated by Xtext from the TURN grammar.

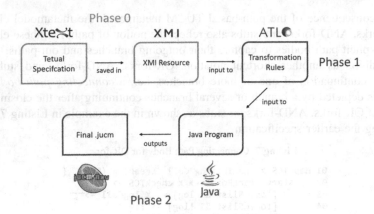

Fig. 8. Transformation phases

Phase 1. The input of this phase is the TURN model in XMI form produced by Phase 0. It involves the execution of transformation rules using the Atlas Transformation Language (ATL; eclipse.org/atl) tool and produces an intermediate URN file as the result of the ATL transformation. This decision is made to address specific differences between the TURN and URN metamodels and the intricacies involved in the transformation of TUCM to UCM.

Phase 2. The input of this phase is the intermediate URN file produced by Phase 1. This phase is implemented with Java and leverages the features provided by the EMF framework. The output of Phase 2 is a valid URN file which can be loaded using the graphical jUCMNav tool, the most comprehensive URN tool available. The implementation involves (i) binding of elements including connects to components, (ii) creating OR-joins that are implicit in the TURN model, and (iii) handling asynchronous connects with a timer. All these cases are handled in Phase 2, because the ATL transformation mixes matched rules (executed once for each instance of a specific type in non-deterministic order) and called rules (executed upon explicit call from other rule). Consequently, not all required target elements may be available when needed in these three specific cases. Hence, we decided to handle them in Phase 2 after the ATL transformation.

Binding elements including connects to components. This is needed when the TURN model contains components with connects or with "from" and "to" attributes, i.e., a component contains all elements between the "from" node and the "to" node. For example, see Fig. 9 where the `Agent` contains a connect between the end point and the timer `getPIN` and all elements from `startPoint` to `failPoint`. After Phase 2, all elements are properly bound to their respective components.

```
      parent Agent: startPoint..failPoint, success
          actor OriginatingUser: enterPIN
```

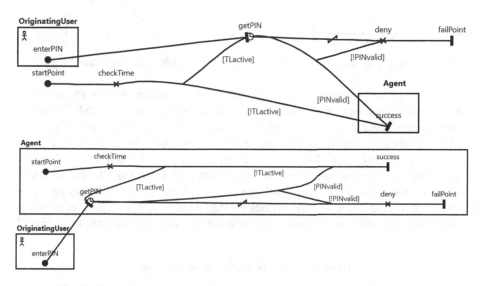

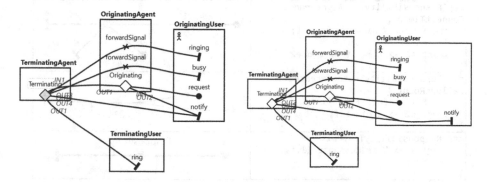

Fig. 9. Teen Line (TL) map after Phase 1 (top) and after Phase 2 (bottom)

Creating implicit OR-joins. Implicit OR-joins are present in a TURN model when end points, failure points, or responsibilities are referred by several elements. If this is the case, an OR-join is inserted before the node and bound to the same component as the node. Since, the jUCMNav tool is flexible enough to allow more than one predecessor for these nodes, we decided to take advantage of it and create OR-joins in Phase 2. For example, see Fig. 10 where `notify` is the end point of two branches.

Fig. 10. Simple connection (SC) map after Phase 1 (left) and after Phase 2 (right)

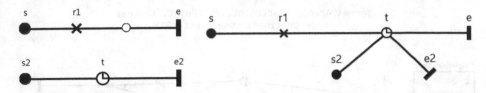

Fig. 11. Map with asynchronous connect after Phase 1 (left) and after Phase 2 (right)

Handling asynchronous connects with timer. The transformation in Phase 1 only adds an empty point with an invisible tag identifying the timer to the UCM. The empty point is then connected to the timer with a proper connect in Phase 2 (see Fig. 11).

The TURN specification and the transformation to URN are tested with a set of rather exhaustive test cases[2]. More than 400 test cases cover all URN model elements, including (i) the combinations of all 12 UCM path nodes, (ii) the UCM component, (iii) the combinations of 6 types of GRL nodes and 3 types of GRL links as permitted by the constraints of URN, and (iv) various validation rules such as number of branches for an AND-fork and unique names. Furthermore, the running example from Figs. 1

Table 1. Sample of responsibility test cases

Test Input	Test Output

map ResponsibilityTestEndPoint {
    start s -> X r1 -> end e.
}
	(diagram: s, r1, e)

map ResponsibilityTestOrJoin {
    start s -> X r1 -> join j -> end e.
    start s2 -> j;
}
	(diagram: s2, j, e, s, r1)

map ResponsibilityTestStub {
    start s -> X r1 -> stub () ->
        end e.
}
	(diagram: s, r1, e, IN1, OUT1)

map ResponsibilityTestAsynchronous
ConnectTimer {
    start s -> X r1 -> trigger t; ->
        end e.
    start s2 -> timer t -> end e2.
}
	(diagram: s, r1, t, e, s2, e2)

map ResponsibilityTestReferenced
FailurePoint {
    start s -> fail f -> end e.
    start s2 -> X r1 -> f;
}
	(diagram: s, s2, r1, f, e)

map ResponsibilityTestFull {
    start s -> X r#"Responsibility" ->
        end e.
}
	(diagram: s, Responsibility, e)

---

[2] The complete set of test cases and the TURN grammar are available at http://www.ece.mcgill.ca/
  ~gmussb1/TURN.

and 2 are also used as a test and cover additionally concerns, URN links, and metadata as well GRL strategies, evaluations, and contribution contexts.

Representative of all test cases, a few test cases for responsibilities are shown in Table 1. The complete suite of test cases for responsibility include tests where a responsibility is followed by each of the possible path body nodes, regular ends, and referenced ends. Other tests vary all optional elements a responsibility may have in TURN. The tests for other model elements follow a similar pattern and are augmented by tests for validation checks.

5   Related Work

There exist various solutions to define concrete syntaxes of DSLs. One of the most popular approaches is HUTN [18], specified as a standard by OMG. It defines a generic concrete syntax, which aims to conform to human-usability criteria. It requires a parser generator and the grammar is automatically generated. An obvious advantage of this approach is that any model can be represented in textual notation at a very low cost. However, HUTN imposes very strict constraints on the notation and is a bit verbose. Users cannot provide their own syntax customizations. We used Xtext to define a custom concrete syntax for URN, where the concrete syntax for GRL is somewhat similar to HUTN but UCM follows a very different approach to define a more compact concrete syntax. Other tools that can be used to define a custom concrete syntax are TCS [12] which uses specifications provided by users to automatically generate editors and tools for model-to-text and text-to-model transformations; and TEF (www2.informatik.hu-berlin.de/sam/meta-tools/tef) which allows defining multiple syntactic constructs for the same metamodel element but requires the user to specify both the grammar and metamodel, which is redundant. An Xtext-based specification, on the other hand, combines the specification of the grammar and meta-model in one single unified representation.

Several languages support textual and graphical syntaxes including the Specification and Description Language (SDL) [8], Message Sequence Charts (MSC) [10], and the Testing and Test Control Notation (TTCN-3) [9], all also standardized by ITU. Two TTCN-3 tools also use an Xtext-based grammar, i.e., T-Rex [22] and T3Q [20]. An effort to create an Xtext-based textual syntax for GRL [1] discusses the challenges faced during the creation of the textual syntax and the conflicts between the reuse of the existing metamodel and the usability of the textual syntax. TURN builds on the lessons learned for GRL. The experience for UCM with TURN is similar to the experience with GRL [1], even more pronounced as the differences of the TUCM metamodel compared to the UCM metamodel are much greater than the differences of the TGRL metamodel compared to the GRL metamodel. A commercial tool, UniqueSoft's Test Architect tool [21], also features a textual notation for UCMs, but does not cover goal models.

Another popular example of a textual language is Umple [5] that integrates the concepts of UML with programming languages such as Java and PHP. Umple models are written using human-readable text seamlessly integrated with algorithmic code and can also be visualized with the UML notation. This model-is-the-code approach helps developers maintain and evolve the code as the system matures. Umple uses its own metamodel and grammar.

There are several tools other than ATL that offer model-to-model transformations. One of the popular implementations is QVT [17], a standard defined by OMG that supports bidirectional transformations. There are two extensions for QVT called QVTd (Declarative) and QVTo (Operational/Procedural). ATL, being a declarative and imperative hybrid, is more expressive with the ability to express any kind of transformations. ATL also executes faster than QVT in most of the cases. Another popular language for model-to-model transformation is ETL [14], which is built on top of a common expression language (EOL) [15]. ETL can transform many inputs to many output models, and can query/modify both source and target models. Other languages include JTL (Janus Transformation Language) [3], a bidirectional model transformation language specifically designed to support non-bijective transformations and change propagation; Kermeta [4], that borrows concepts from languages such as MOF, OCL, QVT, and BasicMTL [23], and is easier to learn due to its java-like syntax; and AToMPM (atompm.github.io), a web based modeling environment which provides model transformations based on T-Core [19], a minimal collection of model transformation operators.

6   Conclusions and Future Work

The Textual User Requirements Notation (TURN) is a textual syntax for the User Requirements Notation published by the International Telecommunication Union. In this paper, TURN is defined as an Xtext grammar, from which an editor and the TURN metamodel are automatically generated. This effort contributes to the standardization of a textual syntax for URN, currently considered by ITU. The differences of the TURN and URN metamodels are discussed. Most notably, TURN uses the notion of *Path*, which does not explicitly exist in URN. Conformance to URN is demonstrated by a multi-phased model-to-model transformation and a rather exhaustive set of more than 400 test cases. As a textual language, TURN addresses scalability issues for very large URN models consisting of thousands of goal and scenario models. Furthermore, layout issues do not need to be considered compared to URN and TURN specifications can be edited quickly, supported by error markers and auto-completion.

In future work, we will endeavour to implement the UCM concepts currently not supported by the Xtext implementation of TURN, i.e., scenario definitions. We will also investigate collaborative modeling with TURN, which is less complex for textual notations compared to graphical notations. From anecdotal experience, we have seen that the textual syntax is well understood after a certain adjustment period for those users familiar with the graphical syntax. It seems to be the case that users initially construct the graphical model from the textual syntax but rely on the graphical model less and less over time. However, the usability and learnability of the proposed textual notation needs to be evaluated more thoroughly with empirical studies.

Acknowledgement. We are indebted to Thomas Weigert for his insightful comments on the advantages and disadvantages of the textual syntax for Use Case Maps.

References

1. Abdelzad, V., Amyot, D., Lethbridge, Timothy C.: Adding a textual syntax to an existing graphical modeling language: experience report with GRL. In: Fischer, J., Scheidgen, M., Schieferdecker, I., Reed, R. (eds.) SDL 2015. LNCS, vol. 9369, pp. 159–174. Springer, Cham (2015). https://doi.org/10.1007/978-3-319-24912-4_12
2. Amyot, D., Mussbacher, G.: User requirements notation: the first ten years, the next ten years. J. Softw. (JSW) 6(5), 747–768 (2011). http://www.jsoftware.us/vol6/jsw0605-1.pdf
3. Cicchetti, A., Di Ruscio, D., Eramo, R., Pierantonio, A.: JTL: a bidirectional and change propagating transformation language. In: Malloy, B., Staab, S., van den Brand, M. (eds.) SLE 2010. LNCS, vol. 6563, pp. 183–202. Springer, Heidelberg (2011). https://doi.org/10.1007/978-3-642-19440-5_11
4. Fleurey, F., Drey, Z., Vojtisek, D., Faucher, C., Mahé, V.: Kermeta Language, Reference Manual. IRISA (2006). http://www.kermeta.org/docs/KerMeta-Manual.pdf
5. Forward, A., et al.: Model-driven rapid prototyping with Umple. Softw. Pract. Exper. 42(7), 781–797 (2012)
6. Grönniger, H., Krahn, H., Rumpe, B., Schindler, M., Völkel, S.: Text-based modeling. In: 4th International Workshop on Software Language Engineering (2007)
7. ITU: Recommendation Z.151 (10/12), User Requirements Notation (URN) – Language definition (2012). http://www.itu.int/rec/T-REC-Z.151/en
8. ITU: Recommendation Z.100 (04/16), Specification and Description Language – Overview of SDL-2010 (2016). http://www.itu.int/rec/T-REC-Z.100-201604-I/en
9. ITU: Recommendation Z.161 (10/17), Testing and Test Control Notation Version 3: TTCN-3 Core Language (2017). http://www.itu.int/rec/T-REC-Z.161-201710-I/en
10. ITU: Recommendation Z.120 (02/11), Message Sequence Chart (MSC) (2011). http://www.itu.int/rec/T-REC-Z.120-201102-I/en
11. Jackson, D.: Alloy: a lightweight object modelling notation. ACM Trans. Softw. Eng. Methodol. (TOSEM) 11(2), 256–290 (2002)
12. Jouault, F., Bézivin, J., Kurtev, I.: TCS: a DSL for the specification of textual concrete syntaxes in model engineering. In: GPCE 2006, pp. 249–254. ACM Press (2006)
13. jUCMNav, version 7.0. University of Ottawa. http://jucmnav.softwareengineering.ca/jucmnav
14. Kolovos, D.S., Paige, R.F., Polack, F.A.C.: The epsilon transformation language. In: Vallecillo, A., Gray, J., Pierantonio, A. (eds.) ICMT 2008. LNCS, vol. 5063, pp. 46–60. Springer, Heidelberg (2008). https://doi.org/10.1007/978-3-540-69927-9_4
15. Kolovos, D.S., Paige, R.F., Polack, F.A.C.: The epsilon object language (EOL). In: Rensink, A., Warmer, J. (eds.) ECMDA-FA 2006. LNCS, vol. 4066, pp. 128–142. Springer, Heidelberg (2006). https://doi.org/10.1007/11787044_11
16. Kosslyn, S.M., Pomerantz, J.R.: Imagery, propositions, and the form of internal representations. Cogn. Psychol. 9(1), 52–76 (1977)
17. Kurtev, I.: State of the art of QVT: a model transformation language standard. In: Schürr, A., Nagl, M., Zündorf, A. (eds.) AGTIVE 2007. LNCS, vol. 5088, pp. 377–393. Springer, Heidelberg (2008). https://doi.org/10.1007/978-3-540-89020-1_26
18. OMG: UML Human-Usable Textual Notation (HUTN). Version 1.0, formal/2004-08-01 (2004). http://www.omg.org/spec/HUTN/1.0/
19. Syriani, E., Vangheluwe, H., LaShomb, B.: T-Core: a framework for custom-built transformation engines. Softw. Syst. Model. 14(3), 1215–1243 (2015)
20. T3Tools, University of Göttingen. https://t3tools.informatik.uni-goettingen.de/trac

21. Test Architect, UniqueSoft. https://www.uniquesoft.com/automated-test-case-generation.php
22. T-Rex – the TTCN-3 Refactoring and Metrics Tool, University of Göttingen. https://www.trex.informatik.uni-goettingen.de/trac
23. Vojtisek, D.: BasicMTL realization guide. Inside the Carroll Research Program and part of the MOTOR project. Technical Report (2004). http://modelware.inria.fr/article.php3?id_article=45

A Comparative Analysis of ITU-MSC-Based Requirements Specification Approaches Used in the Automotive Industry

Kevin Keller[⊠], Jennifer Brings, Marian Daun, and Thorsten Weyer

University of Duisburg Essen, paluno -The Ruhr Institute for Software
Technology, Essen, Germany
{kevin.keller,jennifer.brings,marian.daun,
thorsten.weyer}@paluno.uni-due.de

Abstract. Message sequence charts (MSC) and MSC-like languages play a pivotal role in requirements engineering. Particularly, when it comes to model-based requirements engineering, MSCs are used, e.g., to document scenarios, but also, specifically in the automotive domain, for specifying interaction sequences and the interaction-based behavior of such reactive systems. As the use of natural language requirements is still widespread, there exist various approaches to create MSC-specifications from natural language requirements. In this paper, we report on a comparative analysis to investigate different approaches for MSC-specification generation. To do so, we applied three approaches to an industrial case example from the automotive domain. Our results show that the different approaches lead to correct yet different MSC-specifications that exhibit different characteristics and are thus suited for different requirements engineering purposes.

Keywords: Message sequence charts · Goal-oriented requirement language
Use case maps · Comparative analysis · Requirements engineering

1 Introduction

Message sequence charts (MSC) are commonly used during model-based requirements engineering. MSCs and MSC-like languages are particularly used in the automotive industry [1]. Among others MSC-specifications are generated as part of scenario-based requirements engineering approaches [2, 3], but also to specify the necessary interaction-based behavior of embedded systems. However, in most development projects, requirements are still documented using natural language [4] for various reasons such as ensuring understandability by stakeholders not familiar with modeling notations or to comply with rules of certification agencies. Even as model-based development is becoming more popular, sometimes rules and regulations still demand the use of natural language requirements [5]. Therefore, the need exists to cope with both, natural language requirements and model-based specifications. Hence, MSC-

© Springer Nature Switzerland AG 2018
F. Khendek and R. Gotzhein (Eds.): SAM 2018, LNCS 11150, pp. 183–201, 2018.
https://doi.org/10.1007/978-3-030-01042-3_11

specifications are created on the basis of existing natural language requirements [6]. For this purpose, different approaches are used in the automotive industry to systematically derive MSC-based requirements specifications from natural language requirements specifying the necessary interaction-based behavior of the system under study.

This paper contributes a comparative analysis of three different approaches used in the automotive industry for creating MSC-based requirements specifications out of natural language requirements. To give insights into the strength and weaknesses of the three approaches, this paper reports experiences from their application in the context of an *adaptive electronic light control* from the automotive domain.

This paper is structured according to widely recognized guidelines from [7]. Section 2 gives insight into related approaches and details the three approaches under investigation and the modeling languages used within these approaches. Section 3 elaborates on the study design and Sect. 4 presents results from the application of the three approaches to the case example. Section 5 discusses the findings and draws conclusions. Finally, Sect. 6 concludes the paper.

2 Related Work

This section gives an overview on the related work for the generation of model-based scenario specifications from natural language requirements, the approaches under investigation, and the concrete modeling languages used in our investigation.

2.1 Related Studies

There exist many goal and scenario based approaches [8–10]. Goal and scenario based requirements engineering is an important area, because the coupling of goals and scenarios supports elicitation, validation, and negotiation of requirements [11, 12]. Using goals and scenarios helps requirement engineers to better understand the needs of stakeholders [13]. Another positive aspect of goals and scenarios is the refinement of non-functional requirements through goals. Non-functional requirements are difficult to describe at the beginning and only become more precise when they are refined. This can lead to the detection of different interests of stakeholders as well [14].

In practice natural language is the main presentation form for requirement documents [4]. In such documents the intended behavior of the system is written as a sequence of sentences. *Kof* developed an approach to translate natural language scenarios into executable models using message sequence charts (MSC). The approach was further extended in [15] with heuristics for the analysis of requirements. This allows finding inconsistencies and omissions in the natural language specifications. In [16], an approach is presented, which generates event-based scenarios from natural language requirements. The event-based scenarios are used for deriving test cases of the system. *Sindre and Opdahl* [17] discusses the use of misuse cases as scenarios for detecting and defining security critical requirements in requirements specifications.

In [8], an approach for modeling goals and dependent scenarios is described for an information system. This approach applies the User Requirements Notation (URN).

Goals are used to document all requirements. The scenarios are created based on the task elements in the goal model. *Miga et al.* [18] define a method for deriving MSC from Use Case Maps (UCM).

2.2 Modelling Languages

We used modeling languages defined and standardized by the International Telecommunication Union. This decision was made (a) to avoid gaps between the used languages, which might result in misinterpretation of the findings and (b) because industry partners emphasize the use of standardized languages and the ITU languages have already been found appropriate in previous work [19].

In recommendation Z.151 the ITU URN defines the goal modeling language Goal-oriented Requirement Language (GRL) and the scenario language (UCM) [20]. However, UCM are seldomly used for scenario specifications in the development of embedded systems, as sequence chart like diagrams are preferred by industry. One standardized approach to sequence chart like diagrams are MSC as defined by the ITU in its recommendation Z.120 [21], which are also commonly used for scenario specifications [22]. Investigations among industry partners in German joint research projects showed that industry partners prefer MSCs over UML sequence diagrams or LSCs. This is mainly due industries preference of standards and due to the structuring elements ITU MSCs provide that allow specifying a complete requirements specification (in contrast to rather unrelated descriptions of single scenarios). In previous work we have shown that MSCs are a good language to foster manual validation of industrial specifications [23, 24].

Goal-oriented Requirement Language. GRL [20] is a modeling language for documenting goals, soft goals, tasks, resources and relationships among them; allowing, among others, to document conflicts between different goals. Goals, softgoals, tasks and resources can, furthermore, be assigned to different actors which also enables documenting dependencies between actors with respect to the fulfillment of goals.

Use Case Maps. UCM [20] is a modeling language for documenting scenarios in a way that focuses on causal relationships among responsibilities. In particular, a UCM depicts scenario paths along components (i.e. it is defined which components are involved and where their responsibilities for task executions are).

Message Sequence Charts. MSC [21] define scenarios by documenting the exchange of information between instances. To this end, recommendation Z.120 defines two types of diagrams: basic MSC (bMSC) and high-level MSC (hMSC). While bMSCs define the exchange of messages, hMSCs can be used to define an execution order for bMSCs including alternatives and loops.

2.3 Approaches Under Investigation

The three different approaches all use the same natural language requirements specification as input and result in a MSC-based requirements specification. However, the three approaches make use of different intermediate models (using different modeling languages; see Sect. 2.2) created for the purpose of deriving the MSC-based requirements specification. Figure 1 illustrates the three approaches and their relations. Approach A (NL-MSC) creates a MSC-specification directly from the natural language requirements. Approach B (NL-GRL-MSC) first creates a GRL-goal model from the natural language requirements and then a MSC-specification from the goal model (without consulting the natural language requirements again). Approach C (NL-GRL-UCM-MSC) adds another intermediate step to approach B. UCMs are created based on the goal model and then the MSC-specification is created based on the UCMs.

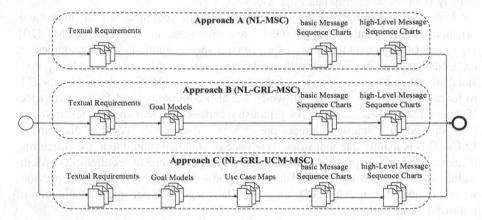

Fig. 1. Procedures of the approaches

Approach A (NL-MSC). Approach A describes the ad-hoc creation of an MSC-based requirements specification from natural language requirements without any intermediate steps as is commonly done in practice [25, 26]. Using this approach requirements engineers tasked with creating MSC-based requirements specifications receive little to no guidance on how to create the MSC-based requirements specification and mostly rely on their intuition and experiences. This approach is meant to be a benchmark to evaluate if structured approaches to the generation of MSC-based requirements specifications lead to better results.

Approach B (NL-GRL-MSC). Approach B describes the creation of an MSC-based requirements specification based on a goal model as is suggested in goal- and scenario-based requirements engineering [27–29]. For each natural language requirement at least one goal is defined. All goals are structured according to their relationships and each goal is assigned to an actor (entity responsible for the fulfilment of the goal). The goal model is further refined until each goal is assigned a task that describes how it is fulfilled. The MSC-specification is then created based on these tasks. For each task a bMSC is defined that describes the execution of the tasks. Subsequently one or more hMSC are defined that structure the created bMSCs according to the goal model.

Approach C (NL-GRL-UCM-MSC). Approach C describes the creation of an MSC-based requirements specification based on an existing UCM-specification as has been proposed in [18]. While the original approach is designed for automated creation of a bMSC-specification, we conducted the approach manually. For each goal from the GRL goal model at least one use case is identified that describes the fulfilment of the goal. Actors from the goal model are represented by agents in the UCM-specification. To create the MSC-specification, a bMSC instance is defined for each agent from the UCM-specification and one action and message is defined for each responsibility from the UCM-specification. Alternatives and loops in the UCM-specification are added to the MSC-specification accordingly using inline expressions. Subsequently, the MSC-specification is structured using a hMSC. As the original approach described in [18] does not explicitly address the creation of a hMSC, we adapted the approach. As each UCM was transformed into one bMSC. The hMSC was created according to the final and initial states in UCMs. If the final state of one UCM is identical to the initial state of another UCM. A flow line was added between the MSC references pointing at the respective bMSCs.

3   Study Design

Section 3 introduces the study design, starting with the research questions in Sect. 3.1. Subsequently, Sect. 3.2 discusses data collection and validity procedures taken. Section 3.3 gives insight into the procedure conducted to create the MSC-specifications using the three approaches and Sect. 3.4 discusses the case and subject selection.

3.1   Research Questions

Despite the increasing popularity of model-based engineering approaches [30] natural language requirements are still common in many development projects [4]. To use the advantages of model-based scenario specifications, such specifications are created based on natural language requirements which are often also needed, among others, as legally binding documents. In this paper, we report on a comparative study from the automotive domain to investigate how to create a model-based scenario specification from natural language requirements.

For each of the three approaches from Sect. 2.3, we want first to determine whether the approach is generally feasible and whether the application of the approach results in a valid MSC-specification. Furthermore, we want to determine benefits and short-comings of different proposed approaches and resulting from the comparison of these, we want to answer the question, which approach is suited best for which purpose of MSC-based requirements specification generation. Therefore, we compare the three resulting MSC-specifications using the SEQUAL framework [31] as reference.

Particularly, we investigate semantical and syntactical quality to investigate the correctness of the specifications. We define:

RQ1:   Does approach A/B/C lead to a syntactical and semantical correct MSC-specification?

To compare the suitability of the approaches for different purposes we investigate the empirical quality of the three resulting MSC-specifications, leading to the research question:

RQ2:   What are the differences w.r.t. the specifications empirical quality of the MSC-specifications generated using the three different approaches.

3.2   Data Collection, Analysis and Validity Procedures

All models have been developed using MS Visio. A Visio Plugin was used that provides shapes of the modeling languages used and provides basic syntactical checks which help prevent syntactical errors. The tool has been developed in the context of research projects to foster the continuous model-based engineering of embedded systems. More information on the Visio Plugin can be found in [32]. For *RQ1*, we investigated syntactical quality, to determine if the specifications are free of syntactical errors; and semantical quality, to ensure that the specifications have no defects and are complete with respect to the natural language requirements. Each specification was checked for syntactical errors by different experts independently. For *RQ 2*, we examined the specifications' empirical quality, to determine if the specifications are easily readable. For determining readability we adapted the structural metrics proposed by [33] originally intended to measure readability of process models. The non-measurable parts of investigation were supported by industry experts to lower threats to generalizability of findings. However, there remain threats to validity, which we discuss in Sect. 4.3.

3.3   Procedure

Model creation started with the MSC-specification for approach A. The models created in each approach were all created by the same person. Thereafter, the same person was responsible for incorporating changes identified as necessary either by our industry partner or by other researchers. First the natural language requirements specification was read and anything unclear was discussed with the industry partner who created and provided the natural language requirements specification. Afterwards an initial MSC-specification was created according to approach A. This initial MSC-specification was reviewed by the creator of the natural language requirements specification and his colleagues. The MSC-specification was then revised and reviewed again. This revision and review cycle was repeated until it was determined that the MSC-specification reflects the natural language requirements specification correctly and completely. This way it was ensured that the MSC-specification does not only contain all aspects defined in the natural language requirements specification but was also structured according to industry needs.

After the MSC-specification from approach A was completed. An initial goal model was created based on the natural language requirements specification. Like the MSC-specification created from approach A, the goal model was reviewed and revised until it was determined that it reflects the natural language requirements specification correctly and completely. Based on this goal model an initial MSC-specification was created according to approach B. Again, the MSC-specification was reviewed and revised. This revision and review cycle continued until it was determined that the MSC-specification reflects the natural language requirements specification.

After the MSC-specification from approach B was completed. An initial UCM was created based on the goal model created in approach B. This UCM was reviewed and revised until it was determined that it reflects the goal model correctly and completely. Based on this UCM an initial MSC-specification was created according to approach C. This MSC-specification was reviewed and revised until it was determined that the MSC-specification reflects the natural language requirements specification.

3.4   Case and Subject Selection

The specification document used in the case study is a natural language specification of an automotive system cluster provided by industry [34]. The automotive system cluster consists of two subsystems the adaptive cruise control (ACC) and the adaptive exterior lighting system (AELS), in this paper we focus on the AELS.

The AELS includes the control of the turn signal, the low beam headlights, the high beam headlights and error handling in case of defective lamps and voltage problems. The control of the turn signal includes activation and deactivation of the left and right direction indicators based on the status of the pitman arm and the hazard warning light switch. When both sides of the direction indicators are activated, the hazard warning lights are activated and the blinking frequency is determined based on the status of the ignition key. During the control of the low beam headlights, the state of the system can be activated or deactivated based on the positions of the light rotary switch and the daytime running light settings. The control of the low beam headlights also includes the control of ambient light and cornering light, which depends on the position of the pitman arm and the current vehicle speed.

Furthermore, the AELS includes the manual control of the high beam headlights as well as the adaptation of the illumination range. With manual control of the high beam headlights, the driver sets a specific illumination range and the system adjusts the brightness. The manual high beam can be switched on or off via the horizontal positions of the pitman arm. On the other hand, the adaptive control of the high beam headlights adjusts the illumination range based on the detection of preceding and oncoming vehicles and their distances to the own vehicle, so that these vehicles cannot be blinded. The adaptive high beam headlights can be activated when the light rotary switch is in the "auto" position and the pitman arm is pressed horizontally backwards.

4   Results

To illustrate our findings this section presents parts of the resulting MSC-specifications (and for approach B and C also parts of the intermediate artifacts). To ensure comparability we present excerpts of GRL, UCM, and MSC models created during application of the three different approaches, which relate to the following two natural language requirements (from [34]). Complete specifications of all models from all three approaches can be found at http://doi.org/10.5281/zenodo.1323516.

> - AL-43: Cornering light: If the low beam headlights are activated and direction blinking is requested, the cornering light is activated, when the vehicle drives slower than 10 km/h. 10 seconds after passing the corner (i.e. the direction blinking is not active any more for 10 seconds), the cornering light is switched in a duration of 1 second (gentle fade-out).
> - AL-139: With activated darkness switch (only armored vehicles) the cornering light is not activated.

4.1   Application of Approach A (NL-MSC)

Figure 2 shows the part of the resulting MSC-specification for the two natural language requirements that was created directly based on the natural language requirements. As can be seen the scenario will be executed when the first condition *Darkness Mode Deactivated* is fulfilled. Otherwise, the scenario terminates without further interactions. After checking the condition, the AELS continues with specific checks and proceeds based on which message it receives from the instance *Turning Light* to activate or deactivate the cornering light. As this approach leads to a bMSC that captures AL-43 and AL139, the corresponding excerpt from the hMSCs shows only one single MSC reference and is thus not shown here.

4.2   Application of Approach B (NL-GRL-MSC)

Figure 3 shows the part of GRL-model created based on the two natural language requirements presented. The goals are derived from the natural language requirements and the tasks were defined to fulfil the goals. The main softgoal *Use Cornering Light* has been decomposed into one task *Detection of Corner Exit* and two goals concerning when corner lighting can and cannot be activated. The task is then further decomposed in two goals concerning the dimming of the cornering light. Finally, all goals are decomposed into one or two tasks.

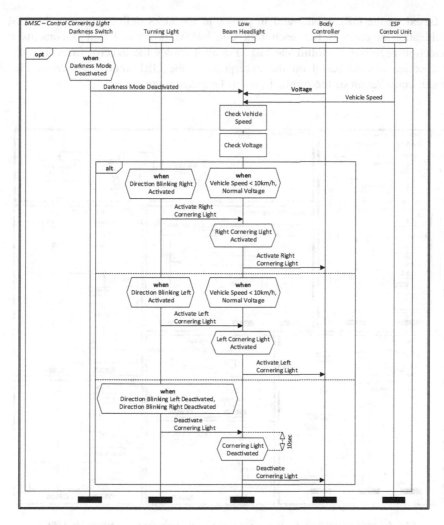

Fig. 2. MSC-specification excerpt created using approach A (NL-MSC)

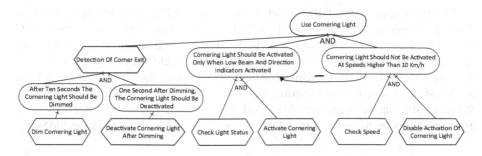

Fig. 3. GRL-model excerpt created using approach B (NL-GRL-MSC)

Based on the GRL-model and in particular the tasks defined therein, the MSC-specification is created. For each task one bMSC is created that documents the interaction necessary to fulfill the task. Figure 4 shows the excerpt from the MSC-specification created based on the excerpt from the GRL model shown in Fig. 3 without consultation of the original natural language requirements.

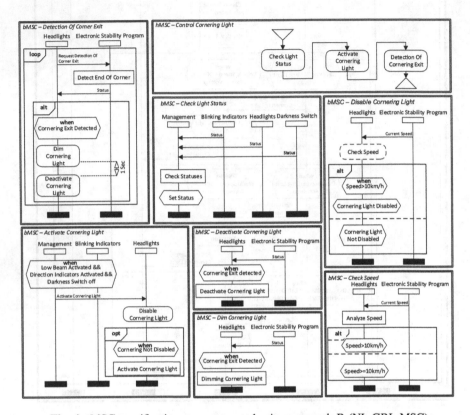

Fig. 4. MSC-specification excerpt created using approach B (NL-GRL-MSC)

For every task in the GRL-model a bMSC is specified. For example, the task *Activate Cornering Light* leads to the bMSC *Activate Cornering Light*, this bMSC starts with a condition, which needs to be fulfilled to continue through the scenario. After that, the bMSC *Disable Cornering Light*, which checks the possibility to activate the cornering light, will be performed. After the creation of the bMSCs for every task, the hMSC for the control of the cornering light is transformed into a structured form. When a bMSC includes another bMSC and the referenced bMSC does not have to be executed anymore, the referenced bMSC do not need to be modeled in the hMSC.

4.3   Application of Approach C (NL-GRL-UCM-MSC)

For approach C the GRL model created by approach B was reused as a basis for the creation of a UCM-specification. Figure 5 shows the excerpt of the UCM created based on the GRL model shown in Fig. 3 without repeated consultation of the original natural language requirements. Three use cases were defined concerning the activation and deactivation of the cornering light *Activate Cornering Light*, *Deactivate Cornering Light* and *Disable Activation of Cornering Light*.

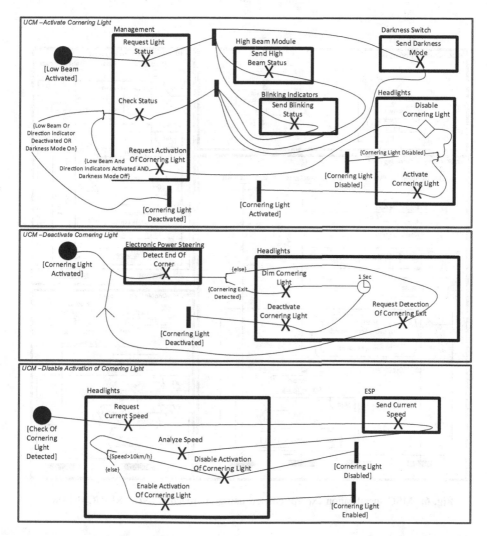

Fig. 5. UCM-specification excerpt created using approach C (NL-GRL-UCM-MSC)

Using approach C based on the UCM-specification the MSC-specification is created using the approach for deriving MSC-specifications from UCM by *Miga et al.* [18]. Figure 6 shows the excerpt from the MSC-specification created based on the excerpt from the UCM model shown in Fig. 5 without consultation of the original natural language requirements nor the GRL model. As can be seen three bMSC and one hMSC are created based on the UCMs. The hMSC includes only two MSC references, because the bMSC *Disable Cornering Light* is referenced in the bMSC *Activate Cornering Light*. This is based on the UCM *Activate Cornering Light*, in which a stub is referenced to the UCM *Disable Cornering Light*.

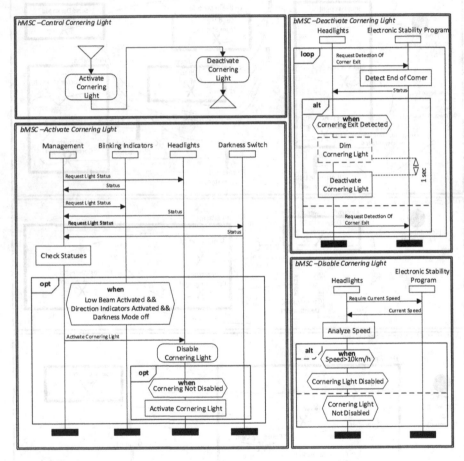

Fig. 6. MSC-specification excerpt created using approach C (NL-GRL-UCM-MSC)

5 Discussion

5.1 Principle Findings

With respect to research question *RQ1* it can be stated that all approaches resulted in a valid MSC-specification. A closer investigation showed that all derived MSC-specifications are consistent and complete, however at different levels of granularity. In this case, completeness refers to the documentation of all relevant aspects of the natural language requirements specification. Nevertheless, there have shown considerable differences with respect to *RQ2*. The resulting MSC-specifications differ with respect to their structural metrics. In particular. we identified differences with respect to (a) the level of detail the MSC-specification describes, (b) the size of the resulting specification, (c) the overall structuring of the hMSC, and (d) the documentation of alternatives. The principle findings based on are briefly summarized in Table 1.

Table 1. Principle findings

	A (NL-MSC)	B (NL-GRL-MSC)	C (NL-GRL-UCM-MSC)
Syntactical quality	No syntactical defects	No syntactical defects	No syntactical defects
Semantical quality	Complete and no further defects	Complete and no further defects	Complete and no further defects
Empirical quality			
Level of detail	High, solution space	Low, problem space	High, problem space
Size	Moderate number of diagrams, large size of single diagrams	High number of diagrams, small size of single diagrams	Low number of diagrams, moderate size of single diagrams
Structure giving elements	hMSC and conditions	hMSC	hMSC
Documentation of alternatives	Related content and alternatives are scattered across different bMSC, connected only via conditions	Related content is divided across bMSCs, but connected by direct flow lines in the hMSC. Alternatives are documented in alternative bMSCs	Closely related content is documented in approximately one bMSC. Minor alternatives are documented in this bMSC, major alternatives in alternative bMSCs

In the following, we discuss these findings in more detail.

Differences in the Level of Details. Compared to the other two approaches the MSC-specification created using approach A (NL-MSC) is more solution oriented. Not only is the system split into various subsystems (e.g., Adaptive High Beam Headlight,

Defect Detection, Instrument Cluster) but also context systems are split into subsystems (e.g., Body Controller, Door Control Unit). Hence, the MSC-specification is used to specify the solution space. In contrast, the specification created using approach B (NL-GRL-MSC) features rather short bMSCs compared to those created using the other two approaches and is rather solution-neutral, specifying the problem space. In particular, the AELS is not considerably divided into its components and, thus, interaction exchange between components is not covered. The specification created using approach C (NL-GRL-UCM) heavily features actions as the approach by [18] requires the definition of an action for each responsibility defined in the use case maps. Like approach B it leads to problem space focused specification. However, the level of details is rather high, i.e. it is differentiated between the components of the AELS and the interactions they need to exchange to fulfill their purpose.

Differences in the Size of the Specifications. We found considerable differences in the sizes of the resulting MSC-specifications. For approach A (NL-MSC) 52 diagrams have been created, thereof 40 bMSC and 12 hMSC diagrams. Approach B (NL-GRL-MSC) resulted in 66 diagrams from which 57 are bMSC and 9 hMSC diagrams. Approach C (NL-GRL-UCM-MSC) resulted in the smallest number of diagrams: 42 diagrams in total, 32 bMSC and 10 hMSC diagrams.

Comparing these numbers, approach A resulted in 23.8% more diagrams than approach C, and approach B in 57.1% more diagrams than in approach C. Considering only bMSCs, approach A resulted in 25.0% more bMSC diagrams than approach C, and approach B resulted in 78.1% more bMSC diagrams.

Regarding the size of the different diagrams, as can be seen by comparison of Figs. 2, 4, and 6, the bMSCs created by approach B are considerably smaller than the others.

Differences in the Structuring of the hMSC. As outlined in Sect. 5.1, approach A (NL-MSC) resulted in a very detailed, solution-oriented MSC-specification. For instance, variables are set in bMSCs that deal with the monitoring of user activity (i.e. use of the pitman arm or the darkness switch), which is quite close to the actual implementation of the AELS. These settings are then referred to in the bMSCs describing the intended behavior of the AELS. Hence, in approach A conditions play an important role for structuring the bMSCs. Another aspect is that approach A makes less often use of structuring alternatives in the hMSC than in the bMSCs. This closely related to the aforementioned finding: In the alternative sections, the current setting of the predefined variables is requested and depending on the outcome different alternatives are executed.

In contrast, the resulting MSC-specification from approach B (NL-GRL-MSC) makes extensive use of hMSC for structuring. This is also reflected in the large number of bMSCs created (see Sect. 5.2). The single bMSCs are extremely short and cover only few messages (which is partly also due to the low level of details, i.e. there is no definition of the detailed interaction taking place between components of the AELS like in approach A. Approach C resulted in a strong hMSC structure linking to bMSCs of moderate size.

Differences in the Documentation of Alternatives. The aforementioned findings also lead to considerable differences when it comes to documenting alternatives. Approach A specifies very fine-grained behavior and therefore is a very close representation of the natural language requirements (i.e. nearly all required functionalities and qualities are documented and the system is defined on a very realistic level) this impacts the documentation of alternatives. Alternatives are scattered across different bMSC diagrams. Due to the extensive use of conditions (to separate monitoring and control activities of the embedded control circuit) these bMSCs are often documented in different branches of the hMSC, which makes it hard to comprehend the overall behavior. In contrast, approaches B and C result in more problem-oriented MSC-specifications, which look more like a typical scenario specified during requirements engineering. However, due to use of numerous small bMSCs in approach B, one scenario is also often divided across multiple diagrams. When it comes to alternatives, approach B heavily relies on the hMSC, i.e. alternatives are documented in bMSCs that follow an alternative path in the hMSC to the bMSCs, which document the original scenario. This allows investigating the alternatives right on the level of the hMSC and saves readers from having to look into the detailed specification of interactions. However, alternatives with very small differences are also documented in separate bMSCs. Approach C documents such small differences in the same bMSC thereby increasing the readability of the overall MSC-specification.

5.2   Threats to Validity

As for all case studies our findings and particular possible conclusions are threatened in their validity. We will briefly discuss the most severe threats remaining.

External Validity. The natural language requirements specification was provided by one industry partner from the automotive domain. While it was not a real specification, due to the need for protection of intellectual property, the specification was carefully designed to be realistic. To ensure this, it was mainly taken from older original specification documents and extended by some properties of newer systems. However, the specification was not a real one. The specification was discussed by different industry partners from different domains (i.e. automotive, avionics, industry automation) and used throughout a joint research project to evaluate different approaches. Hence, we are confident that the case example and the findings from the case example are transferable to the engineering of embedded systems. Nevertheless, we cannot rule out that findings might not be generalizable, which we assume might be particularly true for non-reactive systems, as specifications have been impacted by the idea of control circuits.

Internal Validity. The MSC-specifications have been developed by the authors. Hence, there might be different kinds of researcher bias. While we had no particular interest in having one approach win (as none of these has been proposed by ourselves), it cannot be ruled out that aspects of approaches might have been misunderstood or misinterpreted. In addition, it cannot be ruled out that different modelers applying the approaches come to different MSC-specifications. Furthermore, the resulting MSC-specifications might not be suitable for industry applicability. To avoid this, the resulting specifications have been discussed with industry partners (particularly, with the partner who provided the original requirements). In some cases, we corrected minor aspects in the specifications based on these discussions to better reflect industrial reality.

5.3 Inferences

The direct definition of an MSC-specification on the basis of a natural language requirements document (Approach A) leads to a fine-grained specification of the solution space. For instance, typical system startup routines have been considered during modeling. In these routines measurements are monitored, errors detected, and values measured. In the MSC-specification this has yielded in numerous setting conditions, which were considered later on during system execution. Hence, the direct definition of an MSC-specification can be considered very detailed and realistic, particularly, the specification of the solution space can benefit re-use of the created specification during detailed design. However, closely related contents are distributed across the MSC-specification and are not documented nearby, which is unfortunate from a requirements engineering point of view. Furthermore, as this approach is largely unguided, replicability of results might considerably depend on the modeler.

The definition of the MSC-specification using GRL goal models (Approach B) and GRL goal models and use case maps (Approach C) yielded in a MSC-specification defining the problem space as typically desired in requirements engineering. Comparing these two approaches, the use of use case maps obviously results in more effort needed for creating the MSC-specification. However, this approach is also the most structured and guided, which improves reproducibility and objectivity of produced results. Also, the resulting MSC-specification was beneficial for requirements engineering purposes: High level of detail, but at the same time acceptable complexity of the specification (i.e. low number diagrams at a moderate size of each diagram). Furthermore, closely related content is mostly documented within one bMSC.

Further findings were made through an investigation of syntactical, semantical and empirical quality of the created MSC-specifications. To determine, whether the single approaches are indeed favorable for the different purposes (i.e. approach A for the connection between requirements engineering and detailed design, and approach B for requirements analysis) an investigation of the pragmatic quality is also needed in future work. Pragmatic quality investigates the effect of the model on the user and, therefore, can be investigated using controlled experiments. We intend to use the MSC-specification defined in this paper as input for the experiment materials.

6   Conclusion

MSC-specifications are a vital part of model-based requirements engineering. It is important to understand how best to arrive at such a specification. This is particularly the case, when creating a MSC-based requirements specification from existing natural language requirements. To do so, several approaches exist to create a MSC-specification based on requirements in more or less structured ways. In this paper, we reported on a comparative analysis that compared three MSC-specifications derived by employing three different approaches. We derived the MSC-specification directly from the requirements, by the use of GRL goal models as intermediate model, and by the use of GRL goal models and use case maps as intermediate models. Evaluation of the three MSC-specifications showed that semantical and syntactical quality is comparable: all three approaches lead to defectfree and complete (w.r.t. the natural language requirements specification) MSC-specifications. However, we discovered considerable differences in the empirical quality of the MSC-specifications. Specifications differ in the level of detail and their covering of problem and solution space as well as in size and complexity. Also, the structure giving elements of the MSC-specifications differ as does the way how closely related contents and alternatives are documented. In consequence, the MSC-specifications derived by different approaches seem to be better or worse suited for different purposes. Future work will focus on conducting a controlled experiment to determine pragmatic quality, as this also impacts the models' supportiveness for specific purposes. Furthermore, it is of interest to also investigate the process of creating MSC-specifications more closely, e.g., how long does the creation take, how many iterations are needed, etc.

Acknowledgements. This research has been partly funded by the German Federal Ministry of Education and **Research** under grants no. 01IS16043 V and 01IS15058C. We thank Frank Houdek (Daimler) and our former colleague Felix Föcker (Aldi Süd) for their support during the development of the MSC-specifications.

References

1. Weber, M., Weisbrod, J.: Requirements engineering in automotive development-experiences and challenges. In: Proceedings of the IEEE Joint International Conference on Requirements Engineering, pp. 331–340 (2002)
2. Sutcliffe, A.G., Maiden, N.A.M., Minocha, S., Manuel, D.: Supporting scenario-based requirements engineering. IEEE Trans. Softw. Eng. **24**, 1072–1088 (1998)
3. Zhu, H., Jin, L., Diaper, D., Bai, G.: Software requirements validation via task analysis. J. Syst. Softw. **61**, 145–169 (2002)
4. Kof, L.: From textual scenarios to message sequence charts: inclusion of condition generation and actor extraction. In: 16th IEEE International Requirements Engineering Conference, pp. 331–332 (2008)
5. Osborne, M., MacNish, C.K.: Processing natural language software requirement specifications. In: Proceedings of the Second International Conference on Requirements Engineering, pp. 229–236 (1996)
6. Ali, A., Jawawi, D.N.A., Isa, M.A., Ibrahim, A.O.: Deriving behavioural models of component-based software systems from requirements specifications. In: International Conference on Computing, Control, Networking, Electronics and Embedded Systems Engineering (ICCNEEE), pp. 260–265 (2015)
7. Runeson, P., Host, M., Rainer, A., Regnell, B.: Case Study Research in Software Engineering: Guidelines and Examples. Wiley Publishing, Hoboken (2012)
8. Liu, L., Yu, E.: Designing information systems in social context: a goal and scenario modelling approach. Inf. Syst. **29**, 187–203 (2004)

9. Kim, J., Kim, M., Yang, H., Park, S.: A method and tool support for variant requirements analysis: goal and scenario based approach. In: 11th Asia-Pacific Software Engineering Conference, pp. 168–175 (2004)
10. Kim, M., Park, S., Sugumaran, V., Yang, H.: Managing requirements conflicts in software product lines: a goal and scenario based approach. Data Knowl. Eng. **61**, 417–432 (2007)
11. Rolland, C., Grosz, G., Kla, R.: Experience with goal-scenario coupling in requirements engineering. In: Proceedings IEEE International Symposium on Requirements Engineering (Cat. No. PR00188), pp. 74–81 (1999)
12. Rolland, C., Salinesi, C.: Supporting requirements elicitation through goal/scenario coupling. In: Borgida, A.T., Chaudhri, V.K., Giorgini, P., Yu, E.S. (eds.) Conceptual Modeling: Foundations and Applications. LNCS, vol. 5600, pp. 398–416. Springer, Heidelberg (2009). https://doi.org/10.1007/978-3-642-02463-4_21
13. Pohl, K., Haumer, P.: Modelling contextual information about scenarios. In: Proceedings of the Third International Workshop on Requirements Engineering: Foundations of Software Quality REFSQ 1997, pp. 187–204 (1997)
14. Yu, E.S.K., Mylopoulos, J.: Why goal-oriented requirements engineering. In: Proceedings of the 4th International Workshop on Requirements Engineering: Foundation for Software Quality, REFSQ 1998, Pisa, Italy, 8–9 June 1998, pp. 15–22 (1998)
15. Kof, L.: Requirements Analysis: concept extraction and translation of textual specifications to executable models. In: Horacek, H., Métais, E., Muñoz, R., Wolska, M. (eds.) NLDB 2009. LNCS, vol. 5723, pp. 79–90. Springer, Heidelberg (2010). https://doi.org/10.1007/978-3-642-12550-8_7
16. Cunning, S.J., Rozenbiit, J.W.: Test scenario generation from a structured requirements specification. In: Presented at the Proceedings-ECBS, IEEE Conference and Workshop on Engineering of Computer-Based Systems, pp. 166–172 (1999)
17. Sindre, G., Opdahl, A.L.: Eliciting security requirements with misuse cases. Requir. Eng. **10**, 34–44 (2005)
18. Miga, Andrew, Amyot, Daniel, Bordeleau, Francis, Cameron, Donald, Woodside, Murray: Deriving Message Sequence Charts from Use Case Maps Scenario Specifications. In: Reed, Rick, Reed, Jeanne (eds.) SDL 2001. LNCS, vol. 2078, pp. 268–287. Springer, Heidelberg (2001). https://doi.org/10.1007/3-540-48213-X_17
19. Sikora, E., Tenbergen, B., Pohl, K.: Industry needs and research directions in requirements engineering for embedded systems. Requir. Eng. **17**, 57–78 (2012)
20. International Telecommunication Union: Recommendation Z.151 (10/12), User Requirements Notation (URN) Language Definition
21. International Telecommunication Union: Recommendation Z.120 (02/11), Message Sequence Chart (MSC)
22. Palshikar, G.K., Bhaduri, P.: Verification of scenario-based specifications using templates. Electron. Notes Theor. Comput. Sci. **118**, 37–55 (2005)
23. Daun, M., Weyer, T., Pohl, K.: Detecting and correcting outdated requirements in function-centered engineering of embedded systems. In: Fricker, S.A., Schneider, K. (eds.) REFSQ 2015. LNCS, vol. 9013, pp. 65–80. Springer, Cham (2015). https://doi.org/10.1007/978-3-319-16101-3_5
24. Daun, M., Brings, J., Weyer, T.: On the impact of the model-based representation of inconsistencies to manual reviews. In: Mayr, H.C., Guizzardi, G., Ma, H., Pastor, O. (eds.) ER 2017. LNCS, vol. 10650, pp. 466–473. Springer, Cham (2017). https://doi.org/10.1007/978-3-319-69904-2_35
25. Tang, W., Ning, B., Xu, T., Zhao, L.: Scenario-based modeling and verification of system requirement specification for the European Train Control System, pp. 759–770. Presented at the, WIT Transactions on the Built Environment (2010)

26. Kaindl, H.: A scenario-based approach for requirements engineering: experience in a telecommunication software development project. Syst. Eng. **8**, 197–210 (2005)
27. Rolland, C., Souveyet, C., Achour, C.B.: Guiding goal modeling using scenarios. IEEE Trans. Softw. Eng. **24**, 1055–1071 (1998)
28. Antón, Annie I., McCracken, W.Michael, Potts, Colin: Goal decomposition and scenario analysis in business process reengineering. In: Wijers, Gerard, Brinkkemper, Sjaak, Wasserman, Tony (eds.) CAiSE 1994. LNCS, vol. 811, pp. 94–104. Springer, Heidelberg (1994). https://doi.org/10.1007/3-540-58113-8_164
29. Liu, L., Yu, E.: From requirements to architectural design using goals and scenarios. In: Proceedings of the International Workshop from Software Requirements to Architectures (STRAW), Toronto (2001)
30. Broy, M.: Seamless method- and model-based software and systems engineering. In: The Future of Software Engineering (2010)
31. Krogstie, J., Sindre, G., Jørgensen, H.: Process models representing knowledge for action: a revised quality framework. Eur. J. Inf. Syst. **15**, 91–102 (2006)
32. Keller, K., Neubauer, A., Brings, J., Daun, M.: Tool-Support to foster model-based requirements engineering for cyber-phsyical systems. In: Joint Proceedings of the Workshops at Modellierung co-located with Modellierung , Braunschweig, Germany, 21 Feb 2018, pp. 47–56 (2018)
33. Sánchez-González, L., García, F., Mendling, J., Ruiz, F., Piattini, M.: Prediction of business process model quality based on structural metrics. In: Parsons, J., Saeki, M., Shoval, P., Woo, C., Wand, Y. (eds.) ER 2010. LNCS, vol. 6412, pp. 458–463. Springer, Heidelberg (2010). https://doi.org/10.1007/978-3-642-16373-9_35
34. Houdek, F.: System Requirements Specification Automotive System Cluster (ELC and ACC). Technical Report SyS-LH C34-223 (2013)

Towards Online Collaborative Multi-view Modelling

Nirmal Kanagasabai[1]($\boxtimes$), Omar Alam[2], and Jörg Kienzle[1]

[1] School of Computer Science, McGill University, Montreal, QC, Canada
nirmal.kanagasabai@mail.mcgill.ca, joerg.kienzle@mcgill.ca
[2] Department of Computing and Information Systems, Trent University,
Oshawa, ON, Canada
omaralam@trentu.ca

Abstract. Increasingly, distributed software development teams rely on *online* collaboration tools to work together in real time. Collaborative textual editors are intuitive, since the position of the cursor and the currently selected text, if any, tell other collaborators what part of the text/code a developer is currently focusing on or editing. Model-Driven Engineering (MDE) advocates using models as the primary development artifacts, and to be most effective, the system is described at different levels of abstraction from multiple points of view. This poses additional challenges for online collaboration, as the current focus of the developer and the scope of his changes are often less clear, in particular when the modelling language(s) and views use graphics or have hierarchical or other kinds of dependencies. This paper proposes two algorithms that exploit the metamodels of the involved modelling languages to visualize a collaborator's change in a multi-view modelling environment. The first algorithm determines the most concise way to highlight the elements that are impacted by a change made by a remote developer in the current views of the local developer. The second algorithm delays the deletion of a model element as long as that element is still being referred to from a different view, and notifies the impacted developers, offering them a chance to collaboratively discuss the deletion or undo the deletion if desired. The proposed algorithms are evaluated by applying them on the Reusable Aspect Models (RAM) metamodel.

Keywords: MDE · Online collaboration · Multi-view modelling
Graphical user interface

1 Introduction

MDE advocates software development with models expressed in the right modelling formalism that is suitable for the task at hand. Therefore, an MDE project can involve modellers with a diverse set of expertise who collaborate with each other to produce a complete and coherent system [9] using multiple views and modelling notations. Furthermore, in a complex system, models can quickly grow

ⓒ Springer Nature Switzerland AG 2018
F. Khendek and R. Gotzhein (Eds.): SAM 2018, LNCS 11150, pp. 202–218, 2018.
https://doi.org/10.1007/978-3-030-01042-3_12

in size, deeming the efforts of a single modeller insufficient to maintain and evolve the system. In such projects, collaboration is not an option but a necessity to cope with the growing size of models. As in any collaborative project, modellers need to receive updates about each others' activities. In some cases, real-time (online) updates are necessary, while in other cases, (offline) post-modification updates are sufficient. Online and offline updates can reduce modelling time, duplication of efforts, and inconsistencies between models. However, support for collaboration in modelling tools is limited. Though some modelling environments e.g., GenMyModel [3], AtomPM [24], MetaEdit+ [13], Visual Paradigm [5] provide complex collaboration capabilities, there is a lack of tools that allow different modelling languages to support *online* collaboration.

There are different ways to support online collaboration. While on one hand pessimistic, lock-based approaches guarantee that no editing conflicts or wasted work occur among distributed collaborators, the efficiency of a local developer can be drastically reduced due to locks being held by remote collaborators. Optimistic approaches allow all collaborators to make changes as they please and are far more streamlined, but work only when each local collaborator is sufficiently aware of the current focus of the remote collaborators to avoid potential conflicts. Modern collaborative textual editors like Google Docs and Microsoft Office are based on optimistic collaboration rather than the pessimistic locking approach. In these textual editors, the knowledge of the position of the cursor and/or the currently selected text of the remote collaborators allow the local collaborator to edit the text efficiently without inadvertently undoing the work of remote collaborators.

In MDE, the current focus of a modeller and the scope of his changes are often less clear, in particular when the modelling language(s) and views use graphics or have hierarchical or other kinds of dependencies. This paper proposes two algorithms that allow modellers to streamline online collaboration in multi-view modelling environments. When a model element is changed (created or modified) by a remote collaborator, our first algorithm finds the elements in the current view of the local collaborator that are directly or indirectly impacted by the remote change and highlights them. As a result, the local collaborator is made aware of any relevant changes made by remote collaborators as they are editing the model, and can hence keep track of their current focus. Our second algorithm ensures that model element deletions made by one collaborator do not irreversibly invalidate the work of other collaborators. In essence, the algorithm marks the element as being deleted but effectively delays the deletion until the element is not being referred to anymore from other views.

The remainder of the paper is structured as follows. Section 2 presents background information on collaborative modelling, online vs. offline collaboration, as well as inter-model consistency in multi-view modelling environments. Section 3 describes the challenges that are present in online collaborative multi-view modelling environments. Section 4 elucidates our algorithm that communicates the current focus and intent of a collaborator to other online collaborators. Section 5 explains how we propose to handle highly disruptive deletion operations in a collaborative multi-view setting. Section 6 presents some technical details about our prototype implementation in the context of the TouchCORE tool [22] and presents an evaluation of the effectiveness of the two algorithms on the Reusable Aspect Models (RAM) [15] multi-view modelling formalism. Section 7 discusses the related work, and the last section draws some conclusions.

2 Background

2.1 Online vs. Offline Collaboration

Software development is no longer an individual endeavor. Developers work in teams to collaboratively achieve their project goals. Recently, there have been advances in collaboration tools in software development, such as version control systems (e.g., Git), collaborative editors, and collaborative communication channels (e.g. Slack). Some of these tools focus on *offline collaboration*, e.g., Git. In offline collaboration, developers do not receive real-time updates on each others' activities. Usually, developers collaborate offline after they divide the responsibilities and tasks among themselves. Developers work individually and then merge their changes with the project. Typically, one or several members are responsible for merging the changes and organizing the development branches.

Other tools focus on *online collaboration*, in which the local developer is notified about changes made by remote collaborators in real-time. Collaborative editing tools, e.g. GoogleDocs, Overleaf, or Microsoft Office, intuitively allow for online collaboration by visualizing the positioning of the cursors of the remote collaborators, or by highlighting the text that the remote collaborators have selected or are editing. Other online collaboration tools allow for exchanging messages between developers using a chatbox or sending a sound notification when a collaborator does an activity.

Despite these advances, support for collaboration is limited in the context of MDE. Most modelling tools are single-user and do not support offline or online collaboration [12]. Recently, some modelling tools have emerged that support collaboration. They are discussed in more detail in Sect. 7.

2.2 Pessimistic vs. Optimistic Concurrency Control

In online collaboration, several modellers may concurrently edit a model element, potentially overriding each others' changes or causing conflicts. Some form of concurrency control is needed to either prevent or address conflicts. There are in general two concurrency control strategies, *pessimistic* and *optimistic*. Pessimistic concurrency control serializes the model access, thereby permitting only one modeller to have control over a model element at a given time. The pessimistic approach requires the modeller to request permission to edit a specific model element in advance, typically by acquiring an explicit lock on the element. As models tend to be hierarchical, this approach does not only lock the element being edited, but also the entire containment tree rooted at this element. This approach limits potential concurrency but prevents conflicts from occurring, and hence its main advantage is data integrity.

While the pessimistic approach is useful in situations where there is competition, the assumption in collaborative online modelling is that the different collaborators cooperate to achieve a common goal. Each individual local collaborator is interested in building on the work done by the other remote collaborators as opposed to consciously or inadvertently negate their work. The optimistic approach allows free concurrent access to model elements, and only in case of conflicting updates, actions are required to restore the model to a consistent state. Contemporary real-time collaborative editing tools like Google Apps (Docs, Sheets, Slides, etc.) and Microsoft Office have chosen such an optimistic approach since it allows for closer and more streamlined collaboration. Collaborators are continuously updated about the editing positions and changes made by remote collaborators, which helps them avoid conflicts. In the rare cases where conflict occurs, typically the most recent update overrides the previous one.

3   Online Collaborative Multi-view Modelling Challenges

3.1   Multi-view Collaboration and Running Example

The collaborative platform that this work focuses on is distributed, multi-user and multi-view. Typically, real-time collaboration happens when more than one user is connected online at a given time. From a user's perspective, there is a local user (himself) and one or more remote collaborators who are concurrently editing the same model. The view that the local user is currently looking at is the *active view* of that particular collaborator.

Multi-view, as the name states, allows users to work on distinct views of the same model. The views can either be *orthogonal* (having no elements in common) or *complementary* (presenting the same or overlapping sets of elements). In order to allow the local collaborators to be aware of what the remote collaborators are working on, any remote editing operations that are in progress, or changes made on the underlying model in any of the views should be perceived by all the collaborators. This can be a challenge since not all elements of the underlying model are visualized in all the views.

Another challenging situation occurs when one of the collaborators decides to delete a model element. That model element could still be currently used by a remote collaborator, i.e., referred to by model elements in other views. This can lead to inconsistencies. In a hierarchical modelling language, the deletion of one model element can even lead to further deletions of the contained model elements, which increases the potential for inconsistencies across views.

Figure 1 illustrates a multi-view modelling example where four collaborators are working on a design model of a banking application. Collaborator C_1 is currently working in the structural view, which consists of a design class diagram. Collaborators C_2, C_3 and C_4 are working on three distinct message views, which are sequence diagrams that specify the behaviour of three different operations of the design. We look at a specific case as to how C_1's current action impacts other collaborators. Currently, C_1 is changing the data type of the parameter *interestRate* from *int* to *double*. The data type is *currently being changed*, i.e., C_1 has selected the *int* text and started typing, or double-clicked on the *int* text and is now choosing a new type from a popup menu. The model element has therefore not been changed yet. Hence, for other collaborators, the type is still visualized as *int* and not *double*.

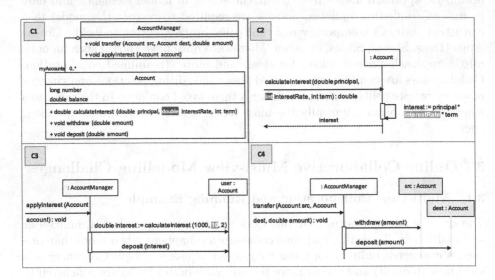

Fig. 1. Collaborative software design modelling example (Color figure online)

3.2   Minimizing Editing Conflicts

Without concurrency control, it is possible that different developers concurrently perform operations that are incompatible, unintentionally causing conflicts or accidentally overriding changes made by others. A natural way of minimizing the occurrence of such situations is to ensure that every collaborator is aware of what the other collaborators are currently working on. While in text editors, the location of the cursor provides a good indication of the current focus of a collaborator, the situation is far more complex in MDE, where many modelling notations are of graphical nature. Hierarchical modelling languages or modelling approaches where systems are developed using multiple views complicate the situation even further. While in single view approaches it would be possible to highlight with different colours the changes made by remote collaborators as they are being made, it is possible that in a multi-view approach, a model element being edited by a remote collaborator in one view is not visualized in the view that the local collaborator is currently looking at. Although the model element that is being edited remotely is not visualized in the local view, the change could have an effect on the task that the local collaborator is working on. For example, in Fig. 1, C_1 changes the type of the parameter *interestRate* from *int* to *double*. In this case, collaborator C_3 might want to adjust the actual value used in the call of the *calculateInterest* operation, e.g., from 10 to 10.2.

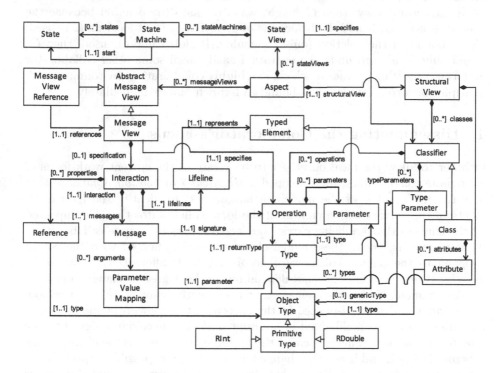

Fig. 2. Excerpt of the RAM metamodel

3.3 Global vs. Local Undo Stack

Most editors provide a useful *undo* functionality that makes it possible to revert the last performed editing action. Unfortunately, providing useful *undo* is challenging in an online collaborative setting. In online collaboration, when two collaborators C_1 and C_2 work in real-time on the same model, the outcome of any performed operation is immediately visible to both C_1 and C_2.

When a collaborator hits the undo button, he may want to revert back to the last change carried out by him (in his view). It is also possible that he wants to undo a change made by a remote collaborator that he disagrees with. To support the first case, a *local* undo strategy must keep track of a local stack of changes for each collaborator, and revert back to the most recent change in that stack. To support the second case, a *global* undo strategy would keep one single global stack, and revert back to the most recent change performed by any collaborator. Both strategies have their shortcomings. With local undo, C_1 cannot undo a change made by a remote C_2. With global undo, C_1 might think he will undo a previous change made by C_2, but actually, a change made by C_3 that happened after the change of C_2 (but possibly in a different view) is undone. For example, in Fig. 1, if C_1 deletes the operation *calculateInterest* in the structural view, then C_3 might want to undo the deletion because the operation is called inside the behaviour of *applyInterest*. If local undo is used, C_3 cannot undo the deletion (only C_1 could). If global undo is used, then C_3 would only be able to undo the operation easily until some other collaborator performs an editing operation, which, in a highly collaborative environment with multiple concurrent modellers is bound to happen almost immediately.

4   Disseminating the Collaborator's Focus

In order to allow the local developer to be aware of the current work focus of his remote collaborators, we developed a *Highlight Propagation Algorithm* that uses the metamodels of the modelling language(s) to identify the model elements in the current active view(s) of the local collaborator that are impacted by the changes that are being carried out across views by remote collaborators. After identifying them, these model elements are highlighted with the colour assigned to the remote collaborator according to 3 different intensity levels, namely, *strong*, *medium* and *light* depending on the degree of change impact.

For example, if *ce* is the element that is currently being edited by a remote collaborator and *ce* is visualized in the current active view(s) of the local collaborator, then *ce* is highlighted in a *strong* shade of the colour assigned to the remote collaborator. This is because the highlighted element is the element that is being changed, and hence the change has the strongest possible impact. If the active view does not visualize *ce*, but displays model elements that directly or indirectly refer to *ce*, they are highlighted with *medium* intensity. The impact, in this case, is relatively lower than the previous case. If neither *ce* nor any model element referring directly or indirectly to *ce* is visualized in the current active view(s), then the algorithm checks whether the current active view(s) display any of the containers of *ce*, or model elements referring to the containers of *ce* and highlights them with a *light* tint. The only situation in which the algorithm will not find anything to highlight is when the current active view(s) are completely orthogonal to *ce*, i.e., any change to *ce* has no impact whatsoever on the current focus of the local collaborator.

Our algorithm is based on the metamodel(s) of the modelling language(s) and exploits the containment hierarchy information as well as the references between model elements that are not within the same containment hierarchy. The pseudocode of the *Highlight Propagation* algorithm that runs locally and independently on the machine of each collaborator is given in Algorithm 1. It uses the following definitions:

$ce :=$ The model element that is being edited by a remote collaborator
$\delta_{ce}^- :=$ Set of model elements that x has references to
$activeView :=$ Current active view of the local collaborator
$GUI_{ce,activeView} :=$ Set of GUI elements that represent ce in $activeView$
$collab_{ce} :=$ Remote collaborator who is currently editing the element ce

The algorithm takes as a parameter the model element ce that is being edited remotely and by whom it is being edited. Lines 3 to 9 handle the case where the element is directly visualized in the current active view. In that case, the element itself is highlighted in *strong* shade, as well as any elements in the current active view that refer directly to the element that is being edited in *medium* intensity. Line 11 invokes the *SearchAcrossViews* function, which uses breadth-first-search to follow incoming references to the element that is being edited until it finds an element that directly or indirectly references the element that is being visualized in the current active view and highlights it with *medium* intensity. Only if this is unsuccessful, then lines 12 to 20 successively try to find elements that are visualized in the current active view that either directly represent or refer to any of the model elements that contain the element being edited.

4.1   Highlighting in the Motivating Example

In the example shown in Fig. 1, C_1, assigned the colour *blue*, is currently changing the type of the parameter *interestRate* of the *calculateInterest* operation of the *Account* class from *int* to *double* in the class diagram view. Looking at the metamodel in Fig. 2, it is the `type` property of *interestRate*, which is an instance of the metaclass **Parameter**, that is being edited. Meanwhile, C_2 is working on the message view of the operation *calculateInterest*. The type of the parameter *interestRate* is also visualized in this view, and is therefore highlighted by our algorithm in *strong blue* to let C_2 know that C_1 is modifying the *int* type of parameter *interestRate* directly. C_3 is in the meantime working on the message view of the operation *applyInterest*, which calls the operation *calculateInterest*, passing 10 as a value to the *interestRate* parameter.

According to the metamodel, this parameter passing requires a *Parameter-ValueMapping*, which in turn holds a reference to the *interestRate* parameter. When our algorithm runs on the machine of C_3, the number 10 will be highlighted in *medium blue*, indicating a less strong potential impact of C_1's change. Finally, C_4 is working on the message view of the operation *transfer*. There is no direct impact of C_1's change to this view – the *interestRate* parameter is not visualized. Also, there is no element that indirectly references the *interestRate* parameter. Therefore, the algorithm looks up the containment hierarchy, and checks whether the operation that contains the changed element, i.e., *calculateInterest* (*Parameter* is contained by *Operation* in Fig. 2), is being directly or indirectly visualized in the view of C_4. As this is still not the case, the algorithm goes further up the containment hierarchy and then checks whether the class *Account* is visualized directly or indirectly in the active view. There are two lifelines, *source* and *destination*, which both are of type *Account*, i.e., in the model, there is a

---

Algorithm 1 Highlight Propagation

1: **procedure** HIGHLIGHTPROPAGATION($ce, collab_{ce}$)
2:      $colour_{strong}, colour_{medium}, colour_{light} \leftarrow$ GETCOLOURSOFCOLLABORATOR($collab_{ce}$)
3:      **if** $GUI_{ce,activeView} \neq \emptyset$ **then**
4:          HIGHLIGHT($ce, colour_{strong}$)
5:          **for each** $re \in \delta_{ce}^{-}$ **do**
6:              **for each** $g \in GUI_{re,activeView}$ **do**
7:                  HIGHLIGHT($re, colour_{medium}$)
8:              **end for**
9:          **end for**
10:     **else**
11:         **if** SEARCHACROSSVIEWS($ce, colour_{medium}$) **then**
12:             $curEl$: ModelElement $\leftarrow$ GETPARENT(ce)
13:             **while** $curEl \neq$ ROOTELEMENT **do**
14:                 **if** $GUI_{curEl,activeView} \neq \emptyset$ **then**
15:                     HIGHLIGHT($curEl, colour_{light}$)
16:                 **else if** SEARCHACROSSVIEWS($curEl, colour_{light}$) **then**
17:                     **return**
18:                 **end if**
19:                 $curEl \leftarrow$ GETPARENT($curEl$)
20:             **end while**
21:         **end if**
22:     **end if**
23: **end procedure**
24:
25: **procedure** SEARCHACROSSVIEWS($me, colour$)
26:     Q: queue of model elements $\leftarrow \emptyset$
27:     $found$: boolean $\leftarrow false$
28:     Q.ENQUEUE(me)
29:     me.MARKASVISITED
30:     **while** $Q \neq \emptyset \wedge \neg found$ **do**
31:         m = Q.DEQUEUE()
32:         **for each** $re \in \delta_{m}^{-}$ **do**
33:             **if** $\neg re$.VISITED **then**
34:                 re.MARKASVISITED
35:                 **if** $GUI_{re,activeView} \neq \emptyset$ **then**
36:                     HIGHLIGHT($re, colour$)
37:                     $found \leftarrow true$
38:                 **else**
39:                     Q.ENQUEUE(re)
40:                 **end if**
41:             **end if**
42:         **end for**
43:     **end while**
44:     **return** $found$
45: **end procedure**

---

reference to the class *Account*. Therefore, the two lifelines are highlighted in *light blue*, indicating that the impact of the change of C_1 on the two lifelines is low.

5 Dealing with Model Element Deletion

In hierarchical and multi-view modelling environments, some model changes can have a significant impact throughout the model. In particular, the deletion of a model element can trigger a *cascading delete* because of containment relationships, or inter-view consistency rules. *Cascading delete* refers to the situation in which the deletion of a model element requires the deletion of other related model elements. For example, deleting the *Account* class in Fig. 1 in turn deletes the *number* and *balance* attributes that the class contains, as well as the *calculateInterest*, *withdraw* and *deposit* operations.

Single-user environments typically provide an *undo* command to address the case where a modeller has inadvertently caused a cascading delete. Unfortunately, *undo* is not very user-friendly in a multi-user setting. As previously explained in Sect. 3.3, neither a local undo stack nor a global undo stack can resolve all situations in a satisfying way. To deal with cascading deletes, we introduce the *Delayed Deletion Algorithm* outlined in Algorithm 2.

de := the element that is to be deleted

δ_{me}^- := Set of model elements that contain a reference to me where removing the reference would violate a lower-bound constraint

C_{de} := Set of elements that are directly or indirectly contained in de

The algorithm relies on a new boolean flag *isDeleted* that is introduced to all the model elements, e.g., by adding it to the metamodel. If a model element de is requested to be deleted, the algorithm checks whether de is being referenced by any other model element. The same check is performed on every element me that is directly or indirectly contained in the model element de. If no reference is found, a standard deletion is performed on de and every me contained in de. However, if even just a single reference is found, no model elements are deleted. Instead, de and every me contained in de are simply marked as deleted by setting the boolean attribute *isDeleted*. The model editor's GUI should treat any model element marked as deleted as though it was actually removed from the model, e.g., by notifying the local collaborator about any now inconsistent references to these model elements. If a collaborator does not agree with the deletion, the GUI should offer the possibility to undelete the elements (by unsetting the *isDeleted* flag.

6 Evaluation

6.1 Prototype Implementation

To evaluate our algorithms, we extended TouchCORE [22], a multi-touch enabled tool for agile software design modelling, with collaboration capabilities. Currently, TouchCORE supports Feature and Goal Models, as well as Class, State

---

Algorithm 2 Delayed Deletion

```
 1: procedure DELAYEDDELETION(de)
 2:     if (δ⁻_de ≠ ∅) then
 3:         DODELAYEDDELETION(de)
 4:     else
 5:         for each (me ∈ C_de) do
 6:             if (δ⁻_me ≠ ∅) then
 7:                 DODELAYEDDELETION(de)
 8:                 return
 9:             end if
10:         end for
11:         DELETE(DE)
12:         for each (me ∈ C_de) do
13:             DELETE(ME)
14:         end for
15:     end if
16: end procedure
17:
18: procedure DODELAYEDDELETION(de)
19:     DE.SETBOOLEANISDELETED
20:     for each (me ∈ C_de) do
21:         ME.SETBOOLEANISDELETED
22:     end for
23: end procedure
```

---

and Sequence Diagrams. For our Multi-View modelling experiments, we focus on the three design views: Structural Views (that visualize class diagrams), Message Views (that visualize sequence diagrams) and State Views (that visualize state diagrams). The structure of these views is described in the Reusable Aspect Models (RAM) metamodel [14].

To enable collaboration, TouchCORE was integrated with Connected Data Objects (CDO), a distributed, shared model repository that persists models in a database. Both CDO and TouchCORE are compatible with the Eclipse Modelling Framework (EMF) [23]. In our prototype, each instance of TouchCORE can establish a session to connect to the shared CDO model repository. All those instances that are connected to the same repository and have loaded the same model element collaborate with one another. Short CDO transactions are used to manipulate the shared models, and EMF notifications are fired from the CDO model repository to ensure that the local model changes whenever it has been updated by a remote collaborator. Despite the fact that CDO offers explicit locks that would make it possible to avoid conflicts or wasted efforts due to concurrent modifications, we decided not to lock any model elements to streamline the collaboration in accordance with the current trends in collaborative environments presented in Sect. 2. The highlighting and deletion algorithms mentioned above implemented in TouchCORE and are in the coming subsection evaluated by applying them on the Reusable Aspect Models (RAM) metamodel.

6.2   Highlight Algorithm Evaluation

As discussed above, the main goal of highlighting model elements is to provide the local collaborator with a sense of what the remote collaborators are currently working on. Concretely, this means that our highlighting algorithm is effective if, when seeing a highlighted model element, the local collaborator knows what the remote collaborator is currently working on and whether or not it interacts with his task. To answer this question, we evaluated how accurately a local user can determine what model element a remote user is editing when a model element is highlighted in his local view.

To this aim, we inspected the TouchCORE GUI for the structural view (class diagram), message view (sequence diagram) and state view (state diagram) editors, and identified a set V of 51 model elements and model element properties from the RAM metamodel (see Fig. 2) that are visualized in at least one of the editors. We then ran our highlight propagation algorithm in reverse on those elements. In other words, given a visualized, highlighted element $e_h \in V$ and a highlighting intensity level – *strong*, *medium* or *light*, we determined the potential elements e_c that could have been edited by the remote collaborator that would cause this highlighting. If there is only one possible element that could have caused the highlighting, then an experienced local collaborator will be able to determine the remote collaborator's focus. Only in cases where more than one possible element can be the cause, the local collaborator cannot determine with certainty what the remote collaborator is working on.

Evaluation Results. It is obvious that if e_h is highlighted in *strong* colour, the only model element that could have been edited remotely that would cause such a highlighting is the element e_h itself. Hence, the local collaborator knows immediately and unambiguously what element is currently being modified and by whom.

For an element e_h to be highlighted in *medium*, it must directly or indirectly refer to some other element. Out of the 51 elements in V, only 24 refer to other elements in the metamodel. Out of these 24, 9 have only one direct outgoing reference, and no indirect references. For these 9 elements, there is therefore a unique model element or property that causes the highlighting. So in the end, only 15 elements have more than one possible cause when being highlighted in *medium*. They are listed in Table 1[1]. 1 highlighted element has *two* potential causes, 6 highlighted elements have *four* potential causes, 6 of them have *six* potential causes and the remaining 2 have *seven or more*.

While this sounds like much, many of the potential causes are knowledge-wise equivalent. A careful inspection of the list reveals that for 6 of them, the

---

[1] The abbreviations used are ORT: Operation Return Type, TP: Type Parameter, IC: Implementation Class, PaT: Parameter Type, AT: Attribute Type, Vis.: Visibility, AE: Association End, RT: Reference Type, MS: Message Signature, RL: Enum Literal, PVM: Parameter Value Mapping, SM: State Machine, TET: Typed Element Type, AS AsTo: Assignment Statement Assign To, CF: Combined Fragment, InCon: Interaction Constraint, MR: Message Returns.

multiple causing elements are close to equivalent considering that the goal is to discover the editing focus of the remote collaborator. For example, when a State is highlighted in *medium* there are *two* potential causes, namely that an incoming or outgoing transition was modified in a different view, or that the signature of the transition was modified. Both cases allow the local collaborator to conclude that the remote collaborator is working on a transition related to the state that was highlighted. The 6 cases that have 4 potential causes also communicate equivalent knowledge to the local collaborator. For example, when the attribute type (AT) is highlighted in *medium*, the remote collaborator must be changing properties of the type definition, e.g., adding a new Enum Literal to a user-defined Enum type. So in the end, out of 51 elements, 36, i.e., *70.58%*, are unambiguous. If knowledge-equivalence is taken into account, only the last 5 elements in Table 1 are actually ambiguous, which increases the unambiguity to 90%.

Table 1. Sample elements highlighted in medium colour

e_h	Elements e_c that could cause *medium* highlighting
State	Transition, Transition signature
IC	RL, Enum, Class, IC
AT	Enum, Class, IC ← RL
GenericType	Enum, Class, IC ← RL
RT	Enum, Class, IC ← RL
ORT	Enum, Class, IC ← RL
PaT	Enum, Class, IC ← RL
MR	AT, PaT ← Enum, Class, IC ← RL
AS value	AT, PaT ← Enum, Class, IC ← RL
InCon	AT, PaT ← Enum, Class, IC ← RL
PVM	Parameter, PaT ← Enum, Class, IC ← RL
MS	Operation Vis, ORT ← Enum, Class, IC ← RL
AS AsTo	AE, AT ← Enum, Class, IC ← RL
Message	Operation Vis, AE, AT, ORT ← Enum, Class, IC ← RL
Lifeline	AE, PaT, AT ← Enum, Class, IC ← RL

We repeated the same analysis for the *light* highlighting. Among the 51 elements in $\mathcal{V}$, only 20 contain other elements and hence could potentially be highlighted in *light*. Out of the 20 cases, 10 of them had a unique cause, 2 of them had *three* possible causes, 1 had *five* possible causes and 7 of them had *six or more* possible causes. The 10 ambiguous cases are listed in Table 2. So in the end, out of 51 elements, 41 cases, i.e. *80.39%*, are unambiguous.

Table 2. Sample elements highlighted in light colour

e_h	Elements e_c that could cause *light* highlighting
ORT	Attribute, Operation, Parameter, TP, AE, RL
PaT	Attribute, Operation, Parameter, TP, AE, RL
IC	Attribute, Operation, Parameter, TP, AE, RL
TP	Attribute, Operation, Parameter, TP, AE, RL
RT	Attribute, Operation, Parameter, TP, AE, RL
Lifeline	Attribute, Operation, Parameter, TP, AE, RL
CF	Interaction Operand, Attribute, Operation, Parameter, TP, AE, RL
Message	Temporary Property, PVM, VS
Transition	Constraint, VS, Parameter
SM	Transition, State, Substitution, Constraint, VS

6.3   Delayed Deletion Algorithm

To evaluate the Delayed Deletion algorithm, we prepared the list of model elements in the RAM metamodel that can be removed or deleted by a collaborator and that could yield inconsistencies because of dangling cross-view references. The idea was to count *how many potential kinds of inconsistencies* can a delete operation on a model element cause. Column 1 in Table 3 lists the model elements that can be deleted by a collaborator in the structural, message and state views of the TouchCORE tool. Column 2 lists the inter-view crossreferences that could cause inconsistencies. The worst case occurs when a *Class* is deleted, as 7 potential inter-view references become inconsistent. For example, the type of a parameter (PaT) could refer to a class that is being deleted. Additionally, though, as per the RAM metamodel, *Classifier*, the supertype of *Class*, contains Operations, Association Ends, Type Parameters and the Operations, which in turn contains Parameters. Class also contains Attributes. Therefore, a delete of a *Class* would remove all these contained elements as well. The total potential kinds of dangling inter-view references when deleting a *Class* is therefore 25!

7   Related Work

To the best of our knowledge, no existing approach provides a highlighting algorithm that can be applied on any multi-view modelling environment. Furthermore, no approach proposes a solution for deleted elements in a multi-view modelling environment.

Support for online collaboration is limited in multi-view modelling environments [11]. Some of the modelling approaches that support real-time collaboration are GenMyModel [3], AtomPM [24], Camel [8], MetaEdit+ [13], Unicase [6], and GEMSjax [10]. With an exception of AToMPM, GenMyModel and WebGME, the other tools focus on single-view workspaces [20]. Some of

Table 3. Evaluation of Delayed Deletion Algorithm

Element	Probable immediate inconsistencies
Classifier	State View Specifies, TP Generic Type, AT, RT, PaT, ORT, TET
Association	Message AsTo, AS AsTo, Structural Feature Value, TET
Attribute	Message AsTo, AS AsTo, Structural Feature Value, TET
Operation	Message, MV, Aspect MV, Transition, Parameter Value, PVM
Parameter	Parameter Value, PVM, TET
Super Type	Classifier
Literal	Enum Literal Value
Message	Message End
State	SM, Transition
Transition	State, Transition Substitution

these approaches use locking such as WebGME [17], which is a web-based collaborative modelling tool. The locked elements indicate which model elements the collaborators are currently working on. However, it is not possible to identify who is working on a model. Our highlighting algorithm does not require locking and visualizes the current focus of the collaborators using personalized colours for each collaborator. The closest approach to our work is Pounamu [25], a modelling approach that that uses synthetic links between domain-specific languages and highlights selected model elements with personalized colours. However, Pounamu does not traverse the metamodels as we do, and does not consider the degree of impact when colouring an element.

Even the tools for UML, which specifies many different kinds of diagrams, have only limited support for multi-view collaboration [11]. Mougenot et al. [19] use partial replication of the system specification and message exchanges to propagate changes among the developers. Bruegge et. al. introduces a framework that uses dedicated modelling artifacts to support collaboration [7]. Michaux et al. [18] represent the state of the model as a sequence of operations that are used to communicate change information between collaborators. All these UML-based approaches do not support highlighting impacted elements as we do and do not the mitigate impact of delayed elements.

Some technologies such as MagicDraw [4] and EMFStore [2] provide support for offline collaborative modelling using version control. The CDO Model Repository [1] provides support for both online and offline collaborative modelling. Rocco et al. provide an overview of these tools and discuss their potentials and shortcomings [21]. However, their simplistic use of locking/conflict management slows down productivity [16]. Our prototype implementation uses the CDO Model Repository for online collaboration without using its pessimistic concurrency control capabilities.

8 Conclusion

This paper introduced two new algorithms that exploit the metamodels of a modelling language to address important challenges in collaborative modelling. The highlight propagation algorithm notifies all online collaborators when a change is being made to the model, and by whom. If the actual element that is being modified is not visible in the active view of the local collaborator, the model element that is impacted by the change is highlighted, if any. The delayed deletion algorithm addresses the problems of inconsistencies that could potentially arise when a model element is deleted by a collaborator without using pessimistic concurrency control techniques.

The two algorithms do not depend on specific language features. They can operate on any modelling language(s) provided they have access to the metamodel of the language(s). We evaluated the effectiveness of the highlighting algorithm on the RAM metamodel, yielding a 100%, 70% and 80% success for communicating the remote change in an unambiguous way for the elements highlighted in *strong*, *medium* and *light* colours respectively.

As future work, we plan to evaluate the effectiveness of our algorithms on metamodels of other multi-view modelling approaches. Furthermore, we will extend our work to multi-model collaborative environments, i.e., approaches in which views are stored in separate models and hence cross-references between views are expressed using more elaborate consistency constraints. Finally, we will perform user studies on the effectiveness and most appropriate duration of highlighting.

References

1. CDO Model Repository. http://www.eclipse.org/cdo/. Last Accessed 2018
2. EMFStore. http://www.eclipse.org/emfstore/. Last Accessed 2018
3. GenMyModel. https://www.genmymodel.com/. Last Accessed 2018
4. Magicdraw. https://www.nomagic.com/. Last Accessed 2018
5. Visual paradigm. https://www.visual-paradigm.com/. Last Accessed 2018
6. Bruegge, B., Creighton, O., Helming, J., Kgel, M.: Unicase an ecosystem for unified software engineering. In: Research Tools, Workshop Distributed Software Development - Methods and Tools for Risk Management, pp. 12–17 (2008)
7. Bruegge, B., Dutoit, A.H., Wolf, T.: Sysiphus: enabling informal collaboration in global software development. In: CAiSE, pp. 139–148. IEEE Computer Society, Washington, DC, USA (2006)
8. Cataldo, M., Shelton, C., Choi, Y., Huang, Y.Y., Ramesh, V., Saini, D., et al.: Camel: a tool for collaborative distributed software design. In: ICGSE, pp. 83–92. IEEE Computer Society, Washington, DC, USA (2009)
9. Combemale, B., DeAntoni, J., Baudry, B., France, R.B., Jézéquel, J.M., Gray, J.: Globalizing modeling languages. Computer **47**(6), 68–71 (2014)
10. Farwick, M., Agreiter, B., White, J., Forster, S., Lanzanasto, N., Breu, R.: A web-based collaborative metamodeling environment with secure remote model access. In: Benatallah, B., Casati, F., Kappel, G., Rossi, G. (eds.) ICWE 2010. LNCS, vol. 6189, pp. 278–291. Springer, Heidelberg (2010). https://doi.org/10.1007/978-3-642-13911-6_19

11. Franzago, M., Ruscio, D.D., Malavolta, I., Muccini, H.: Collaborative model-driven software engineering: a classification framework and a research map. IEEE Trans. Softw. Eng. 1–1 (2017)

12. Gray, J., Rumpe, B.: The evolution of model editors: browser- and cloud-based solutions. Softw. Syst. Model. 15(2), 303–305 (2016). https://doi.org/10.1007/s10270-016-0524-2

13. Kelly, S., Lyytinen, K., Rossi, M.: MetaEdit+ A fully configurable multi-user and multi-tool CASE and CAME environment. In: Constantopoulos, P., Mylopoulos, J., Vassiliou, Y. (eds.) CAiSE 1996. LNCS, vol. 1080, pp. 1–21. Springer, Heidelberg (1996). https://doi.org/10.1007/3-540-61292-0_1

14. Kienzle, J., Al Abed, W., Klein, J.: Aspect-oriented multi-view modeling. In: AOSD 2009, pp. 87–98. ACM Press (2009)

15. Klein, J., Kienzle, J.: Reusable aspect models. In: 11th Aspect-Oriented Modeling Workshop, Nashville, TN, USA, Sept. 30, 2007 (2007)

16. Kolovos, D.S., Rose, L.M., Matragkas, N., Paige, R.F., Guerra, E., Cuadrado, J.S., et al.: A research roadmap towards achieving scalability in model driven engineering. In: BigMDE Workshop, pp. 2:1–2:10. ACM, New York, NY, USA (2013)

17. Maróti, M., Kecskés, T., Kereskényi, R., Broll, B., Völgyesi, P., Jurácz, L., et al.: Next generation (meta)modeling: web- and cloud-based collaborative tool infrastructure. In: Proceedings of the 8th Workshop on Multi-Paradigm Modeling, pp. 41–60 (2014)

18. Michaux, J., Blanc, X., Shapiro, M., Sutra, P.: A semantically rich approach for collaborative model edition. In: Proceedings of the 2011 ACM Symposium on Applied Computing, SAC 2011, pp. 1470–1475. ACM, New York, NY, USA (2011)

19. Mougenot, A., Blanc, X., Gervais, M.-P.: D-Praxis : a peer-to-peer collaborative model editing framework. In: Senivongse, T., Oliveira, R. (eds.) DAIS 2009. LNCS, vol. 5523, pp. 16–29. Springer, Heidelberg (2009). https://doi.org/10.1007/978-3-642-02164-0_2

20. Popoola, S., Carver, J.C., Gray, J.G.: Modeling as a service: a survey of existing tools. In: Tools for Model Driven Engineering (MDETools), a workshop held at Model-Driven Engineering Languages and Systems (MODELS), Austin, TX (2017)

21. Rocco, J.D., Ruscio, D.D., Iovino, L., Pierantonio, A.: Collaborative repositories in model-driven engineering [software technology]. IEEE Softw. 32(3), 28–34 (2015)

22. Schöttle, M., Thimmegowda, N., Alam, O., Kienzle, J., Mussbacher, G.: Feature modelling and traceability for concern-driven software development with touchcore. In: Companion Proceedings of the 14th International Conference on Modularity, MODULARITY 2015, Fort Collins, CO, USA, Mar. 16–19, 2015, pp. 11–14 (2015)

23. Steinberg, D., Budinsky, F., Paternostro, M., Merks, E.: EMF: Eclipse Modeling Framework 2.0, 2nd edn. Addison-Wesley Professional (2009)

24. Syriani, E., Vangheluwe, H., Mannadiar, R., Hansen, C., Mierlo, S.V., Ergin, H.: AToMPM: a web-based modeling environment. In: MODELS 2013 Demonstration, pp. 21–25 (2013)

25. Zhu, N., Grundy, J., Hosking, J., Liu, N., Cao, S., Mehra, A.: Pounamu: a meta-tool for exploratory domain-specific visual language tool development. J. Syst. Softw. 80(8), 1390–1407 (2007)

Collaborative Software Design and Modeling in Open Source Systems

Omar Badreddin[1(✉)], Wahab Hamou-Lhadj[2], Vahdat Abdelzad[3],
Rahad Khandoker[1], and Maged Elassar[4]

[1] University of Texas, El Paso, TX, USA
obbadreddin@utep.edu, rahad.baten@yahoo.com
[2] Concordia University, Montreal, QC, Canada
wahab.hamou-lhadj@concordia.ca
[3] University of Ottawa, Ottawa, ON, Canada
vabde040@uottawa.ca
[4] NASA Jet Propulsion Laboratory, Pasadena, CA, USA
maged.e.elaasar@jpl.nasa.gov

Abstract. The Open source ecosystem creates new pathways for participation and collaboration from a broad and diverse community of developers. As a software system grows, the need to capture its design, often through models, becomes important in order to boost communication and collaboration. In this paper, we report on a study that assesses the open source community's adoption of modeling as a way to capture design and enable collaboration among development teams. The study includes a search of open source repositories to identify modeling artifacts, a survey, a questionnaire, and a set of interviews with open source contributors. Our findings show that there is a low number of modeling artifacts that are included in open source project repositories. However, the survey, the questionnaire, and the interviews suggest that capturing design in models is much more common than what can be inferred by searching the repositories alone. These models are created through collaborations, but often are not shared in the open source repositories. This is due to many factors including the lack of incentives to share modeling artifacts beyond the immediate circle of collaborators and limited collaboration support in modeling tools.

Keywords: Model driven software development · Open source
Collaborative modeling · Empirical investigation

1 Introduction

Open source software (OSS) has demonstrated numerous successes in supporting large-scale collaborative projects. OSS is unique in its support for collaborative development because of its inert ability to attract and sustain a community of users and developers. It is common for an OSS project to include hundreds, and sometimes thousands, of developers contributing to the same project, often with high turnover rates.

However, many OSS projects are developed with little structure, heavily relying on the vigilance of contributors and a few champions. Adoption of UML and other design languages is particularly scarce [1, 6]. This lack of structured development means that

© Springer Nature Switzerland AG 2018
F. Khendek and R. Gotzhein (Eds.): SAM 2018, LNCS 11150, pp. 219–228, 2018.
https://doi.org/10.1007/978-3-030-01042-3_13

OSS often accumulates significant technical debts and suffers from unnecessary and avoidable code complexities [13]. This, in turn, obscures the knowledge embedded in the algorithms and codes, limits reuse, and makes code prohibitively expensive to maintain, upgrade, scale, or extend.

Investigations of open source modeling practices often focus on mining artifacts from open source repositories [9]. These studies provide valuable insights into the types and nature of modeling practices adopted in open source projects. However, such studies are limited in their scope, as some artifacts are not published as part of the open source project. In this paper, we conduct a study that not only investigates open source repositories, but also includes extensive input from open source contributors. Specifically, this study (1) searches repositories to identify modeling artifacts, (2) surveys open source contributors, and (3) collects data from questionnaires and interviews to gain further insights into the practice. This paper extends our previous work on surveying software engineering practitioners [8] and investigating open source development practices [1], including work on open source collaborative design [4].

The rest of the paper is organized as follows. Related work is presented in Sect. 2. The study structure is presented in Sect. 3 where we present the survey, questionnaire and interview design. In Sect. 4 we present the study results and analysis. Threats to validity are discussed in Sect. 5 followed by a conclusion in Sect. 6.

2 Related Work

There are a few studies that focus on collaborative modeling in open source environments. Sack et al. [7] described a methodological framework that combines ethnography, text mining, and socio-technical network analysis and visualization to understand OSS development in its totality. Ho-Quang et al. [3] analyzed open source projects for evidence of modeling. While they found that modeling activities are rather scarce in the open source artifacts, those who do adopt them report increased productivity and code quality. Low adaption of modeling practices particularly in open source projects has also been reported by other studies [1, 2]. Nakagawa presented a case study that established the relationship between software architecture and code quality in open source [11]. Gaar and Teiniker [12] analyzed model-based design collaboration in open source, and demonstrated the potential for using social media platforms to facilitate global model-based collaboration.

Many open source software systems grow organically with little upfront designs [15]. Gregory et al. studied how open source software systems evolve over time [16]. Their study is unique, not only because their focus is the open source software evolution, but also because their study scope is not limited to the open source artifacts alone. They also studied how the open source community evolved along with the software artifacts. In their study, they modeled software teams as collaborative social network of developers.

3   Study Design

Our study includes (1) investigation of open source artifacts, (2) a survey targeting open source contributors and users, and (3) a questionnaire and interview study with open source contributors and users. The aim of the study is to answer the following research questions:

- **RQ1.** To what extent do open source developers collaborate on design and modeling artifacts?
- **RQ2.** What is the nature of the model-based collaborations in open source environments?
- **RQ3.** What are the key incentives and barriers for mode-based collaborations in open source systems?

3.1   Subject Systems

The scope of this study includes 67 open source projects selected based on the following criteria. First, we sorted GitHub repositories based on project size and then selected the first 50 most active projects based on GitHub ranking of project activities [10]. Second, we selected 11 projects based on the following criteria. Using GitHub advanced search, we identified projects written in C++, Java, JavaScript, Shell, C#, and C. This increases the generality of our results and excludes domain-specific languages that may not represent the general open source practices adequately. We excluded all projects that were not active in the last five years. We excluded projects that did not have at least three active contributors and were not cited in any scientific article on Google Scholar. The citation criterion ensures minimum level of maturity of code and excludes in-progress projects. The resulting set was sorted based on project size, and then we selected the top 11 projects. We conveniently added a new system, the Quantum Geographical Information System (QGIS) [5]. QGIS was included because it is the premier geo-analysis tool that is developed by both open and closed source developers. It has a global contributor and user base, with a significant interest from private entities that often support professional developers' contributions. This project sample are identified to represent the general practices of large open source projects. The first 50 projects are listed in [1]. Table 1 lists the additional 12 projects included in this study.

The second set of projects are selected from a pool of projects that are known to have some level of design and modeling activities. We conveniently selected five repositories from a pool of 4,237 identified in [3] to be model-heavy repositories. These 4,237 repositories were selected by mining all GitHub repository artifacts and selecting those that included significant number of UML and modeling elements. From this list, we selected five projects that meet the following criteria, code size is greater than 150 K lines of code written predominantly in an object-oriented language and has GitHub popularity start of at least 4. These repositories represent projects where the team has shared designs and models as part of the open source artifacts. These five repositories are listed in Table 2.

Table 1. Included open source projects

Num.	Name	Commits	Code size	Active contributors
1	Pykep	646	201,430	12
2	Rash	572	148,931	11
3	Epiviz	289	204,528	3
4	Seg3D	2,365	8,574	12
5	BioImageLab	6	15,337	2
6	Sead-virtual-archive	408	200,611	8
7	VEGL-Portal	13,33	72,213	5
8	BEACON Toolkit	101	156	3
9	Mule	61	1,249	2
10	Prov-scaffold	8	2,764	3
11	eo4vistrails	667	18,218	2
12	QGIS	44,029	1.2 m	244

Table 2. Sample of modeling repositories

Repository	Commits	Code size	Primary programming lang.	Analyzed LoC		Active cont'rs
				Count	%	
Marble	9,090	265,546	C++	95,157	36	100
Oryx-editor	2,022	640,127	JavaScript, Java	543,704	85	1
101repo	2,312	183,083	PHP, JavaScript, Java, C#	154,437	84	25
Activiti	7,741	207,339	Java	192,812	93	151
Poi	9,157	450,906	Java	427,326	95	11

3.2   Survey

The survey was conducted online [14]. We sent targeted requests to personal contacts in a wide variety of organizations. We also asked for participation using a variety of Internet forums. The survey consisted of 18 topics. Most of these involved several sub-questions answered using 5-point Likert scales. Responses were in ranges such as strongly disagree to strongly agree, or never to always.

The survey questions were broad in focus and included many questions related to development and design practices and questions about platforms and technologies used. The survey was divided into groups of questions as follows:

- Q1: What is or is not a model? Various options were presented ranging from class diagrams, use cases, to source code. Our objective was to see if participants had a preconceived notion about what they considered a model to be.
- Q2-5: How and when do you model, and using which notations? The objective of these questions was to understand the state of the practice. These questions explore how do the participants go about preforming their modeling and design activities, including whether the participants use models during meeting, use a white board to share and collaborate on the model, etc.

- Q6: How do you approach a new task or feature with respect to requirements, design, modeling, testing and documentation?
- Q7-10: What tools, methods and platforms do you use, and what type of software do you develop?
- Q11-14: To what extent do you use modeling, and how good is it for various tasks.
- Q15-16: What are the principal difficulties you perceive with the model-centric and code-centric approaches?
- Q17: An open-ended free form question for comments about the survey and/or modeling in general.
- Q18: Demographics question with sub-questions about country of origin, education level, and years of experience of the participant.

3.3 Questionnaires and Interviews

We requested short interviews with the survey respondents. When a respondent declined the interview due to time limitation or difficulties in scheduling a suitable time, we sent out a questionnaire. The questionnaire and the interview discussions were moderated by the following questions:

- **Q1:** What kind of contributions do you make to <project name> (code, test, documentations, other)?
- **Q2:** What is the primary goal or motivation of your contributions (for instance: paid effort, support research you do or someone else is doing, or support commercializing or services)?
- **Q3:** How do you go about understanding the code base to make your contributions? Do you refer to documentations, designs, or do you seek information directly from other developers?
- **Q4:** Is there an overall design, architecture, or model that you refer to? How useful is the design or architecture? Is it up to date? Do you collaborate using models with other contributors? If yes, who do you collaborate with and what is the medium of the collaboration? What are the factors that determines this collaboration scope?
- **Q5:** Are software design and modeling artifacts shared as part of the open source project? and why?
- **Q6:** In your opinion, what is required to encourage more contributors to the project? What are the key limiting factors?
- **Q7:** Do you consider <tool name> well designed, and the code is of high quality?

4 Results and Analysis

We have examined 62 projects' code, commits, related documentations such as design artifacts and coding standards. The online survey received 85 complete responses. We have conducted six interviews, and collected questionnaire responses from five contributors. Of the interviewed participants, five were paid professionals contributing to the QGIS project. We shared preliminary results and analysis with two participants and conducted two additional follow-up interviews.

4.1 Evidence for Design and Modeling Artifacts

Investigation of the largest 50 open source projects suggests that modeling artifacts are almost non-existent. Based on the number of files, only 0.03% were XML based. Investigation of these resulting files showed that only 0.01% included XMI specific tags. The examination of related documentations, such as development environment setup guidelines, showed that none of these projects has model-based design descriptions. For the other 12 subject projects (shown in Table 1), we found that they contain negligible modeling artifacts. XML files that included XMI specific tags were almost non-existent (less than 0.01%). Related documentations supported the finding that models and design artifacts are not available.

4.2 Evidence for Design and Modeling Practices

Despite the fact that the examination of artifacts does not directly suggest that modeling is practiced, our questionnaire and interview results suggest a broad set of design and model-based collaborations.

Survey. Participants averaged 10 years of experience, with 50% having more than 5 years of experience, and about 28% having more than 12 years of experience. More than one third of respondents are from the USA. Half of the respondents are from Asia and the rest are from Europe and Africa. 52% of respondents indicated that they either sometimes (42%) or often (10%) engage in design activities on whiteboards. Only 12% indicate that they never use a design tool. Those who participate in design activities reported using a design tool to capture design (78%), transcribe an existing design into a digital format (71%), prototype (60%), brainstorm (45%), and generate some code (72%). 95% of the responses showed interest in using a modeling tool for collaboration. Of those, 60% ranked this capability as very important.

Questionnaire and Interviews. All contributors report code as their primary form of contributions to the open source project. About 27% (3/7) contribute to the test code. Comprehension activities were centered around reading code (95%). Related documentations were not a good source of information for 85% of participants. Interestingly, 36% (4/11) of participants reported engaging in design and model-based collaborations. Those four participants were contacted for follow-up interviewing and we conducted two follow-up interviews. Participants in the interviews were contributors to the QGIS project. Both were professional software engineers compensated for their code contributions. Both participants reported significant design deliberations with other 'key' contributors. For example, one of the participants said: *"we have design documents that I share with my colleagues. We often discuss design decisions in great length."* Those model-based deliberations are often performed offline using personal and business emails. The primary goal of using design models is to plan work packages and resource assignments.

Code quality is a major concern, but design and modeling approaches do not seem to be the primary approach for improving code quality. This can be seen in this passage: *".. we need to do much more code reviews, but we do not have the resources for that. But it is in the plans... do not see how models can improve code quality. Our models are at a higher level, and we do not translate the models to code.*" Furthermore, there is little deviation from the design specifications and implementations. For instance, we obtain this from one of the participants: "*the code matches the design pretty much.. at least for the core components. The corners [plug-ins developed by open source contributors], it is very different.*"

4.3   Characterization of Model-Based Collaborations

As discussed in Sect. 4.1, investigation of open source artifacts does not suggest any significant levels of collaborations on models. In this section, we focus on analysis of the survey and questionnaire/interview data.

Survey. Model-based collaborations on whiteboards and during meetings are the most common venues for model-based collaborations. Of the 40% respondents who reported to participate in collaborative modeling regularly, more than 85% perform these activities on a whiteboard and 54% during meetings. Only 12% share results with close circle of collaborators and none reported publishing results of model-based collaboration along with open source project artifacts.

Questionnaire and Interviews. 36% of participants reported engaging in collaborative design. None of the participants reported using a dedicated design or modeling tool. There was no motivation to use a dedicated modeling or design tool. One said, for example, "*... we do not generate any code or tests from the models.*" QGIS is the only project where design deliberations (not the design models themselves) are made publicly available in the form of meeting minutes.

Lack of mechanisms to enforce design specifications in the code seems to be a major factor limiting incentives to share designs. When probed on reasons for not sharing designs, one participants reported "*.. I share the designs with three collaborators. They know [the project code] and I can trust they will stick to the design specifications. Why would I share designs if there is no way to enforce it?*" Other factors limiting incentives for sharing designs include relevance to other developers, not being part of the build process, and the casual nature of the available designs, and their change fluidity.

We identified two methods of collaborations, namely asynchronous and synchronous collaborations. In asynchronous collaborations, models are stored in Microsoft Word documents and are shared by emails. Changes are often communicated by chats or emails and are implemented in the model as needed. Multiple copies of the models may exist with different contributors and there is no pressing need to ensure model consistency. In synchronous collaborations, models are stored in the cloud, though often not part of the open source project artifacts. Collaborations were limited to only a few concerned developers. One participant expressed "*.. the design specifications are in the cloud and open for anyone. But.. only a few key developers would [care to / invest time to] contribute to the designs..*" Design deliberations can often be lengthy, and can occur over long periods of time.

4.4   Analysis

Our analysis suggests that model-based collaborations in open source is rather limited. When it is performed, it seems that modeling artifacts are only shared with close collaborators and not shared as part of the open source project artifacts. We term this collaboration style as Champions-only Collaboration. In this style, only a few main contributors (or champions) collaborate on design artifacts. Design artifacts may be made available online, but are typically not available for contributions from the broader set of contributors or users. There is often no documentations or guidance on the available designs. Champions collaborate *offline* on models and other design artifacts. This explains, at least in part, why investigations of open source artifacts often suggest little to no collaborative modeling. Participants in our study indicated lack of incentives to share models beyond the immediate circle of collaborators.

5   Threats to Validity

The main threats to validity of our work are summarized below. We also outlined the steps we have taken to help mitigate these threats.

5.1   Question Interpretation

The survey, the questionnaire, and interviews were conducted online. It is possible that some participants may have misunderstood or misinterpreted the question wording. We performed three activities to improve the clarity of the questions. First, we all questions were independently reviewed by two independent researchers. Second, participants often completed an optional feedback questions that included specific feedback on the research instruments itself. Third, we conducted a pilot study to refine question wording to minimize ambiguities.

5.2   Researcher Bias

The goal of the study is to uncover patterns of model-based collaboration. It is possible that the questions or the interviews may have introduced a bias that may have influenced the participants responses. A potential bias may have been introduced if the questions may have influenced participants Reponses. It is also possible that participants may have opted not to participate if the questions were focused on model-based collaboration. To reduce this bias, we selected neutral words whenever possible. Moreover, we presented questions in random order whenever possible.

5.3   External Validity Threat

It is possible the subject repository selected for this study is not an adequate representation for the overall practices in open source projects. To help mitigate this risk, we reported our repository selection process and used objective measures to perform the selection. The selection process included a small number of repositories for in-depth analysis, and a larger repository set that was subject for wholistic analysis. Nevertheless, the external validity threat still exists.

The external validity threat is also present due to the sample of participants in the survey and questionnaire studies. To help minimize this threat, we approached participants from a broad set of venues not limited to open source venues. The collected demographics data reflects diversity in the sample.

6 Conclusion

We conducted a study to understand the nature of model-based collaboration in open source projects. The study included an investigation and analysis of open source artifacts, a survey, a questionnaire and interviews with open source developers. The study included investigations of open source repositories and their artifacts.

The study suggests that model-based collaboration is practiced, but that model-based collaboration artifacts are often not shared as part of the project artifacts. Model-based collaborations are often conducted informally within a small circle of contributors or champions. Designs often do not contribute directly to code and there are little incentives to share design and modeling artifacts beyond the immediate circle of collaborators.

References

1. Badreddin, O., Lethbridge, T.C., Elassar, M.: Modeling practices in open source software. In: Petrinja, E., Succi, G., El Ioini, N., Sillitti, A. (eds.) OSS 2013. IAICT, vol. 404, pp. 127–139. Springer, Heidelberg (2013). https://doi.org/10.1007/978-3-642-38928-3_9
2. Franco-Bedoya, O., Ameller, D., Costal, D., Franch, X.: Open source software ecosystems: a systematic mapping. Inf. Softw. Technol. **91**, 160–185 (2017)
3. Ho-Quang, T., Hebig, R., Robles, G., Chaudron, M.R.V., Fernandez, M.A.: Practices and perceptions of UML use in open source projects. In: Proceedings of the 39th International Conference on Software Engineering: Software Engineering in Practice Track, pp. 203–212. IEEE Press (2017)
4. Badreddin, O.: Umple: a model-oriented programming language. In: Proceedings of the 32nd ACM/IEEE International Conference on Software Engineering, vol. 2, pp. 337–338. ACM (2010)
5. QGIS, D.T.: Quantum GIS geographic information system. Open source geospatial Foundation project, 45 (2011). https://github.com/qgis/QGIS
6. Khandoker, R., Badreddin, O.: Professional coding and modeling practices (2017). https://goo.gl/bQV9Ph
7. Sack, W., Détienne, F., Ducheneaut, N., Burkhardt, J.-M., Mahendran, D., Barcellini, F.: A methodological framework for socio-cognitive analyses of collaborative design of open source software. Comput. Support. Coop. Work (CSCW) **15**(2), 229–250 (2006)
8. Lethbridge, T.C., Forward, A., Badreddin, O.: Problems and opportunities for model-centric vs. code-centric development: a survey of software professionals. In: Proceedings of C2 M: EEMDD (2010)

9. Beller, M., Bacchelli, A., Zaidman, A., Juergens, E.: Modern code reviews in open-source projects: which problems do they fix? In: Proceedings of the 11th Working Conference on Mining Software Repositories, pp. 202–211. ACM (2014)

10. GitHub Developer guide. Available: https://developer.github.com/v3/repos/statistics/

11. Nakagawa, E.Y., de Sousa, E.P.M., de Brito Murata, K., de Faria Andery, G., Morelli, L.B., Maldonado, J.C.: Software architecture relevance in open source software evolution: a case study. In: 32nd Annual IEEE International Computer Software and Applications, 2008. COMPSAC 2008, pp. 1234–1239. IEEE (2008)

12. Gaar, W., Teiniker, E.: Improving model-based collaboration by social media integration. In: 2014 IEEE 27th Conference on Software Engineering Education and Training (CSEE&T), pp. 158–162. IEEE (2014)

13. Alfayez, R., Chen, C., Behnamghader, P., Srisopha, K., Boehm, B.: An empirical study of technical debt in open-source software systems. In: Madni, A.M., Boehm, B., Ghanem, R.G., Erwin, D., Wheaton, M.J. (eds.) Disciplinary Convergence in Systems Engineering Research, pp. 113–125. Springer, Cham (2018). https://doi.org/10.1007/978-3-319-62217-0_9

14. Badreddin, O., Khandoker, R.: Software modeling survey. https://docs.google.com/forms/d/e/1FAIpQLSclPAi-49RXWwtPmbtSfzZBDm6ZBvBwZqhVlzHoybC4pRb1ZQ/viewform?c=0&w=1&includes_info_params=true. Accessed July 2018

15. West, J., Gallagher, S.: Challenges of open innovation: the paradox of firm investment in open-source software. R&d Manag. 36(3), 319–331 (2006)

16. Madey, G., Freeh, V., Tynan, R.: The open source software development phenomenon: an analysis based on social network theory. In: AMCIS 2002 Proceedings (2002), p. 247

The Impact of Integrating Agile Software Development and Model-Driven Development: A Comparative Case Study

Hessa Alfraihi[1,3]([✉]), Kevin Lano[1], Shekoufeh Kolahdouz-Rahimi[2], Mohammadreza Sharbaf[2], and Howard Haughton[1]

[1] Department of Informatics, King's College London, London, UK
{hessa.alfraihi,kevin.lano}@kcl.ac.uk
[2] Department of Software Engineering, University of Isfahan, Isfahan, Iran
{sh.rahimi,m.sharbaf}@eng.ui.ac.ir
[3] Department of Information Systems, Princess Nourah bint Abdulrahman University, Riyadh, Saudi Arabia

Abstract. Agile and Model-Driven Development integration (Agile MDD) is of significant interest to researchers who want to leverage the best of both worlds. Currently, there is no clear evidence or proof for the real impact of such integration. As a first step in this direction, this paper reports an empirical investigation on the impact of integrating Agile and Model-Driven Development on the quality of software systems. To this end, we developed a financial application using Agile MDD, which is further contrasted with three other independent versions of the same application developed using different approaches: Agile method, MDD method, and traditional (manually-coded) method, respectively. We also compared the functionality of the systems and a variety of technical debt metrics measuring the quality of the code and its design. Based on the case study results, we have found that the use of Agile MDD shows some improvements in the product quality and efficiency.

Keywords: Agile development · Model-driven development
Agile model-driven development integration · Case study
Financial applications

1 Introduction

Agile development processes evolved to overcome some of the perceived limitations of the bureaucratic plan-driven approaches [8]. They attempt to be as lightweight as possible in terms of the development process: their primary goal is to deliver a system to the customer that meets his needs, in the shortest possible time, taking account of changes in requirements. This is achieved by having short iterations and developing software incrementally; coping with changes through specific technical practices, and by focusing on customer involvement throughout the development. A variety of agile processes exist that share the same values

© Springer Nature Switzerland AG 2018
F. Khendek and R. Gotzhein (Eds.): SAM 2018, LNCS 11150, pp. 229–245, 2018.
https://doi.org/10.1007/978-3-030-01042-3_14

and principles. The most widely used are Scrum [22] and Extreme Programming (XP) [5].

Model-driven Development (MDD) is another software development approach that has been gaining considerable attention during the last decade [3,17]. Unlike Agile development, MDD provides a capability for a high degree of rigour and formalisation by proposing a paradigm shift from code level to model level. The main aim of MDD is to separate the business logic from its implementation. This allows the developers to focus on solving the problem instead of focusing on its implementation. Particularly, MDD uses models as the primary artifact of the software development and the implementation is generated automatically (or semi-automatically) from the models. MDD promotes faster development with fewer bugs (in principle) by automatic generation of code, easier communication among stakeholders by increasing abstraction in the design, improving maintainability, and generating platform-independent solutions [15].

Agile and Model-driven Development integration (Agile MDD) is of significant interest to researchers who want to utilise the best of both worlds. However, not enough research has been carried out to investigate the impact of their integration [1,6]. More specifically, not much is known about the quality of software developed using an Agile MDD approach. The aim of this paper is to assess the impact of integrating Agile development and MDD through a case study. To that end, a comparison between four independent developments of the same application was performed, with the developments using different approaches: Agile MDD, MDD, Agile, and non-Agile hand-coded development.

The remainder of this paper is structured as follows. After a brief discussion of related work in Sect. 2 and our research methodology in Sect. 3, we describe our Agile MDD process in Sect. 4. In Sect. 5, we report on the case study, while the results are presented in Sect. 6. Section 7 discusses the results followed by listing the limitations of this study. Finally, Sect. 8 discusses the conclusion of the study and highlights areas for future work.

2   Related Work

In our previous work [2] we compare a UML to C code generator developed using Agile MDD, to previously developed code generators (for UML to Java, C++, and C#). These generators were developed using an Agile method with manual coding in Java. The results show a 33% increase in the developer's productivity and a 4 times reduction in size (LOC) for Agile MDD. Likewise, Zhang and Patel [27] compare some components developed using Agile MDD to other hand-coded components developed using Agile method. They noticed a threefold increase in productivity and higher quality in terms of reduced defects density. However, they did not show clear metrics or explain how the comparison was performed.

To the best of our knowledge, there is no case study on Agile MDD that compares the *same* software product in three ways, to one developed using MDD without Agile, to another using Agile development without MDD, and to one developed manually in a traditional way. This study should fill in this gap and provide such comparison.

3   Research Methodology

The high-level goal of our research is to *evaluate the impact of integrating Agile development and MDD*. The research goal was refined into detailed properties, and specific measures for these properties were selected, according to the Goal Question Metric (GQM) methodology [4]. The goal leads to the following research questions:

RQ1: What is the impact of integrating Agile development and MDD on the software product?

RQ2: What is the impact of integrating Agile development and MDD on the software development process?

This research is conducted using the case study method [26]. We designed our study to compare the Agile MDD approach with three different approaches: MDD, Agile, and hand-coded approaches. In particular, the four applications were all implementing the same problem and were completed entirely independently using different development approaches by different developers:

1. A manually-coded version in C++, developed by a financial company.
2. An Agile MDD version, using UML-RSDS, developed by the second author.
3. An MDD approach, using ETL, developed by the fourth author.
4. An Agile approach, using Java, developed by the first author.

In order to answer the RQ1, the properties of quality, efficiency and maintainability of the case study versions were compared. For quality and maintainability, we use measures that are versions of the technical debt [16]. Technical debt is a metaphor referring to immature artifacts in the software development that negatively influence the software quality and maintainability in the long-run [23]. We have selected these technical measures because: (1) they have been used frequently in the literature [10,16]; (2) they are related to the quality of the software product that we intend to investigate, e.g., the complexity, coupling, and design flaws. We have used different measures and metrics to quantitatively compare all the applications by collecting the following data:

- **EAS:** Excessive application size. For MDD specifications a complexity measure can be defined, based on the total number of basic and composite expressions in the specification. For programs, LOC can be used. The threshold for a flaw to be present is a total complexity > 1000, or length > 500 LOC.
- **ENR:** Excessive number of rules ($nrules > 10$). This only applies to transformation languages such as ETL.
- **ENO:** Excessive number of helpers/operations ($nops > 10$).
- **EHS:** Excessive helper/operation size (complexity > 100 or length > 50 LOC). To give a more detailed comparison, we also consider maximum helper/operation size (MHS) within a program/specification.
- **ERS:** Excessive rule size (complexity > 100 or length greater than 50 LOC). Maximum rule size MRS is also considered.

- **EFO:** Excessive fan-out of a rule/operation (>5 different rules/operations called from one rule/operation). Maximum fan out MFO is also considered.
- **CC:** Cyclomatic complexity (of rule logic or of procedural code) (>10). Maximum CC MCC for any rule or code is considered.
- **CBR** Coupling between rules (number of rule/operation explicit or implicit calling relations > $nrules + nops$, or any cyclic dependencies exist in the rule/operation call graph).
- **DC:** Duplicate expressions/code (duplicate expressions or statements with token count > 10).

For efficiency, we measure the total execution time on a sample dataset input of 16 sectors and output of P(S = s) for all values of s $\leq$ 20 (Sect. 5). For size/complexity measures, we assess model-centric and code-centric approaches differently: in Agile MDD and MDD, the measures are applied at the specification level, while in Agile and the original manually-coded approaches measures are applied at the code level. **EAS**, **ENR** and **ERS** are omitted in both the Agile and original applications as they are not applicable. In order to answer the RQ2, we used qualitative measures through an opinion survey, in which the developers were asked to report in a free-form format the main benefits they perceived, along with the issues they faced in each approach.

4   Agile MDD Process Overview

In this section, we provide a brief overview of our Agile MDD approach. A more detailed description can be found in [2]. The development process starts with the *Initialisation* phase and finishes with the *Deployment* phase. After the initialisation phase, the development process follows an iterative cycle. This means that the development process goes through repeated phases until the system meets the customer's needs. The iterative cycle encompasses the following phases: *Requirements and Specifications, Development, Integration and Testing*.

- **Phase 0: Initialisation.** The main objective of this phase is to capture the initial information about the system such as its scope, size, environment conditions and so on. At this stage, strong collaboration with the customer is crucial to gather the required information. Furthermore, the initial requirements of the system are identified and prioritised, and the product backlog is created.
  Each iteration begins with an iteration planning activity to agree on the work to be accomplished in the upcoming iteration (the iteration backlog). The main process of an iteration involves three phases for each task in the iteration backlog:
- **Phase 1: Requirements Specification.** The objective of this phase is to analyse and refine the functional and non-functional requirements from the iteration backlog. Also, any existing components that can be reused in the current development or the potential for new components to be reused in the

future should be identified where possible. Furthermore, the need for specific metamodels and transformations should be identified at this stage.

- **Phase 2: Development.** The objective of this phase is to produce a complete and precise technical specification of the system and to produce (automatically or semi-automatically) an executable system that fulfils the functional and non-functional requirements. The specification should be reviewed and refactored continuously to ensure the best design of the system. Any changes to the requirements should be applied to the modelling level, that might imply changes to some products like models, metamodels, transformation, and updating new elements in the language.
- **Phase 3: Integration and Testing.** In this phase, the developed parts of the system are integrated and tested.
- **Phase 4: Deployment.** When the release has been fully implemented and has reached a stable version, it will then be deployed to the customer.

5   Case Study: Collateralized Debt Obligation (CDO)

The case study concerns the implementation of an application to calculate and evaluate the risk of financial investments known as *Collateralized Debt Obligations* (CDOs) [9]. CDOs are composite investments whereby a portfolio of investments in different companies within different sectors is held as a single combined investment. These companies are usually organised into disjoint groups representing sectors (e.g., insurance, entertainment, telecoms, etc), and there is the possibility of infection of defaults between different companies within each sector [7,9]. Risk analysis of a CDO involves calculating the probability $P(S = s)$ of the total credit loss s in the portfolio. In order to calculate the probability of the financial loss, the following formulas are used from *Hammarlid* [9]: Theorems 1.1, 3.1 and Eqs. 1 and 2. These are listed below. The attribute k represents the index of one sector out of K total sectors, while the attribute n_k refers to the number of companies in sector k that are subject to risk. The attribute p_k represents the probability of a company defaulting in sector k while the attribute L_k represents the loss amount which is lost as a result of each default. The attribute q_k refers to the probability of infection of a default that may occur within sector k.

Theorem 1.1.

$$P(N_k = m) = \binom{n_k}{m} (p_k^m (1 - p_k)^{n_k - m} (1 - q_k)^{m(n_k - m)} +$$

$$\Sigma_{i=1}^{m-1} \binom{m}{i} (p_k^i (1 - p_k)^{n_k - i} (1 - (1 - q_k)^i)^{m-i} \times (1 - q_k)^{i(n_k - m)})$$

This equation gives the probability of m defaults in sector k. Conditioned on an outbreak in a sector, the distribution of the number of defaults is:

Equation (1)

$$P(N_k = m | N_k > 0) = P(N_k = m)/(1 - (1 - p_k)^{nk}) \tag{1}$$

and the probability of credit loss from sector k given an outbreak is:

Equation (2)

$$P(S_k = mL_k) = P(N_k = m | N_k > 0) \tag{2}$$

Theorem 3.1. The overall probability of loss s from the CDO is given recursively by:

$$P(S = 0) = \exp(-\sum_{k=1}^{K} \mu_k) \tag{3}$$

and

$$P(S = s) = \frac{1}{s} \sum_{k=1}^{K} \sum_{m_k=1}^{[s/L_k]} \mu_k m_k L_k P(N_k = m_k | N_k > 0) \times P(S = s - m_k L_k) \tag{4}$$

The same mathematical specification was used for all the four versions of the case study.

5.1   CDO Using Agile MDD Approach

The CDO application has been implemented using UML-Rigorous System Design Support (UML-RSDS) [13]. UML-RSDS is based upon the use case, class diagram, and Object Constraint Language (OCL) notations of UML. These notations are used to write system specifications, and then a design expressed using UML activities is automatically generated from the specifications. Finally, executable code in many programming languages (Java, C++, and C#) can be automatically synthesised from the design. The customer of this application was a financial analyst working in a financial company. The customer's main requirement was to have a precise (but very computationally expensive) and an approximate version of the total credit loss P(S = s) to overcome the limitations of the current application used in the company (lacking efficiency and accuracy). The CDO was developed using the aforementioned Agile MDD (Sect. 4) by one developer who had 10 years experience of UML-RSDS and had no prior experience in financial applications.

The development process began by interviewing the customer to gather the requirements. Both the functional and non-functional requirements were identified and prioritised. Afterwards, the product backlog was created (see Table 1). Since, the financial domain was unfamiliar to the developer, a phase of background research was necessary to understand the problem and to clarify the required computations. The development was organised into four iterations, each of which resulted in the incremental development of the application. The user story US1 was further decomposed into *US1.1: calculate probability of no contagion* and *US1.2: calculate probability of contagion* and were developed during the first iteration. Both US5 and US6 (non-functional requirements) were considered while developing the corresponding functional requirements. Then US2 was performed in development iteration 2. During the development, a further external requirement was introduced by the customer to handle the case of cross-sector contagion (US7), and this was scheduled to be implemented in the third iteration. Finally, US3 and US4 – which both involve manual coding – were developed in the fourth iteration. The system specification (a class diagram and a use case) of the Agile MDD application is presented in Fig. 1.

Table 1. CDO product backlog for Agile MDD approach

ID	User story	Type	Priority
US1	As an investor, I want to compute the probability P(S = s) of a total loss amount of {s} from individual and infectious defaults within a CDO	FR	1
US2	As an investor, I want to calculate the risk probability P(S >= s)	FR	2
US3	As an investor, I want to read the data from a CSV file containing the sectors and companies information	FR	3
US4	As an investor, I want to receive the results in a file	FR	4
US5	As an investor, I want to be able to receive the results in a practical time (less than 30 s for each {s} for a portfolio of 20 sectors and 100 companies)	NFR	1
US6	As an investor, I want the results to be accurate, within 5% of the theoretical exact results	NFR	1
US7	As an investor, I want to handle the case of cross-sector companies and cross-sector infection	FR	2

The specification of the user story US1 has the following postconditions (rules):

```
CDO::
  s : sectors => s.mu = 1 - ( ( 1 - s.p )->pow(s.n) )

CDO::
  ps0 = -sectors.mu.sum->exp()

CDO::
  Integer.subrange(0,20)->forAll( s | PS(s)->display() )
```

The first constraint initialises the *mu* attribute value for each sector. The second then initialises *ps0* using these values. The third constraint calculates and displays *PS(s)* for integer values s from 0 to 20. The operation *PS(s)* computes the Poisson approximation of the loss function, and is itself decomposed into computations of losses based on the possible combinations of failures in individual companies. *P(k,m)* is the probability of *m* defaults in sector *k*, *PCond(k,m)* is the conditional probability of *m* defaults in sector *k*, given that there is at least one default:

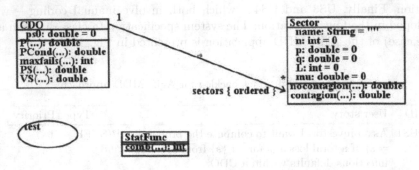

Fig. 1. The system specification for the CDO (Agile MDD application)

```
CDO::
query P(k : int, m : int) : double
pre: true
post:
  result = StatFunc.comb(sectors[k].n,m) *
  ( sectors[k].nocontagion(m) + Integer.Sum(1,m - 1,i,sectors[k].contagion(i,m)) )

CDO::
query PCond(k : int, m : int) : double
pre: true
post:
  ( m >= 1 =>
  result = P(k,m) / ( 1 - ( ( 1 - sectors[k].p )->pow(sectors[k].n) ) ) ) &
  ( m < 1 => result = 0 )
```

These correspond to Theorem 1.1 and Eq. (1) above, respectively. For brevity, we only presented part of the system's specification, from which an executable implementation was automatically generated. The system was a full business success in the sense that it was delivered on time and it was more efficient than the one being used by the company. Subsequently, the final product has been successfully deployed to the customer.

5.2   CDO Using MDD Application Approach

The CDO case study was redeveloped using the same specification of [9], which have been presented above. The developer used EMF/ECORE [25] to specify the metamodels, and the transformation was implemented using the Epsilon

Transformation Language (ETL) [12]. ETL is a hybrid model-to-model transformation language, that can transform many source to many target models. For this case study, single source and target models were used (the metamodel is presented in Fig. 2). This solution was developed by one developer who had 4 years experience of ETL and had no experience in financial applications.

Fig. 2. The metamodel for the CDO (MDD application)

5.3   CDO Using Agile Approach

The CDO application was redeveloped using the Scrum process. The application was implemented in Java and the development process was organised in three iterations (each one-week long). Some Scrum techniques were used such as product backlog, sprint backlog, user stories, requirements prioritisation, sprint planning, sprint review, and frequent customer involvement. The developer had 5 years experience of Java programming and had no experience in financial applications.

5.4   The Original CDO Application

The CDO application was previously developed in C++ and used in a financial company. It was developed using a traditional code-centric approach (waterfall development model). The developer had over 20 years experience in C++ programming and was a financial analyst in that company. This original application is used as a basis for evaluation and comparison.

6   Results

We began our analysis by considering whether the developers in the three new case studies cover the full requirements (the original application was already developed and being used in practice). Both Agile MDD and Agile approaches delivered all the intended functionalities. However, the MDD development delivered an incomplete application, where some main functionalities such as calculating the total loss probability was missing. The main reason behind this failure was the lack of understanding of the requirements, due to the lack of close interaction with the customer. A month later, the developer succeeded to deliver a complete application after clarifying the requirements with the customer. To ensure that all the applications behave similarly, we executed each application on the same data test set of [9]. After the applications had been validated, we compared the original CDO application with the three new versions developed using Agile MDD, MDD, and Agile, with regard to the quantitative measures of Sect. 3. For the Agile application, the measures have been computed using the source code analyser PMD,[1] whereas in the other applications, the measures were computed manually as there is a lack of tool support that can identify the technical debt in model-level artifacts (e.g. models, metamodels, and model transformation) [10].

Table 2 presents the execution time and the size in LOC of the four applications. The efficiency is investigated by measuring the execution time for uploading data input of 16 sectors and output of $P(S \leq 20)$, which involves computing $P(S = s)$ for each s from 0 to 20. The results show that Agile MDD application had the best efficiency (23 ms), while the original manual-code application had the slowest execution time with 231 ms. The Agile and MDD applications had times of 39 and 123 ms, respectively. We also looked at $P(S \leq 50)$, however the two non-MDD applications did not terminate in a reasonable time for this test. The efficiency tests of Agile MDD, Agile and the manual-code applications were carried out on a standard Windows 8.1 with Intel i7 with 3.40 GHz processor, while the MDD test was carried out on Windows 7 PC using an Intel(R) Core(TM) i7 with 3.6 GHz processor due to technical issues. With regard to LOC, we measured the size by counting the number of lines of specifications in case of model-centric applications, while in code-centric applications (i.e, Agile and the original) we counted the number of lines of source code. Thus, the developer using Agile MDD produced only 94 LOC compared to 143, 196, and 129 for MDD, Agile, and the original applications, correspondingly.

Table 3 presents the values for each technical debt metric for the four applications. The metrics of *EAS*, *ENR*, and *MRS* were omitted in both Agile and the original applications as they are not applicable for code-centric estimation. One notable trend we can see is that Agile MDD has a clearly lower *EAS* or complexity (182) than the MDD application (693), whereas they have the same number of rules *ENR*. Regarding *ENO*, all the applications but Agile MDD exceeded the threshold of 10 operations. The other measure maximum *FO* (MFO) appeared to have the same value among all cases. While maximum *RS* (MRS) of the largest rule size (in LOC) did not occur in Agile and the original cases, the measure had a clear difference between Agile MDD (3) and MDD (18). Likewise, for maximum *HS* (MHS), the Agile MDD approach had the smallest value, whilst MDD approaches were better than non-MDD, and Agile approaches were better than

---

[1] https://pmd.github.io/.

Table 2. Execution time and LOC for each application

	Agile MDD	MDD	Agile	Original
Execution time of P(S = s) for all s ≤ 20	23 ms	123 ms	39 ms	231 ms
Execution time of P(S = s) for all s ≤ 50	93 ms	531 ms	>15 min	>15 min
Size(LOC)	94	143	196	129

non-Agile. When looking at the maximum CC (MCC), code-centric applications had the highest value for CC (6) while the lowest value occurred for Agile MDD with a value of 2. CBR is expressed as $CBR_1(CBR_2)$ where CBR_1 refers to the total number of calling dependencies between rules/operations, and CBR_2 is the number of rules/operations which occur in cycles of calling dependencies. The results show that Agile MDD had 11 dependencies between rules/operations and MDD had 13 dependencies between rules/operations (and each approach had two cyclic dependencies). On the other hand, dependencies between operations were 7 and 11 in the Agile and the original applications, correspondingly, with only one cyclic dependency in each case. To identify design flaws, we consider if any bad smell occurs in the application, such as cyclic dependency, duplicated code, or any other violation for the technical debt thresholds. As seen in Table 3, Agile MDD had a lower number of design flaws, although there was not much difference in the flaws density (design flaws/LOC) in the four cases. The MDD applications had similar flaw density to the code-centric solutions, while the Agile applications had lower flaw density than non-Agile applications.

To complement our above quantitative results, the developers were asked to report in an opinion survey the main benefits and issues they perceived in each approach. Starting with Agile MDD approach, development time was reduced due to the direct feedback from the customer during development. In addition, the developer recognised development effort reduction and faster response to changes due to the small size and simplicity of the specification. With respect to the MDD approach, the developer reported as an advantage reduced development effort and high maintainability (related to system revision). On the other side, he faced difficulties in understanding the problem domain at the beginning. Finally, we asked the same question regarding Agile approach. The main benefit perceived by the developer is that frequent costumer involvement assured the application being built meets his needs. In addition, the iterative and incremental nature of the Agile development helped in organising the tasks. Although the application size is small, the developer reported a low maintainability as an issue during the development process. Opinion survey for the traditional code-centric approach was not feasible.

Table 3. Technical debt metrics for each application (flaws underlined)

	Agile MDD	MDD	Agile	Original
EAS (complexity)	182	693	NA	NA
ENR	4	4	NA	NA
ENO	9	11	12	11
MHS	9	18	21	34
MRS	3	18	NA	NA
MFO	3	3	3	3
MCC	2	3	6	6
CBR	11(2)	13(2)	7(1)	11(1)
DC	0	1	2	2
Design flaws	2	4	4	4
Flaws density	0.0213	0.0279	0.0204	0.031

7 Discussion

In this section, we will structure our discussion regarding the impact of integrating Agile and MDD – in terms of the software quality and efficiency – in three ways: Agile vs Non-Agile, MDD vs non-MDD, and Agile MDD vs MDD approaches. In addition, other general insights about integrating Agile and MDD will be discussed.

In terms of efficiency, the application developed using Agile MDD was the fastest. However, the initial efficiency of the solution was too slow, as it took over 2 min to perform the calculation of P(S = s) for all values of s ≤ 20. To address this issue, the recursive operations and other operations with high usage were given the stereotype ≪ *cached* ≫ to avoid unnecessary recomputation. This stereotype means that the operations are implemented using the *memoisation* technique of [18] to store previously-computed results. Likewise, after applying the stereotype *@cached* to the operations in the ETL solution, the efficiency improved significantly from 101 min to 123 ms. Although no caching has been used in either the Agile or original application, they showed better efficiency than the MDD application for $P(S \leq 20)$. The reason of the slowness of ETL is probably that ETL is an interpreted language and hence, it takes longer time to execute an application than UML-RSDS (Agile MDD case) which compiles specifications to a 3GL.

With regard to the product quality, the Agile MDD application had consistently better metrics. The simplest software metric is size (LOC). Smaller size of specification/implementation usually corresponds to a higher quality and reduced maintainability. The Agile MDD application was the smallest of the four versions. The results also show that model-centric approaches have more concise specification size (118.5 LOC in average) compared to non-MDD approaches (162.5 LOC in average). Working at a higher level of abstraction in model-centric approaches plays an important role in the amount of specification the developers need to write. Moreover, the Agile MDD application adopted "simple design" – an Agile practice that encourages minimising the complexity of designs – and this resulted in a smaller size of specification (in particular, the refactoring 'Move operation' was applied to reduce code complexity). The imperative style of ETL resulted instead in a substantially larger specification. Whilst UML-RSDS places operations within classes (as in Fig. 1), the ETL operations are simply listed at one level of scoping in a transformation text. Thus, instead of a sector operation using the *self* object to access sector data, in the ETL version a global lookup for a sector identified by an index precedes any sector-specific functionality, resulting in larger and slower code. For example, the ETL version (written in EOL) of *PCond* is:

```
operation PCond(k : Integer, m : Integer) : Real
{ var secK =
    OUT!Sector.allInstances.selectOne(se|se.id == k);
  if (m >= 1)
  { return P(k,m)/(1-((1-secK.p).pow(secK.n))); }
  else { return 0; }
}
```

Regarding the *EAS* measure, it is interesting to note the significant differences in values between the Agile MDD and MDD applications, although UML-RSDS (Agile MDD case) and ETL (MDD case) have similar expression languages based on OCL. Although none of the applications exceeded the threshold of CC, Agile MDD exhibits the lowest maximum complexity in any operation or rule. Lower complexity should correspond to higher quality and make it easier to understand the specification. Some characteristics of the Agile philosophy support the assertion that programs developed using an Agile process have lower complexity than software developed using non-Agile processes [11]. We can see this is true for the Agile versus non-Agile approaches, although the MDD versus non-MDD distinction for maximum CC is more evident. The adoption of simple design and refactoring in the Agile MDD application resulted in lower complexity and a well-designed system with a lower number of design flaws. Usually, lower complexity tends to reduce the coupling of code or between objects: the higher the complexity the more coupled the code is. Although it has been proved that using *refactoring* contributes in improving code quality by reducing code complexity and coupling [19], the Agile MDD application had more coupling between rules/operations than the Agile application.

Tables 4, 5, and 6 present the average of the values of the metrics for the pairs of approaches: Agile versus non-Agile approaches, MDD versus non-MDD approaches, and Agile MDD versus MDD approaches, respectively. Agile approaches therefore have better values than non-Agile approaches in 8 of the 9 measures while MDD approaches have better values than non-MDD approaches in 7 of the 9 measures. Finally, Agile MDD approach have better values than the MDD approach in all 9 measures.

Agile development relies on frequent interactions with the customer throughout the development process, to share information and provide feedback on what has been done and what to achieve in the next iteration of the development. This Agile characteristic was a significant advantage in our case. Since the financial case study involves highly-complex computations, collaboration with the customer was necessary to ensure that the developer understand the requirements precisely. As a result of lack of customer involvement in the MDD application, the developer did not come to know that there are some missing requirements until the application was delivered to the customer. On the other hand, frequent validation by the customer minimised the risk of building wrong functionalities, in both the Agile MDD and Agile applications. In the case of the original application, the developer was a financial analyst developing a system for his company. Another intrinsic value of Agile development is rapid response to change. For the Agile MDD and Agile applications, we found that the fact that the developer was working in short iterations (in both approaches) and at a higher abstraction level and with concise specifications (in Agile MDD), also made it easier and faster to respond to changes, compared to non-Agile approaches.

The impact of integrating Agile and MDD on productivity is also an important factor to consider. One means to assess productivity is to measure the effort put into development, in person days or hours. In this study, the effort of development was not feasible to measure as the Agile MDD developer spent an initial stage of background research familiarising with the domain concepts and identifying the appropriate mathematical definitions to use. On the other hand, both the MDD and Agile developers were provided with the required background material and a precise problem description and hence spent less time in understanding the problem and started with the development process sooner. The MDD approach was faster than the Agile approach – however incomplete functionality was initially produced by the MDD approach, and the overall effort in the two approaches are similar once the work needed to complete the MDD version is taken into account.

Table 4. Agile versus non-Agile approaches

	Effic.	LOC	ENO	MHS	MCC	CBR	DC	Flaws	Flaws/LOC
Agile	31 ms	145	10.5	15	4	9(1.5)	1	3	0.0207
Non-agile	177 ms	136	11	26	4.5	12(1.5)	1.5	4	0.0294

Table 5. MDD versus non-MDD approaches

	Effic.	LOC	ENO	MHS	MCC	CBR	DC	Flaws	Flaws/LOC
MDD	73 ms	118.5	10	13.5	2.5	12(2)	0.5	3	0.0253
Non-MDD	135 ms	162.5	11.5	27.5	6	9(1)	2	4	0.0246

Table 6. Agile MDD versus MDD approaches for CDO

	Effic.	LOC	ENO	MHS	MCC	CBR	DC	Flaws	Flaws/LOC
Agile MDD	23 ms	94	9	9	2	11(2)	0	2	0.0213
MDD	123 ms	143	11	18	3	13(2)	1	4	0.0279

7.1 Outcome of Research Questions

Regarding the research question RQ1, we found that integrating Agile and MDD has a clear potential in developing small-scale but highly intensive computational applications. There are several improvements visible in the Agile MDD application, specifically in the quality and efficiency of the system (Table 3). Furthermore, our Agile MDD approach specifies a complete application in a single integrated model (class diagram plus use cases), which should facilitate maintainability and responding to change. For RQ2, we believe that building the system using iterative and incremental development helped the developer understand the domain and the requirements better and hence made it more likely that they will build the correct system. Moreover, continuous testing and frequent interaction with the customer resulted in an early discovery of defects or flaws and hence resulted in lower defects compared to the MDD application. MDD approaches have potential benefits of reusability of functionality compared to non-MDD approaches (e.g., the specification of a Sector could be reused from this application in another financial context). By specification at a high level, it is also simple to add a mechanism such as caching by adding a stereotype to an operation. In manually-coded approaches the implementation of caching is non-trivial.

7.2 Threats to Validity

The results of this study are particularly interesting as they resulted from a close-to-industry case study context. However, like most empirical studies, this study has some limitations. The first limitation related to the development team size. Agile methods emphasise on communication, people, and team collaboration. In this research, each of the four applications has been implemented by one developer, and thus it might have a potential impact on the quality of the application developed, and hence impact the evaluation of the case study. However, all developers participated in this study have a good experience working in Agile and/or MDD. Also, other studies in literature show that Agile development can be carried out successfully with solo-developer [20,21]. The second limitation relates to the inevitable differences in languages used for MDD versus non-MDD approaches as it was not possible to find developers who have approximate experience in the same language. Nevertheless, our recent study [14] found that UML-RSDS and ETL are rather similar in terms of fault density over large case studies and thus the impact of this differences on the results should be minimum. Another limitation concerns the generalisation of the results. Although the application used in this study is a real industrial application, implemented according to real customer requirements, we cannot generalise the results to different application types or sizes without more experiments. A possible threat stems from the method of measurement, which have been done partially with tools (i.e. the PMD analyser) and partially manually. Staron et al. [24] have shown that comparison of measures assessed by different tools is error prone. However, the small size of the application made it possible to calculate the values of the measures manually by at least two of the authors. The last threat to the validity is running the test case data on two different operating systems that might affect the evaluation of the efficiency of the applications. Nevertheless, the specification of the two operating systems is very similar and has almost negligible impact on the results.

8   Conclusion

The aim of this paper was to provide a better understanding of how integrating Agile development processes and MDD could impact on the properties of the developed software. We have compared the experiences of four different independent development teams using different development methodologies. The results show some indicators that Agile MDD has improved the efficiency and the quality. We believe that this study is an early step in understanding the impact of integrating Agile development and MDD. Certainly, more research is required to further investigate its benefits or disadvantages. To this end, we intend to replicate this study using larger case studies with larger development teams using the same transformation and programming languages. Moreover, more measured properties such as productivity, time-to-market and comprehensibility of the developed code/specification should also be measured in future studies.

References

1. Alfraihi, H., Lano, K.: The integration of agile development and model driven development: a systematic literature review. In: Proceedings of the 5th International Conference on Model-Driven Engineering and Software Development, MODELSWARD (2017)
2. Alfraihi, H., Lano, K.: A process for integrating agile software development and model-driven development. In: 3rd Flexible MDE Workshop (FlexMDE) Co-located with ACM/IEEE 20th International Conference on Model Driven Engineering Languages & Systems (MoDELS 2017), CEUR Workshop Proceedings, Austin, TX, USA, pp. 412–417. CEUR-WS.org (2017)
3. Atkinson, C., Kuhne, T.: Model-driven development: a metamodeling foundation. IEEE Softw. **20**(5), 36–41 (2003)
4. Basili, V.R.: Software modeling and measurement: the goal/question/metric paradigm. Technical report (1992)
5. Beck, K.: Extreme Programming Explained: Embrace Change. Addison-Wesley Professional, Boston (2000)
6. Burden, H., Hansson, S., Zhao, Y.: How MAD are we? empirical evidence for model-driven agile development. In: Proceedings of XM 2014, 3rd Extreme Modeling Workshop, Valencia, Spain, vol. 1239, pp. 2–11. CEUR (2014)

7. Davis, M., Lo, V.: Infectious defaults. Quant. Financ. **1**(4), 382–387 (2001)
8. Fowler, M.: The new methodology. Wuhan Univ. J. Nat. Sci. **6**(1), 12–24 (2001). Mar
9. Hammarlid, O.: Aggregating sectors in the infectious defaults model. Quan. Financ. **4**(1), 64–69 (2004)
10. He, X., Avgeriou, P., Liang, P., Li, Z.: Technical debt in MDE: a case study on GMF/EMF-based projects. In: Proceedings of the ACM/IEEE 19th International Conference on Model Driven Engineering Languages and Systems, pp. 162–172. ACM (2016)
11. Knippers, D.: Agile software development and maintainability. In: 15th Twente Student Conference (2011)
12. Kolovos, D.S., Paige, R.F., Polack, F.A.C.: The epsilon transformation language. In: Vallecillo, A., Gray, J., Pierantonio, A. (eds.) ICMT 2008. LNCS, vol. 5063, pp. 46–60. Springer, Heidelberg (2008). https://doi.org/10.1007/978-3-540-69927-9_4
13. Lano, K.: Agile Model-Based Development Using UML-RSDS. CRC Press, Boca Raton (2017)
14. Lano, K., Rahimi, S.K., Sharbaf, M., Alfraihi, H.: Technical debt in model transformation specifications. In: Theory and Practice of Model Transformations (2018)
15. MacDonald, A., Russell, D., Atchison, B.: Model-driven development within a legacy system: an industry experience report. In: Proceedings of 2005 Australian Software Engineering Conference, pp. 14–22. IEEE (2005)
16. Marinescu, R.: Assessing technical debt by identifying design flaws in software systems. IBM J. Res. Dev. **56**(5), 9:1–9:13 (2012)
17. Mellor, S.J., Clark, T., Futagami, T.: Model-driven development: guest editors' introduction. IEEE Softw. **20**(5), 14–18 (2003)
18. Michie, D.: Memo functions and machine learning. Nature **218**(5136), 19 (1968)
19. Moser, R., Abrahamsson, P., Pedrycz, W., Sillitti, A., Succi, G.: A case study on the impact of refactoring on quality and productivity in an agile team. In: Meyer, B., Nawrocki, J.R., Walter, B. (eds.) CEE-SET 2007. LNCS, vol. 5082, pp. 252–266. Springer, Heidelberg (2008). https://doi.org/10.1007/978-3-540-85279-7_20
20. Nyström, A.: Agile solo-defining and evaluating an agile software development process for a single software developer (2011)
21. Pagotto, T., Fabri, J.A., Lerario, A., Gonçalves, J.A.: Scrum solo: software process for individual development. In: 2016 11th Iberian Conference on Information Systems and Technologies (CISTI), pp. 1–6. IEEE (2016)
22. Schwaber, K., Beedle, M.: Agile Software Development with Scrum. Prentice Hall, Agile Software Development (2002)
23. Seaman, C., Guo, Y.: Measuring and monitoring technical debt. In: Advances in Computers, vol. 82, pp. 25–46. Elsevier, UK (2011)
24. Staron, M., Durisic, D., Rana, R.: Improving measurement certainty by using calibration to find systematic measurement error—a case of lines-of-code measure. In: Madeyski, L., Śmiałek, M., Hnatkowska, B., Huzar, Z. (eds.) Software Engineering: Challenges and Solutions. AISC, vol. 504, pp. 119–132. Springer, Cham (2017). https://doi.org/10.1007/978-3-319-43606-7_9
25. Steinberg, D., Budinsky, F., Merks, E., Paternostro, M.: EMF: Eclipse Modeling Framework, 2nd edn. Pearson Education, London (2008)
26. Yin, R.K.: Case study research: design and methods. SAGE **2003**(181), 15 (2003)
27. Zhang, Y., Patel, S.: Agile model-driven development in practice. IEEE Softw. **28**(2), 84–91 (2011)

Author Index

Printed in the United States
By Bookmasters